SLOW TRAVEL

Yorkshire Dales

Local, characterful guides to Britain's special places

Mike Bagshaw
Updated by Rob Ainsley

T0182497

EDITION 3
Bradt Guides Ltd, UK
The Globe Pequot Press Inc, USA

Third edition published June 2024
First published 2014
Bradt Travel Guides Ltd
31a High Street, Chesham, Buckinghamshire, HP5 1BW, England
www.bradtguides.com
Print edition published in the USA by The Globe Pequot Press Inc, PO Box 480, Guilford,
Connecticut 06437-0480

Text copyright © Bradt Travel Guides Ltd, 2024
Maps copyright © Bradt Travel Guides Ltd, 2024; includes map data
© OpenStreetMap contributors
Photographs copyright © Individual photographers, 2024 (see below)
Project Managers: Emma Gibbs and Anna Moores
Cover research: Pepi Bluck, Perfect Picture

ISBN: 9781804692165

British Library Cataloguing in Publication Data
A catalogue record for this book is available from the British Library

Photographs
© individual photographers and organisations credited beside images & also from picture
libraries credited as follows: Alamy.com (A); Dreamstime.com (DT); Shutterstock.com (S);
Superstock.com (SS)

Front cover Langcliffe Scar and Ribblesdale (Guy Edwardes/AWL Images)
Back cover Knaresborough (Joe Choosong/S)
Title page Craven, near Settle (Pete Stuart/S)

Maps David McCutcheon FBCart.S. FRGS

Typeset by Ian Spick, Bradt Guides
Production managed by Gutenberg Press Ltd, printed in Malta
Digital conversion by www.dataworks.co.in

Paper used for this product comes from sustainably managed forests, recycled and controlled
sources.

AUTHOR

Although a Lancastrian by birth, **Mike Bagshaw** has spent the last 40 years living and working in Yorkshire and currently resides with his wife in the North York Moors near Whitby. Now retired from a career teaching outdoor education to North Yorkshire schoolchildren, he is relishing the opportunity to travel to wild places around the world as a naturalist and explorer. When at home,  he divides his time between writing nature columns for newspapers and magazines and volunteering for local wildlife and conservation bodies.

CONTRIBUTING AUTHOR

Caroline Mills, author of the Nidderdale chapter, is a freelance writer of travel guides, including the Bradt guide *Slow Travel Cotswolds*, and contributes to various national magazines on travel, food and gardens. Though not officially of Yorkshire stock, she has many family connections with the county she classes as her second 'home'. Caroline writes, 'It has been great to return "home" for this guide. When you live in an area, it's easy to take your  surroundings for granted and stop exploring. Returning to Yorkshire, I've visited with a fresh pair of eyes and have been able to talk with residents about places they didn't know were on their doorstep.'

UPDATER

Rob Ainsley is a cycling writer and blogger who has got wet riding all over Yorkshire. Born and bred in the county, he lives in York, but is usually away cycling somewhere. His name appears in various magazines such as *Cycle* and *Cycling Plus*, usually in a small point size up the side. In researching this update, he spent a very happy few months re-exploring the Dales using his four and a half bikes, boots, and occasionally an inflatable canoe – all in the Slow Travel way. Rob's cycling blog 'Yorkshire Ridings' is at ⊘ e2e.bike.

AUTHOR'S STORY

On the face of it, a Lancastrian 'townie' writing about rural Yorkshire is an unusual phenomenon, but the truth is that I have spent more of my life in this adopted county than in the one of my birth.

My first experience of Yorkshire, a seaside holiday in the late 1960s, was a shocking one; for a ten-year-old boy used to the Gulf Stream waters of north Wales, swimming in the North Sea came as a very rude awakening.

Fast forward a few years and I am back in Dentdale, where we teenagers enjoyed residential stays in the school's country cottage. With hindsight, those first exposures to real country life – windswept hills, clean rivers and undisturbed wildlife – were life-changing experiences, for which I am eternally grateful.

That initial love affair with the Yorkshire Dales has been consummated every Easter since, for 40 years, accompanied by a handful of like-minded school friends, and during that time we reckon to have visited just about every hilltop and decent pub available. That, coupled with my 30 years living and working in the North York Moors, led me to believe that I knew pretty much all there was to know about North Yorkshire. How wrong I was.

The welcome opportunity to write this guide has allowed me to see familiar places in a new light, and discover corners I had unwittingly missed. It also gave me the incentive to go and do some of those things that I'd always promised myself, like watch an early-morning black grouse lek, or brave the descent of Gaping Gill cavern. Best of all, it's rekindled my desire to go out exploring, and see what else I might have missed in this wonderful county.

ACKNOWLEDGEMENTS

A big thank you goes to all those people that have helped me with this book. The Yorkshire contributors who shared a little of their lives and passions and allowed me to quote them; Caroline Mills for contributing a chapter of writing; and everyone in the Bradt team for being so professional and patient.

DEDICATION

To my fellow 'Lads at Dent'...
Roger, Andrew, Grant, Phil, Bri, Pete, Gaz, Ste, Mart and Ian,
with priceless memories of half a lifetime's Dales exploration.
Mike Bagshaw

FEEDBACK REQUEST

At Bradt Guides we're aware that guidebooks start to go out of date on the day they're published – and that you, our readers, are out there in the field doing research of your own. You'll find out before us when a fine new family-run hotel opens or a favourite restaurant changes hands and goes downhill. So why not tell us about your experiences? Contact us on ✆ 01753 893444 or ✉ info@bradtguides.com. We will forward emails to the author who may post updates on the Bradt website at ⬨ bradtguides.com/updates. Alternatively, you can add a review of the book to Amazon, or share your adventures with us on Facebook, X or Instagram (@BradtGuides).

SUGGESTED PLACES TO BASE YOURSELF

These bases make ideal starting points for exploring localities the Slow way.

KIRKBY STEPHEN page 53
One of the few towns in the Dales accessible by rail, this northern gateway to the national park is a great base from which to explore its new Cumbrian corner.

KELD/THWAITE/MUKER pages 146, 147 & 148
If it's rural isolation you want then Upper Swaledale is the place. Empty fells all around but a surprising range of accommodation available.

SEDBERGH page 62
This historic home of Quakerism and modern book town sits comfortably at the foot of the Howgill Fells and within sight of the Three Peaks.

HAWES page 173
There's lots going on in the capital of Upper Wensleydale itself but it's also at a handy crossroads with easy access to Swaledale, Garsdale and Ribblesdale.

CLAPHAM page 74
Rail links to Skipton and Lancaster and a gentle bike ride to the busier Ingleton. As for walking – you've got a show cave, Three Peaks and classic limestone pavements, all a short stroll away.

SKIPTON page 108
It calls itself the 'Gateway to the Dales', which aptly describes its good bus and train links to Three Peaks country, Craven and Wharfedale. Don't just travel from here though – Skipton itself has lots to offer with canals, a steam railway and one of the best castles in the country.

Durham

Appleby-in-Westmorland

Barnard Ca

Cumbria

Kirkby Stephen

CHAPTER 4
page 142

Keld

CHAPTER 1
page 44

Thwaite

Muker

Sedbergh

Ure

Hawes

CHAPTER 5
page 170

North Yorkshire

Kirkby Lonsdale

CHAPTER 2
page 68

Ingleton

Clapham

CHAPTER 3
page 102

Wharfe

Settle

Grassington

Embsay & Bolton Abb Steam Railw

Lancashire

Skipton

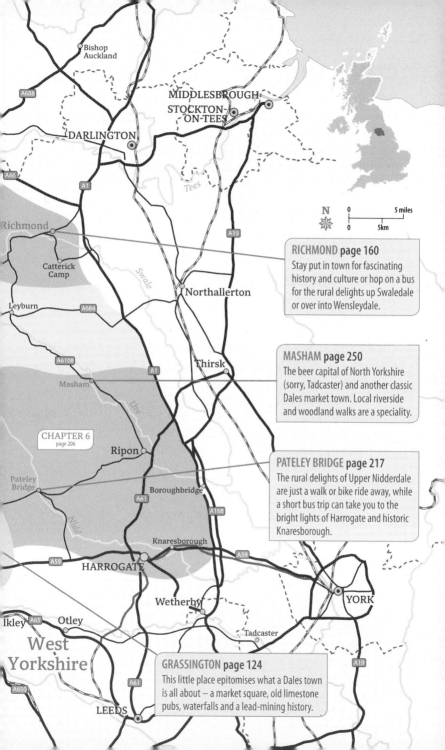

RICHMOND page 160
Stay put in town for fascinating history and culture or hop on a bus for the rural delights up Swaledale or over into Wensleydale.

MASHAM page 250
The beer capital of North Yorkshire (sorry, Tadcaster) and another classic Dales market town. Local riverside and woodland walks are a speciality.

PATELEY BRIDGE page 217
The rural delights of Upper Nidderdale are just a walk or bike ride away, while a short bus trip can take you to the bright lights of Harrogate and historic Knaresborough.

GRASSINGTON page 124
This little place epitomises what a Dales town is all about – a market square, old limestone pubs, waterfalls and a lead-mining history.

N

0   5 miles
0   5km

CHAPTER 6
page 206

West Yorkshire

CONTENTS

YORKSHIRE DALES

North Yorkshire is England's largest county, and an astonishingly diverse region. This book covers the western half of the county, that area of the Pennines traditionally known as the Yorkshire Dales, with all but one of its valleys sitting predominantly in the national park of the same name. Nidderdale was left out in the cold on the park's inception, but has since been rightly granted its own status as a National Landscape so I feel that it deserves its place here.

In 2016, the Yorkshire Dales National Park was extended to the west, growing in area by a quarter. The new territory took in some parts of historic Westmorland and even Lancashire: some of the Howgill Fells and the Orton Fells are now 'in the Yorkshire Dales'. They're covered in this book, together with gateway towns such as Kirkby Lonsdale and Kirkby Stephen.

I have been far more flighty with borders in the east, allowing much of Lower Wensleydale to feature in the Nidderdale chapter because of its failure to make the national park. The towns of Harrogate and Knaresborough and Ripon, North Yorkshire's only city now that York is a separate unitary authority, also made it in because they are close by and jolly fine places. In the south I stuck with the county boundary – so apologies to Ilkley and Otley. The eastern half of the county of North Yorkshire has been dealt with separately in *Slow Travel North York Moors & Yorkshire Wolds*.

What makes the Yorkshire Dales so special? Why is it visited so much and written about so often? The answers to these questions lie not just in the obvious observations of space, natural beauty and breathtaking landscape; it involves the culture of the place as well – the people. Dales folk are often old-fashioned but proud of it; they see it as an attribute, not a fault. While many places are rediscovering the values of the traditional, real and genuine, and renewing connections with their

history and landscape, many parts of the Dales never lost them in the first place.

So-called progress has brought us cheap, mass-produced goods sold in supermarkets the size of villages and even bigger shopping malls. Thankfully, a backlash is taking place, and rural North Yorkshire is at the forefront of the push to preserve those things that make places different, interesting and, well, real. Folk are fighting hard to keep their village shops open, promote locally produced, high-quality food and drink, and encourage their own artists and artisans. These are the special people – the brewers, potters, shopkeepers, cheesemakers, farmers, wood-carvers, butchers, bakers and candlestick makers – that have managed to capture a little of the essence of their corner of this singular county, and enable you to feel it, smell it, taste it or even take a little of it away with you. I hope this book inspires you, not just to read about the Yorkshire Dales, but to live it – to come and meet these people, spend some Slow time where they live and get to know it as they do.

Climb a few hills, stroll through the woods and meditate in a ruined abbey, eat a pork pie from the village butcher by the river, and finish the day in an old stone pub, with a glass of your favourite tipple and a crackling fire to toast your feet on. A Yorkshire Dales version of the board game Monopoly appeared in 2024; you, however, can enjoy the real thing.

A DALES TIMELINE

For the Yorkshire Dales there have been four milestone events. The first of these moments was a long one, the Carboniferous period, lasting 140 million years in fact. During this time, the overwhelmingly dominant rock of the Dales, its limestone, was laid down, as multi-layered coral reef in a shallow tropical sea.

Ten thousand years ago, the next big event was drawing to a close, as the Devensian ice finally retreated, to reveal the shapes it had carved into the underlying land surface: classic U-shaped valleys, ice-plucked crags with cascading waterfalls and bare, soil-less hilltops.

The first real human impact came in the Bronze Age, when a vast, blanketing wildwood was cleared for agriculture and, finally, all the newly revealed features were named by the Vikings just over a thousand

---

◄ **1** The village of Askrigg (page 181). **2** Sheep at Scar House Reservoir (page 211).

years ago. Fell, dale, foss, ghyll and beck are all pure lingua-Scandinavia, as are most of Yorkshire's town and village names.

Obviously, a lot has happened since the Danes arrived – castle-building in Norman times, lead mining, and the Industrial Revolution for instance – but 1954 will always be a particularly important year with the formation of the Yorkshire Dales National Park. As in all 14 other national parks, the authority is charged with maintaining and enhancing the landscape, nature, culture and history of the park, for us visitors, and the people that live in it, to enjoy. In striving towards these ideals, it has made itself a champion of all things traditional and sustainable, and a tremendous source of information and expertise for

THE SLOW MINDSET

Hilary Bradt, Founder, Bradt Guides

We shall not cease from exploration
And the end of all our exploring
Will be to arrive where we started
And know the place for the first time.
T S Eliot, 'Little Gidding', *Four Quartets*

This series evolved, slowly, from a Bradt editorial meeting when we started to explore ideas for guides to our favourite part of the world – Great Britain. We wanted to get away from the usual 'top sights' formula and encourage our authors to bring out the nuances and local differences that make up a sense of place – such things as food, building styles, nature, geology, or local people and what makes them tick. Our aim was to create a series that celebrates the present, focusing on sustainable tourism, rather than taking a nostalgic wallow in the past.

So without our realising it at the time, we had defined 'Slow Travel', or at least our concept of it. For the beauty of the Slow movement is that there is no fixed definition;

we adapt the philosophy to fit our individual needs and aspirations. Thus Carl Honoré, author of *In Praise of Slow*, writes: 'The Slow Movement is a cultural revolution against the notion that faster is always better. It's not about doing everything at a snail's pace, it's about seeking to do everything at the right speed. Savouring the hours and minutes rather than just counting them. Doing everything as well as possible, instead of as fast as possible. It's about quality over quantity in everything from work to food to parenting.' And travel.

So take time to explore. Don't rush it, get to know an area – and the people who live there – and you'll be as delighted as the authors by what you find.

TOURIST INFORMATION

For **information** about the Yorkshire Dales National Park before you visit, go online to the park authority's website, ⊘ yorkshiredales.org.uk, or get hold of a copy of their annual guide/newspaper, *The Visitor*.

those of us that wish to go Slow in the Dales. What it does particularly well is enable travel and discovery without a car; in particular, cycling is strongly encouraged, both on roads and off-road on mountain bikes (⊘ cyclethedales.org.uk).

Rural economies round Britain in the 2020s are facing serious challenges, and the Yorkshire Dales area is no exception. Many pubs, cafés and shops, already hit by pandemic restrictions, are grappling with huge increases in energy bills, difficulty getting staff, and customers with less money in their pockets.

But there's resilience too, and while around one in five places have closed since the last edition, several new, vibrant and positive ones have opened up in places such as Keld (page 147), Ingleton (page 82) and Clapham (page 75). Some of the lost pubs are, it's hoped, being rescued by community or benefactor buyouts, to be run as a local resource: the one in Redmire (page 191) is a recent example.

HOW MANY DALES?

A good question. Various figures are quoted, usually in the order of 20 to 30. Last time we looked, Wikipedia listed 57 specifically in the Yorkshire Dales region. (There are many more in other parts of Yorkshire.) Yet more named dales lurk in the recesses of maps, especially old ones. But here, going roughly north to south, is a brief list of the main dales, and their side-dales, that we cover in this book.

Swaledale (River Swale) The most scenically dramatic in its upper reaches. Flattens after going through Richmond and eventually joins the Ure north of York. *Side-dales:* West Stonesdale, Arkengarthdale.
Wensleydale (River Ure) Wide, lush and expansive: the cream of the Dales. After Leyburn, meanders on the level through Masham and Ripon. The river changes name to the Ouse after the Swale joins it, and then flows through York to the Humber. *Side-dales:* Raydale, Bishopdale, Coverdale.

Wharfedale (River Wharfe) Raw, steep-sided and remote at first, before passing pretty villages. Goes through Grassington, Bolton Abbey and Ilkley before ultimately joining the Ouse south of York. *Side-dales:* Littondale.

Airedale (River Aire) The most enigmatic: after its lofty genesis at Malham Tarn, it disappears underground to re-emerge in Malham village. Passes through Skipton before its long passage through Leeds and across the plains towards the Humber at Goole.

Nidderdale (River Nidd) Often overlooked, the Nidd starts off at remote, aerial reservoirs and passes through off-piste villages to Pateley Bridge. After Knaresborough's spectacular gorge, it winds laconically across farmland to join the Ouse just north of York.

Dentdale (River Dee) Heads through Dent and past Sedbergh on its way to the Lune. Nearby, heading southwest and ultimately to the Lune, are Kingsdale and Barbondale. North of Dentdale, running roughly parallel to it, is Garsdale (River Clough).

FLOWERS OF THE DALES

Lime-rich soil, a history of traditional non-intensive agriculture and lots of rain: these are the three blessings bestowed on the Yorkshire Dales that allow a fabulously rich flora to bloom in the spring and summer months.

Down in the valleys, away from the biting wind and chance of a late blizzard, early **March** can see odd pioneers like butterbur and coltsfoot appearing on roadside verges, but late March is when the real display starts. A bright, crisp, early-spring-day stroll along an old sunken lane like Thoresby Lane near Castle Bolton (page 188) or Howgill Lane near Appletreewick (page 129) can be an ideal way to celebrate the end of winter. Yellow celandines and white wood anemones pepper the track bank like scattered stars, still-furled cuckoo-pint flowers arrow their way upwards, and the humble moschatel, a particular favourite of mine, hides behind more extrovert blooms. I love alternative country names for flowers, and the moschatel's pseudonym of 'town hall clock' is an elegantly descriptive one. The flower stalk stands vertical and produces at its tip four outward-facing green circular flowers all at 90 degrees to their neighbour, and a fifth as an afterthought pointing straight upwards. All they need are tiny numerals and hands and the model would be perfect.

---

1 Visit Skipton Woods to experience the fragrant wild garlic displays. 2 The lady's slipper orchid – the rarest flower of them all. 3 Harrogate's cherry blossom display in late April. 4 Visit in June for trademark verge and hedge blues like nettle-leaved bellflower. ▶

In late **April** part of The Stray in Harrogate becomes 'Little Japan', as dozens of cherry trees blossom and people picnic under the dense pink canopy (page 231).

May is the time for the woodlands of the region, when the great floral carpets are unrolled; white drifts of wild garlic or ramsons and a lilac mist of incomparable bluebells. There cannot be many better displays anywhere in the country than Skipton Woods (page 110) or Hag Wood near Richmond (page 161). Out in the fields, hawthorn hedges paint lines of white May blossom up hillsides, and wet roadsides dance with bobbing heads of water avens.

If you can only visit the Dales once in the year to experience its flowers, then **June** has to be the time. This is when the display is at its peak: daylight hours are at their maximum and plant growth is so fast you can almost hear it. This is when the iconic limestone flowers appear, trademark verge and hedge blues like meadow cranesbill and nettle-leaved bellflower, traditional hayfield species including yellow rattle and betony, and the real stars of the show, the orchids. Many of the family are lime-loving (calcicoles) so it is no surprise that more than ten species of orchid grow within the national park. All are beautiful, none is very common and some are extremely rare.

The **lady's slipper orchid** is arguably the best-looking and without doubt the rarest flower of all: only one native wild lady's slipper orchid plant exists in Britain and it grows in a secret ash-wood location somewhere in the Craven and Wharfedale locale. In pre-Victorian times this orchid was also found in Derbyshire, Durham and Cumbria but was never common. Wholesale picking for markets and uprooting for collections was its downfall, the attraction, of course, being its stunning appearance. The maroon perianth crowns the golden-yellow shoe-shaped lip which gives the plant all of its names; *Cyripedium calceolus* literally means 'little shoe of Venus', and 'Mary's shoe' is a vernacular Yorkshire name.

Now other lady's slippers grow in one or two dales and Cumbrian woods but these are all artificially propagated from seeds collected since 1987 from the one 'wild' plant. Natural England is co-ordinating this Species Recovery Programme, which is now starting to blossom – literally. It takes 11 years for a lady's slipper plant to flower once established, and in 2000 the first of the new scheme's offspring did just that near Ingleton. Let us hope that the efforts of the scientists are successful – that these magnificent flowers return to their old haunts, no longer secret and guarded, and we can all marvel at the plant that so nearly disappeared.

WILDLIFE OF THE DALES

Animal life in the Yorkshire Dales could never be described as superabundant; we've lost far too much of our native woodland for that. But it is special. The limestone that encourages calcium-loving plants is also the building material for snails' shells so, not surprisingly, the Dales has an impressive **gastropod** species list, including the very rare round-mouthed whorl snail.

Some other unusual invertebrates are here as well, not because they need the limestone itself but because they like the plants that grow on the limestone. The **rock-rose leafhopper**, for instance, feeds only on rock-roses adorning the limestone pavements of the Craven region and the **wall mason bee** has an inordinate fondness for the pollen of another local plant, bird's foot trefoil.

The exposed hilltop environment of the Dales is what attracts the fantastically named **cloud-living spider**, found only here, Scotland and Siberia. This is also the habitat of choice for many of the area's iconic **birds**: curlews, red grouse, golden plovers and lapwings, now scarce in lowland England, thrive up here, while short-eared owls and merlins hunt over the grasslands for voles and small birds respectively. The small birds concerned aren't the sparrows and tits that us valley-dwellers are familiar with, but upland specialists like wheatears, meadow pipits and, that secretive member of the finch family, the twite. High up in a wooded ghyll, you may even catch sight, or more likely hear the jaunty song, of our mountain blackbird, the ring ouzel.

The nymphs of mayflies and stoneflies can only live in oxygen-rich, unpolluted waters, and rivers don't come any more pristine than the spring-fed torrents of the Yorkshire Dales. The resulting aquatic insect richness is harvested by underwater predators, brown trout and bullheads, and waterside birds like grey wagtails and dippers – for me, the latter is the signature bird of the Yorkshire Dales. Another clean-water fusspot living here, but gone from many other parts of the country, is our native **white-clawed crayfish** which is still doing well because its arch rival, the invasive signal crayfish, is largely absent from the rivers of the Dales.

Top of the aquatic food chain is the **otter**. This fabulous animal was in serious trouble not so long ago, having been pushed to the brink of extinction in England by the same organochlorine poisons that nearly did for the peregrine falcon (page 90). Its recovery in the last 20 years has been nothing short of remarkable, and otters are now thriving in all of the region's rivers. Having said that, they are very rarely seen due to their extreme shyness and largely nocturnal habits – footprints and droppings are often the only visible evidence of their presence.

Other mammals that do particularly well in the Yorkshire Dales are **bats** and that is due in no small part to the abundance of caves here. Ten different species live in the region and, while some do roost in buildings and hollow trees, most are very happy in big, dry caverns. With over 2,000 cave entrances to choose from, it's not surprising that there are many bat colonies scattered around the Dales, with those in the Ease Gill cave system near Kirkby Lonsdale big enough to be of international importance.

It's one thing knowing that interesting and exciting animals exist in the Yorkshire Dales but it's another getting to see them. You have to be in the right place at the right time, and below is my list of seven recommended places and times to see the best of the region's wildlife.

MALHAM COVE & TARN

The RSPB viewpoint telescopes, trained on the resident peregrine falcons' nest high in the cove (page 113), are justifiably famous (☉ Easter–Aug) but there are a wide variety of other birds to see here, particularly along the wooded banks of Malham Beck below the cove and on Malham Tarn itself.

NOSTERFIELD LAKES

Wetland habitat is sparse in North Yorkshire, which makes this local nature reserve all the more important. The Lower Ure Conservation Trust manages a series of flooded gravel pits which support a rich community of wildlife all year round but with particularly good numbers of winter ducks, geese and swans. As these newly created habitats mature they will only get better (page 248).

SNAIZEHOLME VALLEY

Most of the Yorkshire Dales is grey-squirrel territory but our native reds are holding on in a few coniferous woods in the northwest of the region. One of northern England's 17 refuges for the reds is in the tiny Snaizeholme Valley, just southwest of Hawes (page 173). It's cyclable from Hawes, but the road can be a bit busy. The easiest way to get there is on the shuttle bus from the town's National Park Visitor Centre (for a small charge; book online at ⊘ littlewhitebus.co.uk) but there are public footpaths in the woods if you want to pick up a trail leaflet from the centre and make your own way. A 2½-mile circular walk takes you to the viewing hide. The squirrels are there all year round and the bus operates on demand.

STAINFORTH FORCE

Since the cleaning up of the Humber Estuary, salmon have re-colonised all of the major Dales rivers. The River Ribble flows west into the Irish Sea so never lost the 'king of fish' and Stainforth Force (page 106) is still the best place in the county to watch their annual migration in October and November as they leap up the waterfall and head upstream.

STRID WOOD

Where the River Wharfe has cut a gorge through the hills north of Bolton Abbey, steep slopes support the richest ancient oak wood in the Dales. In addition to the birds mentioned on page 121, these woods also support a healthy population of badgers, roe deer and at least three species of bat. Best visited in early summer.

SUNBIGGIN TARN

One of the most incredible wildlife spectacles to be seen anywhere in the world is the pre-roost synchronised flight of a flock of starlings – a phenomenon known as a murmuration. One of the country's largest involves tens of thousands of birds and occurs at Sunbiggin Tarn near Kirkby Stephen (page 50). Fortunately for us, murmurations are fairly predictable events, happening at dusk on most autumn and winter evenings.

UPPER WHARFEDALE ESTATE

Moorland birds can be seen just about anywhere in the Yorkshire Dales above the 500-metre contour line, but many of the heather-covered hilltops are managed grouse moors. When the hills surrounding the village of Buckden, which make up the Upper Wharfedale Estate (page 137),

were donated to the National Trust, it was on the proviso that no sport shooting would take place there. Consequently, predator control and heather burning no longer take place on the estate. The result is a rich and undisturbed blanket-bog ecosystem, particularly on Cray Moss and Yockenthwaite Moor, and a much better chance of seeing birds of prey and carnivorous mammals like stoats and weasels – and red grouse of course.

SHEEP OF THE DALES

My first sighting of a **Wensleydale** sheep was as a teenager on a family trip, as I leaned over a wall near Hawes – and it remains one of the oddest-looking farm animals that I've ever seen. Wensleydales are the tallest British breed of sheep, but they still manage to grow a full-body set of dreadlocks, so long that they trail on the ground, and make the most valuable sheep's wool in the world. Sometimes called 'poor man's mohair', it is prized by local knitters; the breed almost became extinct in the 1970s, but was saved by the Rare Breeds Survival Trust.

For sheer numbers though, no breed of sheep can match the **Swaledale**, not just in Yorkshire but in all of upland northern England. The high fells and moors are dominated by these hardy, black-faced and horned ewes to such an extent that a Swaledale sheep's head was chosen as the emblem of the Yorkshire Dales National Park. These days they are crossed with Texel rams to produce good meat lambs, but back in the 1940s they were usually purebred.

Transport was more traditional then as well, as Stanley Thackray, the last living drover in Wharfedale, remembers: 'We would walk the sheep and cattle down the dale roads to market in Skipton, yes – our animals and some neighbours', for fourpence an animal. My father had a very good dog in the 40s so we were often called on, especially after another drover, Old Jossy, died. Joe Ibbotson had a cattle wagon, but there was no petrol, it being the war years, so walking the beasts was the only way.

◀ **1** Starling murmuration at Sunbiggin Tarn. **2** The exposed hilltop environment of the Dales attracts curlews among other iconic birds. **3** Badgers may be spotted at Strid Wood. **4** Otters are now thriving in all the region's rivers. **5** Red grouse is another iconic species drawn to this exposed environment.

It all stopped about 1950 when folk got hold of petrol again, and the roads became too busy – yes.'

Times have changed. These days the price of lamb is so low that most hill farmers can only survive with the help of large government subsidies and each sheep costs the taxpayer more to produce than its meat and wool are actually worth. This ridiculous and unsustainable situation has prompted some commentators to suggest a drastic scaling-down of hill-sheep farming. The removal of hundreds of thousands of sets of nibbling teeth would save millions of pounds and also allow the natural vegetation of the Yorkshire Dales to return. Perhaps in a hundred years' time the Three Peaks will float majestically above a sea of forest and the emblem of the national park will be an oak tree.

DRY STONE WALLS

The ubiquitous mortar-free walls that keep the sheep in are an iconic element of the Dales landscape, with a whole vocabulary of their own: 'smoots' and 'lunkies', for example, are types of hole built into the walls, sized to allow specific animals to pass through.

If you want to try the ancient craft for yourself, two-day courses are available from the Yorkshire Dry Stone Walling Guild (⊘ ydswg.co.uk) based in places such as Ripon and Leyburn.

THERE'S LEAD IN THEM THERE HILLS

Yorkshire lead can be found in the paint on the frescoes of Pompeii, in the plumbing of classical Rome and on the medieval roofs of Antwerp and Bordeaux. The fascinating story of how it found its way to all of these places starts millions of years ago. Geological movements caused thousands of small cracks to form in the limestone surface of the north Pennines, which filled with mineral-rich hot water from deep below the earth's crust. When it cooled it deposited crystals of various minerals, including galena or lead sulphide, and this is the ore that has been extracted on a small scale for thousands of years. We know that the Romans delved here because a block or 'pig' of lead was found stamped with the Emperor Trajan's name. Later, the rich monasteries at Fountains, Rievaulx and Jervaulx kept records of their 15th-century trade with Belgium and France.

Lead mining went large-scale between 1650 and 1900, and its impact on the landscape and rural society was devastating. Valleys that had previously only known woodland crafts and sheep farming now became brutal and polluted industrial centres. Forests were felled and hillsides shaved of peat to fuel the furnaces, and miles of tunnel were blasted out underground. One particularly destructive practice was called 'hushing', where a beck was dammed to form a reservoir above a hillside with a known lead vein. The dam was deliberately breached to cause a flash flood which would scour off all the surface soil and rock, thus exposing the valuable seam beneath.

Thousands of outsiders moved into the Dales, living in squalor for the most part, sometimes ten or twelve to a two-roomed cottage with shared beds slept in on a rota. A whole sub-culture developed, almost with its own language. A young miner would, for instance, strike a 'bar-gain', or join a 'gang' who would work underground on a 'stope'. 'Bouse' would be taken out by 'kibble' or 'whim' to fill a 'bouseteam'. This was emptied on to the 'dressing floor', the 'deads' were rejected and the remainder was 'spalled' and 'bukkered' to make it small enough to be sieved in a 'hotching tub' and then the 'slime' collected in a 'running buddle'. The ore was then 'smelted' and cast into a 'pig'. Got that? Good. Working life started at ten years old and ended on average (life that is) at 45. Life expectancy was so short because of long working hours, bad air in the mines, poisonous fumes from the smelters, tuberculosis from cramped living, and general poverty. Some miners were so poor they knitted clothes as they walked to work, to sell for a few extra pennies.

Faced with this human cost, I can't help feeling that the collapse of lead mining in the early 20th century was a blessing. Virtually no veterans with a first-hand memory of the industry survive, and the economy of the Dales has returned to sheep and, latterly, tourism. Socially, outside of museums and archives, it's as if nothing had ever happened, but up on the fellsides, scars will take longer to heal. The problem is that the lead that still remains in the 'hushed' areas and vast spoil heaps, being poisonous, stopped the vegetation regenerating. The moors around Greenhow in Nidderdale and above Grassington in Wharfedale are grim, bare and uninviting places, but nothing compared with the north side of Swaledale. The walking-guide guru Alfred Wainwright deliberately routed his Coast to Coast Walk through the worst of the damaged landscape because he felt people needed to see the consequences of irresponsible land use.

Every cloud does have a silver lining though, and in this case it is *Minuartia verna*, the spring sandwort, a beautiful and rare plant; rare, that is, virtually everywhere except on lead-mine spoil heaps. This is one of the few British plants tolerant to high levels of lead, and its neat cushions are sometimes the only life in a heavy metal desert.

DARK SKIES

Stargazing (⊘ yorkshiredales.org.uk/stargazing) – or astro-tourism, to give it its formal name – depends on night skies relatively free from human light pollution, and the Yorkshire Dales is one of the few places in England that fits the bill. The national park was granted International Dark Sky Reserve status in 2020 and holds a **Dark Skies Festival** every February around half-term, during which visitors can enjoy talks,

TEN DALES OUTDOOR SWIMMING SPOTS

Here are ten of our favourite outdoor swimming spots in the Yorkshire Dales, in north-to-south order. Informal car parking is nearby unless stated.

Near Sedbergh (River Rawthey) ⚲ SD634908 /// clincher.quietest.output. Stay at Holme Farm campsite in Sedbergh and you have gentle and refreshing river dips on-site.

Wain Wath Force (River Swale) ⚲ NY833015 /// amphibian.collides.sudden. Compact, scenic falls and pool right on the B-road a mile west of Keld.

Kisdon Force (River Swale) ⚲ NY898010 /// dreamers.egging.duos. A spectacular half-mile rocky path down the valley from Keld gets you to a series of slippery falls very popular for dips. Park in Keld.

Cotter Force (Cotterdale Beck) ⚲ SD850915 /// explains.glider.flocking. Just 400yds off the A684 along a level-access path is this secluded amphitheatrical gem of a falls and pool.

Semer Water (River Bain) ⚲ SD921875 /// alarming.crusaders.online. Shallow but inviting freshwater lake amid green hills that you'll probably have to yourself. Waterside parking for a fee at eastern end.

night hikes and canoe trips, and participate in (well-gloved) hands-on telescope sessions.

Clear (and therefore cold) nights in autumn and winter are the best times to stargaze, at places such as the Tan Hill Inn (page 157) or Lime Tree Observatory (page 248).

Various free astronomy apps can show you round the night sky on your phone, as it appears at your exact location and time – essential if you want to identify planets or spot the International Space Station. The BBC *Sky at Night Magazine* (⊘ skyatnightmagazine. com) has more details on what to see each month and which apps to download.

The Dales is also one of the best locations in England for spotting the **Northern Lights**, though the appearance of an aurora can only be tentatively predicted a couple of days or even hours beforehand. See the 'Space Weather' section of the Met Office website (⊘ metoffice.gov. uk) for day-before forecasts, and Lancaster University's Aurorawatch (⊘ aurorawatch.lancs.ac.uk) for current activity. To stand a chance of seeing anything, you need a perfectly cloudless sky looking due north near the horizon. The subtle purple and green glows are more

---

Ingleton Lido (River Doe) Sammy Ln, Ingleton LA6 3EG ⊘ 01524 241147 ⊘ ingletonpool. co.uk. Fancy something with facilities, outdoors but not 'wild'? Ingleton's open-air lido is heated outside of winter. Entry fee; park in village.

Stainforth Force (River Ribble) ♀ SD818672 ▦ elect.licks.depth. Rocky bridgeside falls very popular for family picnics and paddles in summer – and with spawning salmon in autumn.

Janet's Foss (Gordale Beck) ♀ SD911635 ▦ barrel.dearest.penned. Fairy-glade falls and pool a short rocky walk from the road, just a mile from Malham.

Burnsall (River Wharfe) ♀ SE029617 ▦ animated.hazelnuts.promotes. Half a mile up the riverside path from Burnsall village green at Loup Scar is this popular family dipping spot. Park in village.

Bolton Abbey (River Wharfe) ♀ SE075541 ▦ deck.stooping.blockage. Sprawl on the riverside green amid the free-to-visit abbey ruins; dip, splash, try the stepping-stones and enjoy an ice cream.

pronounced on a camera than to the naked eye, so don't expect a firework display. It's a subtle experience, but a magical one.

WILD SWIMMING

All the main rivers in the Dales have hidden corners where the water is clean, clear and the right depth and safe enough to swim in, and the Wharfe and Swale in particular boast some of the best wild bathing in the country. If you want advice on where to swim, then see ⌀ wildswimming.co.uk or ⌀ river-swimming.co.uk, or join the 'Dales Dippers' Facebook page for hyper-local, up-to-the-minute information and tips.

SAVOURING THE TASTE

Agriculturally, the Yorkshire Dales is primarily a pastoral region, so it's no surprise that the best-known local produce originates from cattle or sheep. Milk from local dairy herds that isn't drunk (by calves or humans) has, for hundreds of years, been the main ingredient of a variety of local **cheeses** that often take the name of their valley of production. Wensleydale is by far the most well known but Coverdale, Swaledale and Ribblesdale all have their own distinct recipes, and a trio of artisan dairies are still making the proper stuff. The Wensleydale Creamery (page 174) is in Hawes, as is the much smaller Ribblesdale Cheese Company (page 176), while Reeth in Swaledale is the home of Lacey's Cheese (page 154). Beginners' courses in cheesemaking can be done at Ribblesdale and Lacey's and also at the Courtyard Dairy near Austwick (page 74), which also boasts a wonderful cheese shop and museum. One other excellent cheese shop deserving a mention is the Churchmouse at Barbon (page 91).

A local Dales dairy product less traditional Yorkshire than cheese, but just as popular, is **ice cream**. Delicious farm-produced ice cream can be slurped at Sedbergh (page 66), Bolton Abbey, Richmond (page 167), Austwick (page 74), Aysgarth (page 188) and Risplith (page 242).

Not all the cattle in the Dales belong to dairy herds; higher up the fellsides beef cattle predominate and the best limestone **beef** can be bought direct from the producers at Town End Farm in Malhamdale (page 119) and Springhill Farm near Masham (◼ Springhill Beef

SQUIDBEAK

🖉 squidbeak.co.uk

Pubs and restaurants open and close with alarming regularity and good chefs move on, leaving a recommended place average and their new kitchen brilliant but unknown. Wouldn't it be great if there were a website run by truly independent food enthusiasts who keep abreast of what's happening gastronomically in Yorkshire, and keep us informed? Hurrah, there is!

Squidbeak is run by Jill Turton and Mandy Wragg, two professional restaurant critics who both live in Yorkshire and share a love of unpretentious, high-quality food. The website (which, incidentally, took its name from a sarcastic graffitied recipe in a posh restaurant – 'Squidbeak of a bum-arse on a bed of bum gravy') doesn't just cover eateries, but also Yorkshire produce, recipes and places to stay.

and Lamb). When it comes to meat though, it's **lamb and mutton** for which this part of the country is famed – there are nearly half a million sheep here, after all. Every Dales town or village butcher will sell locally reared lamb, and maybe mutton if you're lucky. Swaledale Butchers (🖉 swaledale.co.uk) sells high-quality meat from several small-scale, sustainable Dales farms.

Great quality **fish** can also be found in the Dales: rainbow trout from Kilnsey Trout Farm (page 134) and, perhaps surprisingly so far from the coast, fresh sea fish at the Punch Bowl Inn in Low Row (page 152) and Whitby lobsters at the Sportsman's Arms in Wath (page 217). Notable seafood restaurants are The Fleece, Addingham (page 124) and the Wensleydale Heifer, West Witton (page 193). For top-quality **restaurant food** across the board it's hard to beat Where There's Smoke, in Masham (page 254).

The climate of the Yorkshire Dales doesn't lend itself to wine or cider production, so **beer** tends to be the tipple of choice, with a dozen or so breweries operating in the area. They range from household names like the Theakston and Black Sheep breweries of Masham (page 252) down to barn-behind-the-pub micro-breweries like the wonderful Dark Horse Brewery in Hetton (page 112).

Learning how to cook like the experts has become a very popular activity in recent years, and two venues here offer **cookery schools** all year round: Bettys in Harrogate (page 232) and Swinton Park near Masham (page 249).

FOOD FESTIVALS

Cookery workshops are often on offer at **food festivals** and the annual gastronomic events that happen in the Dales region:

Harrogate Food & Drink Festival Harrogate ⊘ harrogatefoodfestival.com
⊙ Jun & Aug
Yorkshire Dales Food & Drink Festival Skipton ⊘ yorkshiredalesfoodanddrinkfestival.
com ⊙ Jul
Taste Cumbria Kirkby Lonsdale ⊘ tastecumbria.com ⊙ Sep
Cheese Festival Across the Dales region ⊘ yorkshiredales.org.uk ⊙ Oct

FARMERS' MARKETS

Apart from farm-gate stalls and honesty-box eggs and jam by the roadside, farmers' markets are probably the best source of genuinely local, Slow produce. They generally take place once a month during summer.

Grassington The Square ⊙ Mar–Sep 3rd Sun
Harrogate Cambridge St ⊙ 2nd Thu
Masham Market Pl ⊙ Apr–Oct 1st Sun
Orton Market Hall ⊙ 2nd Sat
Skipton The Canal Basin ⊙ 1st & 3rd Sun

More general weekly markets are held all year round in various places. They usually include a few farmer's outlets among the stalls.

Hawes Burtersett Rd ⊙ Tue
Leyburn Market Pl ⊙ Fri
Reeth Market Sq ⊙ Fri
Ripon Town Sq ⊙ Thu & Sat
Sedbergh Joss Lane Car Park ⊙ Wed
Settle Market Pl ⊙ Tue

AGRICULTURAL SHOWS

The **Great Yorkshire Show** at Harrogate's showground in July is one of Britain's most spectacular celebrations of rural life (⊘ greatyorkshireshow. co.uk). The four-day event transforms the normally quiet venue into a marqueed, thronging small town, with shops and restaurants selling local food and drink interspersed with arts and crafts emporia, tractor exhibitions, log-cabin makers and much more. Events range from bird-of-prey demos to international-quality showjumping competitions in the main ring.

Perhaps the most characteristic experience is wandering around enormous livestock display and parade spaces, spotting rare or distinctive breeds of cattle, sheep and pigs. Chatting to exhibitors is one of the joys of the event, and gives a vivid immersion into modern Dales life.

There are several other agricultural shows round the region during the summer. Though smaller in scope, they are lively and welcoming

SLOW ENCOUNTERS

Chance meetings are all part of the Slow Travel experience: you have the time to talk to locals, to get a feel for the place and its people. Yorkshire Dales folk are a down-to-earth lot, practical, open, friendly and collaborative – and often chatty. You will encounter many regional British accents these days in addition to native Yorkshire tones; the era of impenetrable country dialects varying from dale to dale are long gone. To hear what we've lost, visit ⊘ dialectandheritage.org.uk.

While updating this edition, I had several Slow encounters that seemed to personify the atmosphere of the Yorkshire Dales. Here are three of them:

I was mountain-biking a rough bridleway through a hilltop farm near Malham when it started bucketing down with rain. I dived into an open-fronted farm building to wait out the shower – and saw the farmer marching determinedly towards me. I prepared excuses and apologies… only to find he'd come to offer me tea and cake, and friendly, useful

route advice. When the rain stopped, I set off, refreshed, with the pedalling equivalent of a spring in my step.

Cycling the Swale Trail early one autumn morning, I came across a rifle-toting local out shooting rabbits. He had a couple of them suspended from a bar across his shoulders, destined for local pubs. When he learnt I was staying at the nearby youth hostel, he cheerily offered me one of them as a gift, saying it would make a grand stew. I reluctantly declined: I might not have made myself popular in the hostel kitchen having had a dead animal in my pannier all day on a hot, bumpy ride.

On another occasion, I hesitated to set off on my bike back to the train station after visiting a stately home, seeing that a storm was brewing. A passing local driver, noticing me gaze anxiously at the black skies, stopped unbidden and gave me a lift, my bike stowed in the back of her car amid bags and piles of farm equipment. Half an hour later, we'd swopped addresses and life stories.

celebrations, with plenty of chance to savour a genuinely Slow Dales atmosphere. Don't come in your best shoes!

Gargrave Show ⬦ gargraveshow.org.uk ☉ Aug
Kilnsey Show ⬦ kilnseyshow.co.uk ☉ Aug
Malham Show ⬦ malhamshow.co.uk ☉ Aug
Reeth Show ⬦ reethshow.co.uk ☉ Aug
Ripley Show ⬦ ripleyshow.co.uk ☉ Aug
Wensleydale Show (Leyburn) ⬦ wensleydaleshow.org.uk ☉ Aug
Moorcock Show ⬦ moorcockshow.co.uk ☉ Sep
Muker Show ⬦ mukershow.co.uk ☉ Sep
Nidderdale Show (Pateley Bridge) ⬦ nidderdaleshow.co.uk ☉ Sep

THE DALES ON SCREEN

The Yorkshire Dales are a frequent setting for fictional and reality television series, and often form the backdrop in feature films.

The most striking screen appearance of the region has been in two versions of *All Creatures Great and Small*, both light-hearted dramatisations of the books by James Herriot that recount tales of a vet's life working in the Dales and nearby Yorkshire Moors in the mid-1900s.

The original BBC series (1978–1990) was mainly filmed in Askrigg (the 'Darrowby' of the books; page 181) and Bainbridge, though various locations in Swaledale, Wensleydale and others were used at times. The Red Lion pub in Arkengarthdale (page 157) appears in some scenes, while the 'Drover's Arms' of 'Darrowby' was the King's Arms in Askrigg. In Channel 5's current version, running since 2020, 'Darrowby' is Grassington (page 124) – the 'Drover's Arms' is The Devonshire in the town square (exterior scenes) and the Green Dragon in Hardraw (interior scenes; page 179).

The durable ITV soap *Emmerdale* is now shot in an artificial village outside Leeds, but back when it started in 1971 it was filmed in Littondale (page 139), with 'The Woolpack' pub the Falcon Inn, in Arncliffe.

Perhaps the most notable of the various reality TV series based in the region is *Our Yorkshire Farm*, which ran on Channel 5 in the 2010s and followed the working lives of Amanda and Clive Owen (and their nine children) at remote Ravenseat Farm, up a track from Swaledale, west of Keld (page 146).

As for **feature films**, *Harry Potter and the Deathly Hallows* (2010) was filmed in Malham Cove and Kirkby Malham. A memorable scene in *Robin Hood Prince of Thieves* (1991), when Robin battles Little John, took place at Aysgarth Falls (page 186); Robin also bathes in Hardraw Force at one point (page 179). *Calendar Girls* (2003) was filmed in and around Kettlewell (page 136) but the girls themselves stripped off in Rylstone (page 112).

For more on filming locations, see the 'Filming' pages of ⊘ yorkshiredales.org.uk.

CAR-FREE TRAVEL

Most people get here and travel around within the area by car. However, a growing number of visitors to the Dales are doing it without their cars. Car-free travel is at the root of the Slow mindset, and this edition was researched through summer and autumn entirely by train, bus and bike. Planned well and done properly, this can be a really liberating experience. The national park authority (⊘ yorkshiredales.org.uk) is very supportive of this idea – not surprisingly, it wants more people in the park but fewer cars, so it has a whole section of its website devoted to encouraging this.

TRAINS

As you would expect from a mountainous region, railways tend to skirt the edges, getting you to outlying towns and villages like Skipton, Settle, Clapham, Northallerton, Harrogate and Knaresborough, but not into the interior. The one glorious exception is the Settle to Carlisle line (page 107), which ploughs straight through the middle of the Dales, giving access to Horton in Ribblesdale, Dentdale, Garsdale/Wensleydale heads and Kirkby Stephen.

A couple of short, private railways add to the picture, but because they are not fully linked to the National Rail system, they are not of huge use to car-free travellers. The operator of the Embsay line is working hard to join it up to Skipton, as is the Wensleydale Railway Association to Northallerton, but these are very long-term projects.

We could moan at length about the inadequacies of our National Rail system (and I often do) but one aspect they need hearty congratulations for is the free-transport-of-bikes rule.

This facility opens up so many doors for cyclists, who either don't own a car or are tired of doing circular routes back to the starting point. Using the train to gain altitude and save your legs is a good ploy; you could, for instance, take your bike on the train to Ribblehead and freewheel back to Settle or Clapham via Ingleton. Likewise, Dent Station gives a nice quiet run down to Sedbergh and Oxenholme Station beyond. Garsdale Station allows a similar downhill trip to Kirkby Stephen.

You need to book a cycle space in advance if going to Northallerton, but all the other stations mentioned here are serviced by Northern Trains, for which you can simply turn up and walk your bike on. There's an official limit of two cycles per train, but in practice nobody seems to mind more than that, as long as common sense is employed and nowhere gets blocked.

BUSES

Without a bike in tow you also have the bus network at your disposal. There's a handy summary of services under 'Visit the Dales' on ⬄ yorkshiredales.org.uk.

Probably the best deal on offer is the **Dales Rover Ticket**, giving you unlimited bus journeys for the day within the Dales, and deals from many local businesses like cafés, pubs, B&Bs and attractions. If they display a 'Dales Bus Discount Scheme' sticker, you will get some freebie or other, even if it's only a cup of tea.

Ingleton Twelve buses a day from Lancaster (80, 81, 82, 580, 581, 583) and ten from Settle and Skipton (580, 581, 583).

Kirkby Lonsdale Ten buses a day to Settle and Skipton (580/581) and 12 to Lancaster (81, 82).

Leyburn Five buses a day from Bedale (155) and seven from Richmond (159). Four buses a day along Wensleydale to Hawes (156).

Masham Four buses on Tuesdays, Wednesdays and Fridays from Bedale (144) and five a day (except Sundays) from Ripon (138, 159).

Pateley Bridge Eight buses a day (three on school days only) from Harrogate (24).

◀ 1 Dry-stone walling – an iconic part of the Dales landscape. 2 Wild swimming at Wain Wath Force. 3 Sampling the flavours on offer at the Harrogate Food Festival. 4 Tours of Wensleydale Creamery involve some sampling. 5 Scenes from the Great Yorkshire Show.

Richmond Very regular buses from Darlington (X26, X27, 29, 34) and three buses a day from Northallerton (55). Three buses a day to Reeth (30).

Ripon Very regular buses from Leeds, York and Harrogate (22, 36) and five a day from both Thirsk and Northallerton (70).

Sedbergh Not well served. A few services a week to Kirkby Stephen, Penrith and Kendal; check ⊘ westerndalesbus.co.uk.

All the other smaller places up the Dales are served by the **Dales Explorer Bus** (⊘ dalesbus.org). Almost every hamlet gets a visit at some point, even if it is just once a week in summer, like poor old Scar House in **Nidderdale**. Many routes operate weekdays and all year round, but quite a few extra leisure services are put on for the summer months (Easter to October); these are usually only Sundays and bank holidays. The four-hour Sunday trip from York to Hawes on the 875 Dales Bus, for instance, is one of Britain's most scenic bus journeys.

BOAT TRIPS & WATERSPORTS

Unless you count the rowing boats on the River Nidd at Knaresborough, the Leeds and Liverpool Canal at Skipton is the one and only **boating venue** in the Dales, but it does offer a variety of options. You can join half-hour or one-hour trips in and around town, or hire a boat for a day, weekend or entire week. Westwards is the more rural and unspoilt direction to sail from Skipton, but even this choice turns away from the Dales and into the lowlands on its journey towards Lancashire; a tour of farm country – nice and certainly Slow, if tame.

Canoeing and **kayaking** are possible on some rivers, but the access situation is complex. You need to know what you're doing, in which case you're probably already a member of British Canoeing (⊘ britishcanoeing.org.uk), which can advise on options in detail. The River Ure between Hack Falls and Sleningford Mill is a popular five-mile paddle. **Canals** are more straightforward, and there's easy access and pleasant paddling to be had on Ripon Canal (page 243) and the Leeds and Liverpool Canal between Gargrave and Settle (page 110).

Sailing, **stand-up paddleboarding** and **windsurfing** are also possible on Semer Water (page 183) for a small fee. The reservoirs at Embsay

1 The Dales area offers some of Britain's most rewarding cycling, at whatever pace. 2 The Dales' waterways attract kayakers and canoeists, such as here at Linton Falls (page 126). ▶

and Grimwith are other options. For more information, consult the Yorkshire Dales Sailing Club (⌀ yorkshiredales.sc). Note that Malham Tarn is off-limits to all watersports.

Aquatic activities of various types are available at **How Stean Gorge activity centre** (page 215). These include kayaking on Scar House Reservoir (on which it has exclusive access) or paddleboarding along Ripon Canal.

Pennine Cruisers Coach St, Skipton ⌀ 01756 795478 ⌀ penninecruisers.com. Half-hour public cruises around the back of Skipton castle. Daily self-drive hire of a 30ft narrowboat for up to ten people, also evenings. Half-week and full-week holidays with four or eight berths.

Skipton Boat Trips Coach St, Skipton ⌀ 01756 790829 ⌀ canaltrips.co.uk. One-hour public cruises on a 58ft narrowboat (Mar–Nov daily). Catered private charters available. Also has narrowboats for day hire.

Snaygill Boats Bradley ⌀ 01756 795150 ⌀ snaygillboats.co.uk. A similar day and holiday hire service to Pennine Cruisers, but from a village two miles away.

CYCLING

The Yorkshire Dales has always been a popular destination for road cyclists, many of them pedalling along the two well-established touring routes that pass through the region. The Way of the Roses route, 170 miles coast to coast from Morecambe to Bridlington, traverses the region from west to east. Some keen types do it in one long summer day; three or four days is more like it for most people. Meanwhile, the Pennine Cycleway also spans the Dales, but from south to north, on its 355-mile odyssey between Derby and Berwick-upon-Tweed. The two routes cross at Settle.

Another very popular loop entirely within the area is the 130-mile Yorkshire Dales Cycleway. It is designed to be started and finished at Skipton but as it is circular it can, of course, be initiated anywhere along its length. An optional extra 20-mile section was added in 2016 to sample the new part of the national park in the west. The Park has produced a handy little pamphlet, *Cycling in the Yorkshire Dales National Park*, to introduce these routes but by far the best source of information is their website ⌀ cyclethedales.org.uk.

Yorkshire's already-strong cycling tradition received a boost in 2014 when the first two days of the Tour de France took place in the county. The first stage showcased the Dales: a 110-mile pedal starting in Leeds, travelling up most of Wharfedale and down most of Wensleydale, with a brief visit to Swaledale before finishing at Harrogate. The verges were packed with onlookers, and the sight of the peloton vaulting Buttertubs Pass through cheering

BIKE FACILITIES IN THE YORKSHIRE DALES

In the list below, 'e' denotes e-bikes available for rent.

	Hire	Shop	Repairs
3 Peaks Cycles Settle	✓ e	✓	✓
360 Cycleworx Bedale		✓	✓
Arthur Caygill Cycles Richmond		✓	✓
Aurelius Cycles Gargrave		✓	✓
Chevin Cycles Harrogate		✓	✓
Chevin Cycles Skipton		✓	✓
Coast to Coast Cycles Kirkby Stephen		✓	✓
Dales Bike Centre Reeth	✓ e	✓	✓
Dave Ferguson Cycles Skipton		✓	✓
Escape Bike Shop Ingleton		✓	✓
Grassington e-Bikes Grassington	✓ e		
J D Tandems Gargrave	✓	✓	
Moonglu Ripon		✓	✓
Nidderdale Cycle Hire Pateley Bridge	✓		
North Yorkshire e-bikes Knaresborough	✓ e		
Prologue Cycling Harrogate		✓	✓
Sedbergh e-Bike Hire Sedbergh	✓ e		
Specialized Harrogate		✓	✓
Stage 1 Cycles Hawes	✓ e	✓	✓
Stif Cycles Pateley Bridge		✓	
Vern Overton Cycles Harrogate	✓		✓
Yorkshire Bike Company Grassington		✓	✓

TEN TOP ROAD BIKE RIDES

Here is a list of ten of our favourite one-day circular bike rides in the Yorkshire Dales, ranging from ten miles to 60-plus. They're all fairly strenuous apart from the first, but very rewarding in terms of views, and almost all on quiet roads.

Harrogate train station to Ripley, Knaresborough and back on NCN7 and NCN626 (19 miles; page 236)

Reeth to Keld and back along Swaledale (different sides out and back; 25 miles)

Ingleton – Chapel le Dale – Ribblehead – Stone House – Dentdale – Dent – Kingsdale – Ingleton (31 miles)

Reeth – Swaledale – Keld – Tan Hill Inn – Arkengarthdale – Langthwaite – Reeth (35 miles)

Reeth – Redmire – Wensleydale – Askrigg – Hawes – Buttertubs – Thwaite – Swaledale – Reeth (36 miles)

Sedbergh – Dentdale – Dent – Gawthrop – Barbondale – Kirkby Lonsdale – Middleton – Sedbergh (43 miles)

Malham – Gargrave – Leeds and Liverpool Canal – Skipton – Embsay – Bolton Abbey – Wharfedale – Grassington – Arncliffe – Malham Tarn – Malham (44 miles)

Leyburn – Middleham – Coverdale – Kettlewell – Cray – Bishopdale – Aysgarth – Castle Bolton – Wensley – Leyburn (45 miles)

Hawes – Oughtershaw – Wharfedale – Kettlewell – Littondale – Arncliffe – Stainforth – Ribblehead – Hawes (53 miles)

Masham – Middleham – Coverdale – Kettlewell – Wharfedale – Grassington – Appletreewick – Pateley Bridge – Nidderdale – Lofthouse – Masham (63 miles)

crowds was a memorable spectacle. If you want to emulate the route and ride it yourself, visit the excellent cycle.travel website (⬧ cycle.travel/route/tour_de_yorkshire).

The success of those first two days inspired the Tour de Yorkshire, an annual cycle race round the county that attracted top international riders when it ran from 2015 to 2019. Sadly, for various reasons including the effect of pandemics, it has not run since.

A colourful legacy of that 2014 Tour, and the Tours de Yorkshire, is the sight of bicycles painted yellow (sometimes blue) decorating buildings, shops, farms, roadsides and trees. They were put up by locals to celebrate the races going past, and are now part of the landscape.

If you fancy exploring the Dales by bike but are put off by the hills, hiring an **e-bike** could be for you. Their battery-powered motor provides assistance to your pedalling, rather than replacing it, and the maximum help comes when you most need it, so you can actually relish whizzing up hills or into headwinds.

ACCESSIBILITY IN THE DALES

Stiles, steps, gates, steep rocky paths, narrow winding staircases in ancient buildings – the Dales present mobility challenges to all visitors, but especially users of wheelchairs or walking aids. However, the situation is improving every year, with more and more visitor attractions, outdoor routes and accommodation becoming accessible. Skipton's recently reconfigured Museum and Visitor Centre (page 110), for instance, prides itself as being convenient for everyone, while Aysgarth Falls (page 186) has a good level-access path, and The Burgoyne in Reeth (page 153) offers a wheelchair-positive room.

The excellent website Access the Dales ($\oslash$ access-the-dales.com) lists wheelchair-friendly places to eat, drink and stay, and has details of seven or eight wheelchair hubs across the Dales. Here, in places such as Richmond, Aysgarth Falls, Malham and Nateby (Kirkby Stephen), you can borrow trekking wheelchairs to take you over the toughest terrain.

HOW THIS BOOK IS ARRANGED

MAPS

The colour map at the front of this book shows the area of land that falls within each chapter. The chapters themselves begin with a more detailed map bearing numbered points which correspond to numbered headings in the text. Featured walks have an even larger scale map accompanying them.

By far the most complete and useful maps for walking, cycling, horse-riding and general sightseeing are the OS 1:25,000 scale Explorer series. Those covering the region described in this book are:

• OL2 Yorkshire Dales – Southern & Western areas.
• OL19 Howgill Fells & Upper Eden Valley.
• OL30 Yorkshire Dales – Northern & Central areas.
• 298 Nidderdale.

Other maps specifically designed for hillwalkers, fell runners or cyclists, with bags of useful extra information, are produced by Harveys (⊘ harveymaps.co.uk). Their Dales titles include:

AN ACCESS PIONEER

Campaigner and motivational speaker Debbie North, the woman behind Access the Dales (page 39), has a simple mission: to open the countryside to everyone. She and her team are dedicated to increasing the availability of all-terrain wheelchairs in the Yorkshire Dales, ensuring that people with disabilities can freely explore and experience what she calls 'the healing wonders of nature'.

'Back when we gained charity status in August 2022', says Debbie, 'we had ambitious plans for three wheelchair hubs. Fast forward to October 2023, and we've proudly established seven hubs, with three more on the horizon in the Forest of Bowland National Landscape. It's been an incredible journey. The welcoming reception from the Dales community has been heartwarming. The positive feedback from those we've assisted reaffirms that we're making a meaningful difference in people's lives.

'One of the most special stile-free walks for me is on the fells above Nateby, close to Kirkby Stephen. When my husband Andy and I lived there, we cherished exploring these open-access fells together. Although I've since moved homes following Andy's passing in 2021, I still frequent these hills. They hold a trove of cherished memories, and being there allows me to spend quiet moments alone, reminiscing about our happy times together.

'That's why we've established a hub at Rakehead Farm in Nateby – to provide others with a chance to relish a similar experience. The breathtaking 360-degree views encompass the Lake District, the North Pennines, Wild Boar Fell and the Howgills, making it an extraordinary spot for anyone seeking the beauty and tranquillity of these hills.

'At the wheelchair hub located at Richmond Swimming Pool, visitors have the fantastic opportunity to borrow a mobility scooter. They can then relish a delightful stroll along the old railway line leading to Easby Abbey. The pathway is even, offering a smooth and picturesque walk on a well-maintained track. Tea and cake at The Station makes for a perfect conclusion to the experience!'

Debbie is always on the lookout for passionate individuals to join Access the Dales, as trustees or volunteers. You can contact her through the Access the Dales website.

• Mountain Map 1:40,000 Yorkshire Dales.
• Superwalker 1:25,000 – four maps covering the whole area except some of the new parts of the national park.
• Dales Way 1:40,000.
• Nidderdale Way 1:40,000.
• *Eight Walks Centred On* series – day walks around popular Dales towns and villages including Grassington, Pateley Bridge, Reeth, Settle, Skipton, Sedbergh and Hawes.
• Yorkshire Dales for Cyclists 1:100,000. With information about shops, repair and hire as well as some town plans.

Also, look out for the classic series of local walk maps hand-drawn in black and red ink by Arthur Gemmell, and unchanged in style for nearly half a century.

In this book, *III* denotes a 'What3words' location (⌖ what3words.com). The system, which you can consult online or via apps, uniquely encodes every 10ft × 10ft square in the world by a combination of three words. It can be a quick and accurate way of locating somewhere off the beaten track, especially for emergency services (who recognise the format). For instance, the summit of Pen-y-ghent is at 'headboard.manages.parent'.

ACCOMMODATION

Bed-and-breakfasts, pub rooms and **country hotels** abound, many of them stylish and well-appointed. There are over a hundred campsites in the Dales area. However, many sites these days only offer large expensive pitches aimed at car-campers, with electric hookups. Websites such as ⌖ ukcampsite.co.uk and ⌖ pitchup.com can help with your requirements. There's plenty of opportunity for **glamping**; search Sawdays (⌖ sawdays. co.uk) or Canopy and Stars (⌖ canopyandstars.co.uk).

If you want to keep things basic (and reasonably cheap) but also stay indoors, your main options are **hostels and bunkhouses**; the Dales has about two dozen, most easily found by a Google search. Unfortunately many cater only for pre-booked groups now. Honourable exceptions exist though, including the hostel at Kirkby Stephen and Broadrake Bunkbarn near Ribblehead. Many bunkbarns have closed, but a few new ones are opening, such as that planned for Hudswell, outside Richmond.

The **YHA hostels** at Hawes, Reeth (Grinton), Kettlewell, Ingleton and Malham still have dorm beds for individuals, at least, and are ideally set up for Slow travel. Check the YHA website (⌖ yha.org.uk) for special offers in winter, when you can often snap up a bed for less than the price of a pub dinner. For other hostels and bunkhouses, try ⊘ yorkshiredales. org.uk and ⊘ independenthostels.co.uk.

Special stays

The places to stay listed in each chapter are a personal selection of bed and breakfasts, campsites, self-catering cottages and one or two very special hotels – places that struck us for their location, friendliness or character, or a mixture of all three.

The hotels, bed and breakfasts and hostels are indicated by the symbol ♠ under the heading for the nearest town or village in which they are located; self-catering options by ⌂. Camping options, which cover everything from full-on glamping to no-frills pitches, are indicated with a ⋏ symbol.

FOOD & DRINK

Recommended places for food and drink include restaurants, cafés, pubs, farm shops, delis and suchlike. Inclusion is my choice alone with no charge having been paid by the outlet. My selection criteria are quality, value and 'Slow' credentials such as home-grown vegetables or meat from named local farms. Food miles are important but I was willing to make exceptions – seafood restaurants for instance.

I'm very fussy about my pubs and like them to be as 'unimproved' as possible, not exclusively foodie and a genuine part of the community that they are in – in short, a proper local. As for beer, I will not allow keg or smooth-flow liquids to pass my lips, so you can rest assured that every pub or inn included serves cask beer, usually brewed locally.

OPENING HOURS

In listings, you can assume shops, cafés, tourist information offices, attractions and so on are open every day unless we state otherwise (with the ☉ symbol).

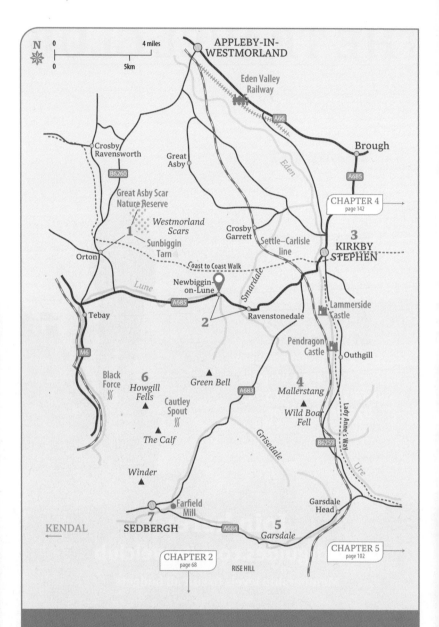

N

| 0 | | 4 miles |
| 0 | 5km | |

APPLEBY-IN-
WESTMORLAND

Eden Valley
Railway

A66

Brough

Crosby
Ravensworth

B6260

Great
Asby

A685

Great Asby Scar
Nature Reserve

CHAPTER 4
page 142

*Westmorland
Scars*

Crosby
Garrett

Settle–Carlisle
line

1

3

KIRKBY
STEPHEN

Sunbiggin
Tarn

Orton

Coast to Coast Walk

Newbiggin-
on-Lune

A685

Smardale

Lune

Lammerside
Castle

Tebay

2

Ravenstonedale

M6

Pendragon
Castle

Outhgill

Black
Force

6

Green Bell

A683

4

Mallerstang

*Howgill
Fells*

Cautley
Spout

*Wild Boar
Fell*

The Calf

Grisedale

B6259

Lady Anne's Way

Ure

Winder

Garsdale
Head

KENDAL

7

Farfield
Mill

SEDBERGH

A684

5

Garsdale

CHAPTER 2
page 68

RISE HILL

CHAPTER 5
page 102

THE CUMBRIAN CORNER

1
THE CUMBRIAN CORNER

The northwestern corner of the Yorkshire Dales National Park is made up of three separate upland massifs, each with a very different character: the Howgill Fells, Baugh and Wild Boar Fells, and the Westmorland Scars. Most of the watercourses here drain southwestwards into the River Lune but in the north the beautiful River Eden flows in the opposite direction through Kirkby Stephen on its way towards Carlisle and the Solway Firth.

Despite the name, very little of this section of the Yorkshire Dales National Park – which gained the 'Cumbrian corner' when it was extended in 2016 – is actually 'in Yorkshire'. (Much of it comes from the historical county of Westmorland.) Boundary changes over the years have caused many an identity crisis. Today Sedbergh, for instance, is in the historical county of Yorkshire (since time immemorial), the ceremonial county of Cumbria (since 1974), but the council area of Westmorland and Furness (since 2023)!

As well as being the newest part of the national park, the Cumbrian corner is without doubt the quietest. Even at the peak of the tourist season when thousands of people are queueing to climb the Three Peaks and Wensleydale's tea shops are bursting at the seams, it is still possible to stride along Mallerstang Edge or explore the flora of Great Asby Scar National Nature Reserve without seeing another person all day.

SELF-POWERED TRAVEL

CYCLING

For road cycling I think this is a region of two halves – the southern section poor and the northern bit brilliant. My preferences are based on the availability of traffic-free country lanes with no monstrous gradients, so the network of quiet, minor roads around the Westmorland Scars suits me down to the ground. Sustrans agree and have their route 68 passing through Great and Little Asby and Orton on its way south, but could just as easily have routed it through Maulds Meaburn, Crosby Ravensworth and Crosby Garrett.

There's a thrilling circular 23-mile mountain bike route taking you to Smardale, Whygill Head and Great Asby. For details, pick up the leaflet 'Kirkby Stephen Cycle' from the town's Tourist Information Office.

There are far fewer roads in the more mountainous south and they are generally big and very busy – not everyone's cup of tea. The one exception is a minor road that skirts the western side of the Howgill Fells, following the Lune Valley from Sedbergh to Tebay. If you ignore the close-up view of the M6 it is a delight and makes the continuation of the Sustrans route 68 mentioned above. The return to Sedbergh from Ravenstonedale along the A683, passing Cautley Spout, actually isn't too bad: the road is not that busy and is downhill almost all the way. The only other road route I would consider here is a lazy downhill-only stretch from Garsdale Head to Kirkby Stephen, having first taken my bike uphill to the start on the Settle–Carlisle train. Off-road biking here is generally sparse, although some disused railways near Kirkby Stephen can be ridden.

HORSERIDING

The Pennine Bridleway passes though the Mallerstang Valley and over Wild Boar Fell to terminate (or start if you choose to go north to south) at Ravenstonedale. There are plans to extend the route up into Northumberland when funding allows.

WALKING

Four **long-distance footpaths** pass over the land covered in this chapter, two of which were first described by the famous Alfred Wainwright. His **Coast to Coast Walk** was designed to be travelled west to east and, after traversing the Lake District, it enters the Yorkshire Dales National Park at the tiny hamlet of Oddendale, near M6 junction 39. For the next 20 or so miles it crosses the Westmorland Scars, returning to 'civilisation' again at Kirkby Stephen. Mr Wainwright's other long-distance route, **A Pennine Journey**, crosses the Coast to Coast at Kirkby Stephen; to the north it then heads off to Hadrian's wall but southwards visits Garsdale Head via the valley of Mallerstang before skirting Baugh Fell and the Howgills en route to Sedbergh, all within this region. The **Dales High Way**, as its name suggests, doesn't skirt anything but deliberately scales the highest ground available between Saltaire and Appleby. Here it does a full traverse of the Howgill Fells from Sedbergh to Newbiggin-on-Lune then does the same over Asby Scar. The last long-distance walk of the four celebrates the achievements of the remarkable 17th-century aristocrat Lady Anne Clifford. The 100 splendid miles of **Lady Anne's Way** link many of the grand buildings she was responsible for renovating between Skipton and Penrith, and travels along the valley of Mallerstang en route.

All manner of **shorter walks** are available, many following the banks of the Rivers Lune, Rawthey, Clough and Eden or the trackbeds of old railways. Fortuitously, some of the most pleasant stretches of river are very accessible from towns and villages; a delightful loop of the **River Rawthey** can be followed just south of Sedbergh town centre with another opportunity beside the River Eden as it cascades through a gorge to the east of Kirkby Stephen. You can cross the Rawthey at the footbridge south of Sedbergh, but the old railway bridge south of Brigflatts is fenced off.

If you would like the riverbank to yourself, the section of the Dales Way following the **River Lune** upstream from the A684 bridge west of Sedbergh always seems quiet as does the lovely wooded stretch of the **River Clough** by Farfield Mill (page 65). More challenging short walks, with some serious gradients and testing navigation, particularly in poor weather, can be found anywhere in the Howgill Fells (page 60).

THE WESTMORLAND SCARS & KIRKBY STEPHEN

1 ORTON & THE SCARS

In the Neolithic and Bronze Ages, our ancestors tended to live away from swampy valley bottoms, settling higher up where soils were thin enough for them to clear forests easily. They must have loved the area that we now call the Westmorland Scars because their cairns, stone circles and remains of settlements seem to be everywhere here. Apart from sheep and walkers, these limestone plateaus are deserted nowadays and human settlements have grown up around the fringes of the limestone scars at Crosby Ravensworth, Great Asby, Crosby Garrett and, marginally the largest of all, Orton.

I like Orton – it manages to be bustling and purposeful yet peaceful at the same time. Although granted a market town charter in the Middle Ages, it decided to remain a village and this air of modesty has remained with it to this day. That said, with its church, chapel, cafés, pub and thriving post-office-cum-shop, Orton isn't short of facilities for locals or visitors. Many of the latter come very specifically on the second Saturday of the month because this is when Orton's highly regarded farmers' market takes place. Another big draw for those with a sweet tooth is the chocolate shop on Front Street. Just south of the Orton Scar Café, opposite the toilets, the bus shelter has a free book exchange/library and 'four seasons' murals, and makes a handy place to snack or hide from the rain.

Great Asby Scar Nature Reserve

This rocky plateau and its attendant grass-dominated flora constitute one of the UK's richest but most vulnerable ecosystems. The Yorkshire Dales boasts the lion's share of the country's karst topography (as geographers call it) and internationally famous examples sit on the flanks of the Three Peaks and at the top of Malham Cove. Here in the new, northwest corner of the national park is another huge and little-known area of limestone pavement sometimes known as the Westmorland Scars. In his seminal walking guide *A Coast to Coast Walk*, Alfred Wainwright described it as, 'rarely visited and relatively unknown, almost a blank on the map, yet for the observant a region of immense fascination'.

Although continuous for 15 square miles, different sections of it go by various names – Orton Scar, Grange Scar, Little Asby Scar and Gaythorne Plain, for example. The large central section known as **Great Asby Scar** has been designated a National Nature Reserve primarily to

---

1 Great Asby Scar. 2 & 3 Dark red helleborine and Solomon's seal can be found in the karst landscape of this area. 4 Sunbiggin Tarn. ▶

protect and conserve the geological features of the pavement itself, but also some rare and very particular plants that thrive in this environment.

"Great Asby Scar is also home to the most impressive prehistoric archaeological site in the region: Castle Folds."

Botanists get particularly excited by the angular Solomon's seal, dark red helleborines and autumn gentians that grow in the 'grykes' between eroding limestone blocks. As an added bonus, Great Asby Scar is also home to the most impressive prehistoric archaeological site in the region: Castle Folds is a fortified Romano-British settlement near the high point of the scar affording glorious views in all directions for those that make the effort to get there.

When Mr Wainwright first designed his coast-to-coast route in 1973, this section posed him severe navigational headaches due to its lack of public rights-of-way. Today, open access legislation allows us to explore anywhere on these heights at will, but great care needs to be taken negotiating the loose rock and extreme convolutions underfoot.

Sunbiggin Tarn

Lakes tend to be few and far between in limestone areas where water disappears underground through the porous rocks of the hillsides. Sunbiggin Tarn's rarity makes it popular with wildlife and visiting humans alike. In summertime, a large colony of black-headed gulls nest here as well as significant numbers of other waterbirds, like wigeon, gadwall, little grebe and water rail. At other times of year it's an important migration stop-off for many other birds – ospreys often call in for a fish supper. Among birdwatchers this place is probably best known for its spectacular autumn starling roost displays (page 21).

¶¶ FOOD & DRINK

The Butchers Arms Crosby Ravensworth CA10 3JP ℰ 01931 715500 ♦ thebutcherscrosby. co.uk. This old hostelry was saved from closure in 2011 by a locals' buyout and is now run very successfully as a community pub. Visitors are made extremely welcome and the food is excellent.

The George Hotel Orton CA10 3RJ ℰ 01539 624071. A large, traditional country inn with accommodation (including self-catering and camping). Very welcoming, particularly for walkers and cyclists, with local beers and hearty pub grub from locally sourced ingredients. A community buyout was being debated at the time of writing.

Kennedy's Fine Chocolate Orton CA10 3RU ⌀ 01539 624781 ⌀ kennedyschocolates. co.uk. All manner of chocolates are handmade here and you can watch the production process through a viewing window in the attached conservatory coffee house. Luxury chocolate cake and hot chocolate drinks are the best sellers in the café, as you would expect.

Orton Scar Café Orton CA10 3RQ ⌀ 01539 624421 ☺ Mon–Sat. Homemade cakes, quiches and light lunches. Popular with cyclists.

Tebay Motorway Services M6, CA10 3SB ⌀ 01539 624511 ⌀ tebayservices.com. When the M6 motorway was built through their farm in 1972, the Dunning family took the opportunity to provide probably the 'greenest' and 'slowest' motorway service station in the country, and they still do. On-site is a hotel, café and farm shop, and there's also a duck pond, mountain views from the picnic tables – and free showers!

The Three Greyhounds Great Asby CA16 6EX ⌀ 01768 351428 ⌀ asbyparish.org.uk/the-three-greyhounds. A lively and welcoming village pub with regular quizzes and live music. Food is very good value pub grub, with treats from the pizza oven particularly popular.

2 RAVENSTONEDALE & NEWBIGGIN-ON-LUNE

These are two places that are almost one: sister villages barely a mile apart that have lots in common but retain their own individual characters. They both fall within the parish of Ravenstonedale and each bears a long and convoluted name that locals can't be bothered with, so shorten for convenience. Ravenstonedale has become 'Rissendle' and, more often than not, Newbiggin's 'on Lune' gets dropped in conversation. Geographically, the 'on Lune' bit is actually quite important as St Helen's Well, just north of the village, is the official source of this historic river.

Both villages sit just off (but aren't spoilt by) the busy Kirkby Stephen to Kendal Road and each has easy access to the beautiful Howgill Fells to the south. Footpaths from each village meet nearly 2,000ft up at the summit of Green Bell. **Ravenstonedale** is the bigger of the two but its village shop and post office are sadly gone. The parish church dedicated to St Oswald and built in 1744 is here with the remains of a small Gilbertine monastic house founded in 1131 adjacent – what you see is mostly the foundations of some rooms of the house with walls standing a couple of feet high. In keeping with the family theme, there was a Ravenstonedale

"These are two places that are almost one: sister villages barely a mile apart that have lots in common."

A Smardale circuit

❄ OS Explorer map OL19; start at Newbiggin-on-Lune ♀ NY703054; 7½ miles; generally easy on well-defined tracks

Car parking on the north side of the busy A685 is limited, so you're best off finding somewhere on-street in Newbiggin. The start of the walk proper is where the access lane to Brownber House crosses the course of the dismantled Stainmore railway line. Here a Cumbria Wildlife Trust illustrated board gives information about the first half of the walk ahead.

Navigation for the first three miles is easy – just follow the flat track bed of the former railway and marvel at the wildlife engineering that you pass on the way. Summer visitors will be treated to a spectacular floral display on the grass verges which in turn attracts many butterflies, including the very rare Scotch argus. Wooded areas are home to red squirrels, pied flycatchers and redstarts. There's also awe-inspiring dry stonework on the cuttings and lime kilns and the magnificent Smardalegill viaduct.

Our walk leaves the line at the hamlet of **Smardale** and heads westwards for a mile along a quiet country lane to the village of **Crosby Garrett**. This is a sleepy and peaceful place (except when trains go past on the Settle to Carlisle line) but unfortunately for walkers it has no café or pub. Turn left in the village and walk under the viaduct to reach the open access land on **Crosby Garrett Fell**, where you can wander where you wish of course, generally southwards taking you back to Newbiggin. Adventurers may wish to 'bag' **Nettle Hill** (1,253ft) but the easiest return route is along the bridleway to the left of the high land. After a mile, a footpath

railway station but it was sited in Newbiggin. Westwards from the old station, the 'new' A685 follows the trackbed of the old railway all the way to Tebay.

⅋ FOOD & DRINK

For its size, Ravenstonedale is well-endowed with places to eat. Just as well, as Newbiggin now has none.

Black Swan Hotel CA17 4NG ✆ 01539 623204 ⊕ blackswanhotel.com. The south end of Ravenstonedale boasts this large, rambling Victorian building, overlooking the intriguingly named Scandal Beck. The chef and owners pride themselves on serving top-quality, locally sourced and seasonal food served with well-selected beers and wines. There's also a range of rooms, plus glamping yurts.

branches left to bring you back to the railway line via an area of hillside called **Severals**, which has extensive Romano-British earthworks – remains of field systems and settlements.

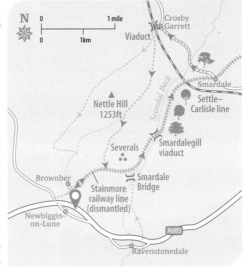

Alternatives

Ravenstonedale can be used as an alternative start point to Newbiggin by following the footpath alongside Scandal Beck to Smardale Bridge. Also, as this is a circular route it can be started at any accessible point en route and done in the opposite direction; starting at Crosby Garrett has the advantage of allowing a beer or a brew halfway. For a shorter stroll, Newbiggin or Ravenstonedale to Smardalegill viaduct, and back on the other side of the beck, fits the bill admirably and affords magnificent views of the viaduct itself.

King's Head Hotel CA17 4NH ✆ 01539 623050 ⌚ kings-head.com. The Black Swan may just pip it in the food quality stakes (though they are both brilliant) but this 500-year-old building feels more like a proper pub to me, with a Lancashire outlook to its beer selection. Up at the north end of the village, the King's Head also has its own watercourse to overlook, the pretty Stone Gill.

3 KIRKBY STEPHEN

🏠 Riverbank Cottage

Half of Kirkby Stephen's name clearly refers to its impressive parish church, sometimes referred to as the Cathedral of the Dales. Where the 'Stephen' bit comes from is more of a mystery as the church has never been dedicated to the saint of that name and no historical Stephen has ever been connected with the town. The most probable explanation is a

linguistic mistake – an Anglo-Saxon word meaning moorland is 'Stefan' and 'Church-village-by-the-moor' would be an appropriate name for this place.

Kirkby Stephen feels thriving, with its range of independent shops, places to eat and drink, and lively local arts scene. Each July it hosts the **Westmorland Dales Festival** (⊘ visituppereden.org.uk), with themes ranging from food, music and storytelling to vintage tractors. The Tourist Information Centre is friendly and helpful, and its leaflet on the Heritage Trail is worth picking up. Unfortunately, the volume of traffic on the A685 in the centre can detract from its appeal.

For me, to see the best of Kirkby Stephen you need to get off the High Street and into its less frequented lanes and alleyways, particularly to the east towards the river. The River Eden is Kirkby Stephen's secret delight – travelling through the town by car you get no sight of it at all but a stroll down the strangely named Stoneshot will take you behind the Market Square and down to **Frank's Bridge**. This attractive two-arched packhorse bridge over the river has one end attached to a building which was once a brewery, and the brewer was called Francis Birbeck – hence the name.

"To see the best of Kirkby Stephen you need to get off the High Street and into its less frequented lanes and alleyways."

The road junction at the south end of the centre has a curious old direction sign, giving distances in furlongs (eighths of a mile).

The parish church

Kirkby Stephen Parish Church is hidden away behind tall Georgian buildings lining the town's main thoroughfare with an attractive, pink sandstone entrance porch the only clue to its presence. 'The Cloisters', as they are known, are a relatively late addition to this very old, but much-altered and added-to, church. Once through the cloisters' arch you're transported back in time and into an oasis of peace and quiet. Traffic noise is magically gone and, across a lime-tree-lined lawn, sits the lovely sandstone church.

◀ **1** Kirkby Stephen with the parish church – the Cathedral of the Dales – in the background. **2** The Smardalegill viaduct can be seen on the Smardale circuit detailed on page 52. **3** Look out for redstarts in wooded areas along the Smardale circuit. **4** The village of Ravenstonedale.

RAILWAYS AROUND KIRKBY STEPHEN

A hundred years ago the smell of coal smoke and the sound of steam engines must have filled the air above Kirkby Stephen, as no fewer than three railway lines converged on the town at that time. In 1962 Dr Beeching put paid to the Eden Valley line from Penrith and the Stainmore line that ran between Lancaster and Durham. The Settle–Carlisle line still very famously operates, calling at Kirkby Stephen. The current main station was the old 'Kirkby Stephen West', and is actually well over a mile southwest of the town (train travellers take note!). Enthusiasts also run heritage trains on a very short stretch of old Eden Valley line under the auspices of the Stainmore Rail Company ($\oslash$ kirkbystepheneast.co.uk), based at the old Kirkby Stephen East railway station.

The legacy from this rail-rich past is the abundance of disused lines in the area which now double as excellent foot- and cycleways. Disused railways are always havens for wildlife but two here are so good they have been designated as nature reserves and put in the care of the Cumbria Wildlife Trust. Waitby Greenriggs, at the junction of the Eden Valley and Stainmore lines just west of Kirkby Stephen, is particularly good for orchids and other grassland flora while Smardale is nationally famous for its red squirrels and butterflies (page 52). The Trust does not allow cycling or horseriding on its reserves but both are permitted on the Northern Viaduct Round walk, a three-miler starting and finishing at Kirkby Stephen marketplace. This walk is also wheelchair-accessible (if you avoid the kissing gate at the start – ask in the Tourist Information Office for details) with route details from the Northern Viaduct Trust ($\oslash$ edenviaducts.org.uk).

Inside are remnants of **Saxon stone crosses**, from when the church itself was thought to be a wooden structure, and a striking artefact from its Viking period. The Loki Stone is a decorated, rectangular stone block bearing a horned carved figure in chains thought to represent Loki, the Norse god of mischief (Tom Hiddleston to our younger readers).

Most of the present church is medieval, including two unusual separate chapels at the eastern end, both dedicated to local aristocratic families. The **Wharton Chapel** on the north side contains the tomb of Thomas, first Lord Wharton, who in 1566 founded Kirkby Stephen Grammar School (now the library in Vicarage Lane next door). On the opposite side of the chancel, the older **Hartley Chapel** houses the remains of two families, the Hartleys and the Musgraves. Sir Andrew Hartley was hung, drawn and quartered as a traitor in 1323 and his forfeited estates passed to the Musgraves. Legend always had it that the last wild boar in England was killed by Sir Richard Musgrave in the 1400s on a nearby hill, known subsequently as Wild Boar Fell. Intriguingly, when Sir Richard's tomb was opened during restoration in 1847, a boar's tusk was found inside, lending some credence to the story.

A very old tradition has resulted in a **clock chime** anomaly from the church bell tower. After the 20.00 hour chimes, an additional bell is rung to sound the night-time curfew, known locally as the Taggy Bell. If children weren't home by this time they were

"After the 20.00 hour chimes, an additional bell is rung to sound the night-time curfew, known as the Taggy Bell."

threatened with the 'Taggyman'. This tradition was celebrated when the old White Lion pub on Market Street was renamed the Taggy Man.

SPECIAL STAYS

Riverbank Cottage ⌂ cottages.com/cottages/riverbank-cottage-cc131162. If you don't mind a two-mile hike from Kirkby Stephen station – or organising a taxi – this is a genuinely Slow option. Thanks to the Settle–Carlisle line you can get to this part of the Dales car-free, and then explore it unencumbered. The cottage sleeps two and overlooks the bridge and the river: you can feed the ducks from the window. Kirkby Stephen's plentiful indie eating and drinking is a short stroll away, within enough options to keep you exploring for several evenings.

FOOD & DRINK

The marketplace in Kirkby Stephen has a good no-nonsense café in the **Mulberry Bush** (✆ 01768 371572), and the **Century** (✆ 01768 372828) is a great-value Chinese restaurant and take-away. Cosy new micropub the **La'l Nook** (✆ 07506 075625 ☺ Tue–Sun) has a good range of beers, while the **Sports & Social Club** (✆ 01768 372332) lets you take your own food to its beer garden, which offers views of Nine Standards Rigg. **Owen's Farm Shop** (Sandwath CA17 4HE ✆ 07972 485794 ☺ Tue–Sun), half a mile west of the centre, is a great place for local produce and has a café.

The Bay Horse Winton CA17 4HS ✆ 01768 371451 ⌂ thebayhorsewinton.co.uk. An old, whitewashed stone building in an attractive village. The menu is mainly traditional and hearty – slow-cooked Cumbrian pork belly for instance – and beers are from local breweries. Children are well catered for.

Black Bull at Nateby Nateby CA17 4JP ✆ 01768 371588 ⌂ nateby-inn.co.uk. Wainwright's Coast to Coast and Pennine Journey walks cross nearby so, not surprisingly, the pub is very popular with walkers for both dining and accommodation (the baths are much appreciated). The menu is an imaginative range of English dishes. Very dog-friendly.

PAUL HARRIS PHOTOGRAPHY

PETE STUART/S

GAZ ATKINSON PHOTOGRAPHY

PHIL HARLAND/DT

MALLERSTANG & GARSDALE

4 MALLERSTANG

Mallerstang is a nebulous area of land covering much of the upper Eden Valley and surrounding hillsides from the watershed near the headwaters of the River Ure (the North Yorkshire–Cumbria boundary) down to Kirkby Stephen. The name is a combination of Celtic and Norse, meaning 'Landmark Hill' and probably refers to the distinctive pyramidal summit of Wild Boar Fell (2,323ft). The ascent of this lovely hill is one of my favourite hikes in the Dales. The eastern side of the valley is made up of a long limestone escarpment known as Mallerstang Edge, the traverse of which makes another fabulous, quiet day's walk. **Wild Boar Fell** to the west is relatively unfrequented but this side of the valley is positively deserted – in all my years exploring here I have never seen another walker.

There is no village of Mallerstang, just a scattering of farms and the tiny, homely hamlet of Outhgill, but evidence of an important human historical presence stands in the ruins of two Norman castles. **Pendragon Castle**, on the banks of the River Eden just north of Outhgill, is the larger of the two with a spurious legendary connection to King Arthur. The castle isn't old enough for that to be true but it was one of Lady Anne Clifford's restoration projects in the 17th century (page 110) and the Lady Anne's Way footpath goes right past the door. The castle has been uninhabited for hundreds of years and is now a romantic ruin. Mallerstang's other castle, two miles downstream from Pendragon, dates from the same time but is even more ruinous. **Lammerside Castle** was built by the Wharton family who abandoned it when they moved to nearby Wharton Hall in the 1600s, and the fabric of the building has steadily degenerated ever since.

5 GARSDALE

This most northwesterly of the Yorkshire Dales holds the odd double distinction of being one of the most visited of the park's valleys but also the least known. The main road west out of busy Wensleydale snakes along the whole length of Garsdale, from top to bottom, but hundreds,

---

◀ 1 Ruinous Lammerside Castle, Mallerstang. 2 Garsdale is a stronghold for red squirrels. 3 Wild Boar Fell summit, Mallerstang. 4 A view of Wild Boar Fell from Garsdale Head.

RED SQUIRRELS

Garsdale is isolated enough to be one of the harassed red squirrel's few islands of refuge from its aggressive and disease-carrying cousin, the grey. This is one of a number of woodland areas in northern England where active management is taking place to help the beleaguered reds. Mature cone-bearing Scots pines and larches are encouraged instead of the oaks and hazels preferred by the greys, and any non-native intruders that get in are trapped and killed – controversial but necessary.

Look out for ginger 'tufties' in Grisedale, Dodderham Moss above Dent Station, the platforms at Garsdale station, and Coat Weggs Woods near Garsdale church. There is also a Red Squirrel Trail at Snaizeholme, near Hawes (page 173).

For information on the Red Squirrels Northern England partnership see ⬧ rsne.org.uk.

sometimes thousands, of people a day pass through, on their way to scenic Wensleydale, or the wild and peaceful Howgills, unwittingly bypassing a landscape with all the same attributes in humble Garsdale. Key to this phenomenon is that there is no village in Garsdale to tempt visitors to stop, and few side roads to draw them off the A684 and slow them down.

It takes a conscious effort to pause and explore here, but try it, because the rewards are rich. The two best opportunities are where minor roads leave the A684, one at Tom Croft Hill, only two miles east of Sedbergh, which gives access to Rise Hill (also known as Aye Gill Pike), from the old road to Grisedale. This small side valley and footpaths following the gorgeous River Clough, and the other higher up the dale, is often labelled the 'Dale that Died' after a 1970s television programme of the same name which documented the last days of the farming families of the dale. It is a deserted place now but great walking country, especially since open access legislation has made the surrounding hills available for walkers.

"It takes a conscious effort to pause and explore here, but try it, because the rewards are rich."

THE HOWGILLS & SEDBERGH

6 THE HOWGILL FELLS

The Howgills are a very discrete range of hills, geologically separate from the Yorkshire Dales proper, and with the River Lune (and more obviously the M6 motorway) providing the boundary with the mountains of the Lake District. Such is the gentle rounded aspect of these hills from a distance that a friend of mine once likened them to a giant plate of dumplings. Alfred Wainwright was less obsessed with food, and in his book *Walks on the Howgill Fells* preferred the metaphor 'a huddle of squatting elephants'. This is very different country, and what makes it so is an absence of things rather than a list of attributes: no roads or buildings, virtually no trees except in the deepest creases and, most striking of all, no walls – not a single one. This makes for a particularly liberating place to walk in, as you can genuinely just wander where you fancy, terrain permitting – and make no mistake, despite the distant gentle impressions, some serious gradients lie hidden away.

"The most accessible Howgill is most definitely Winder, a mere morning stroll from Sedbergh, albeit a very steep one."

The most accessible Howgill is most definitely Winder, a mere morning stroll from Sedbergh, albeit a very steep one, but longer treks allow you to lose yourself in this special place. For a nice, easy stroll into the heart of the Howgills without too much climbing, the walk along the beck from near the Cross Keys to Cautley Spout waterfall is highly recommended. The ascent of the Howgills' highest point, The Calf (2,220ft), via Cautley Spout waterfall and then down to Sedbergh, makes a fine day's walk, but the plum route for me is Black Force via Carlingill Beck.

Unfortunately, it starts with a six-mile drive/taxi ride/hitched lift on the minor road from Sedbergh, through the hamlet of Howgill to Carlingill Bridge ❄ OS Explorer map OL19 ♀ SD624996). But within minutes of starting, the M6 is out of sight and your only company is grazing dales ponies, wheatears protesting loudly from boulder-tops, and dippers feeding by (and in) the water. You are forced to criss-cross the beck as the valley walls close in (it may be impassable after heavy rain) and finally reach the spot of the day, where Black Force Beck tumbles down its ravine to join you. Scan the skyline for ravens and peregrine falcons.

Both routes to the tops involve some serious scrambling, up the side of either Black Force or Carlingill Beck and then you are back on gentle grassy slopes again. The route from there is your choice; back to the car via Uldale Head or Linghaw (three miles in total), or over some elephants' backs (Bush Howe and The Calf) to Sedbergh (seven miles in all).

🍴 FOOD & DRINK

Cross Keys Inn Cautley LA10 5NE 🖉 01539 620284 ⬧ cautleyspout.co.uk ⊘ Fri–Sun all day & Mon lunchtime. In a 400-year-old building that looks its age, this pub has been unlicensed since 1902 and has the status of a temperance inn. It is still run on Quaker lines and is owned by the National Trust. Delicious rustic meals (rabbit pie with black pudding and bacon is the best seller) and a book café. Alcohol is not on sale but you can bring your own for free. Usefully placed for walks to Cautley Spout waterfall and also recommended for B&B.

Fat Lamb Hotel Crossbank CA17 4LL 🖉 01539 623242 ⬧ fatlamb.co.uk. This 350-year-old coaching inn is an archetypal country pub serving traditional Dales fare. It might have a Ravenstonedale postal address but in reality it's in the middle of nowhere, with its own nature reserve behind the building. Dog-friendly accommodation available, and wheelchair-accessible rooms.

7 SEDBERGH

The little-known River Rawthey squeezes its way between the Pennine hills of the Yorkshire Dales and the Howgill Fells just to their west. On its northern bank, just before it spills into the grand River Lune, sits Sedbergh, a market town with a castle mound and venerable bowed buildings lining a cobbled main street. Sedbergh is a very self-contained little place, comfortable in its own skin. Until recently it was really only known to walkers or mountain bikers with designs on the southern Howgills, or those with connections to the prestigious private school whose buildings dominate the land between the main street and the river. Sedbergh School, founded in 1525, has by necessity moved with the times and now has modern facilities, day pupils and a significant proportion of girl students. Thirty-five years ago, when I was a schoolboy myself and visiting Sedbergh on a school trip, things were far more traditional. The male-only boarders were ripe for our astonished ridicule as we leant over the school wall and saw the 'posh kids' all in shorts – right up to 18-year-old sixth-formers!

These days, mention the name Sedbergh and many people will think of books, because this is officially England's book town and partner to Hay-on-Wye in Wales (where it all started) and Wigtown in Scotland. The town's rebranding has been brilliantly orchestrated by

1 A weaving workshop at Farfield Mill. 2 View towards the village of Sedbergh. 3 Cautley Spout Waterfall, Howgill Fells. 4 Carlingill Beck, Howgill Fells. 5 It is thought that the Society of Friends was founded at Fox's Pulpit near Sedbergh. ▶

FARFIELD MILL

RADOMIR REZNY/S

JOHN ROBERTS IMAGES/S

KEVIN EAVES/S

GEORGESIXTH/DT

SWIFTS IN SEDBERGH

If ever a totem bird was needed for your typical English country town it would have to be the swift. For me, their 'devil bird' screams as they race each other between the houses is the soundtrack of summer. Sadly, UK swift populations have crashed in recent years, but Sedbergh remains one of their strongholds and this is in no small part down to the efforts of the Sedbergh Community Swift Group (⊘ sedbergh.org.uk). Under the hugely enthusiastic leadership of Tanya Hoare, they monitor the nesting sites under eaves of tall buildings, put up extra nest boxes where needed and raise awareness with talks and events. As with every really successful community project, local children are also involved. The nest boxes are made by design technology students at Sedbergh School, and footage of swift nestlings shown on BBC *Springwatch* was taken from a box fitted with a camera at Settlebeck Primary School in the town.

a group of local residents who realised after the 2001 foot-and-mouth disease outbreak how vulnerable rural communities dependent on farming were. 'This has been so good for the town', said Carol Nelson, manager of the project. 'It's brought more people in, which supports and safeguards the future of the shops that really matter – the butcher, grocer, hardware shop, post office and the like – but it also allows us to celebrate the glory of books. The sort of books people buy in a book town aren't your throwaway airport novellas, but important ones that you are prepared to keep, read to your children and which eventually become old friends.' It's not just literature that is thriving here either: the town has a really active music scene with its own brass band, choral society, orchestra and biennial music festival in June.

Quakers in Sedbergh

Less well known than its contribution to books is Sedbergh's importance in the beginnings of the Quaker movement. In 1652, George Fox, the founder of the Society of Friends, preached in and around the town to hundreds of local folk. His sermon from a rock on Firbank Fell, now known as **Fox's Pulpit**, is widely held to be the founding moment of the Society. Twenty-two years after these events, local 'Friends' built a meeting house at **Brigflatts** by the river, half a mile west of Sedbergh. It has survived the intervening 400 years as the oldest meeting house in the north of England, its plain, wood-bench-simplicity testimony to the minimalist Friends' philosophy. You are welcome to go inside and enjoy some peaceful moments, and the building is open all year. Brigflatts is only a mile's stroll away from Sedbergh town centre along the riverside Dales Way, with a seat in the peaceful burial ground another ideal spot for a moment of meditation before the return path across the fields.

Farfield Mill

Garsdale Rd, LA10 5LW ✆ 01539 621958 ⏣ farfieldmill.org ⏲ Wed–Sun; free entry

As in many other parts of the country, the local Quaker movement was associated with Victorian industry, and in the mid 19th century Sedbergh boasted five water-powered woollen mills. The best preserved of these by a long way is Farfield Mill, just east of Sedbergh on the way to Garsdale.

For years, Joseph Dover toiled away as manager of Hepplethwaite Mill, to the west of Sedbergh, dreaming of owning his own mill. Finally, in 1836 he had saved the necessary £490 to buy land at Farfield on a bend of the River Clough, and start construction. A year after the mill was completed, Joseph died but his two sons developed the business into a lucrative concern that remained within the Dover family for 100 years.

The mill ceased operating in 1992 and was subsequently renovated by the Sedbergh and District Buildings Preservation Trust. It now operates as a multi-use venue – part weaving museum and part 'Slow' shopping mall, selling books, art and craft work, and lots of textiley things. You can sign up for a weaving, painting or craft workshop or just admire the work of the experts featured in whatever the current exhibition happens to be. A great place to spend a wet afternoon.

⫴ FOOD & DRINK

The **Black Bull**, **Red Lion** and **Dalesman** are close to each other and all do food and local cask ales.

Black Bull Inn Main St ✆ 01539 620264 ⏣ theblackbullsedbergh.co.uk. Reopened in 2018 under its original name (it was just The Bull for many years), this is now an unashamedly luxurious coaching inn catering mainly for posh parents of Sedbergh School students. It serves excellent food from the Ratcliffe–Matsunaga kitchen and boasts a wildflower beer garden.

Green Door Sweet Shop Main St ✆ 01539 620089. Do you ever yearn for the nostalgic taste of pear drops, Pontefract cakes and sherbet lemons? Then enter the Green Door because they are all here, with hundreds more besides, and a range of exotic chocolates.

Gun Dog Coffee Shop Main St ⌂ thegundogcoffeeshop.co.uk. Proper coffee and homemade light lunches and cakes during the day, and a cosy bistro in the evening. Take-away curries at weekends.

Howgill Fellside Ice Cream Lock Bank Farm, Howgill LA10 5HE ✆ 07985 654832 ⌂ howgillfellicecream.co.uk. Ice creams and sorbets made on-site at the farm using milk from their own herd. Mouthwatering flavours include raspberry cheesecake and whisky and marmalade. Enjoy them at the farm's outside tables – a new seating area inside is promised – or from the Spar in Sedbergh.

Smatt's Duo Café Main St ✆ 01539 620552 ⌂ smattsduo.co.uk ⊙ Mon & Thu–Sat. If you were a couple called Sue and Matt and you ran a café, what would you call it? Exactly. This place always seems busy, basically because it's very welcoming and very good. My local food contacts (Biddy 'n' Griff) rate their full English breakfast as the best this side of the Dales.

BOOKSHOPS

Sedbergh has five bookshops (and even the bus shelter offers shelves for browsing or borrowing). See also ⌂ sedberghbooktown.co.uk.

Clutterbooks 77 Main St ⊙ Mon–Sat. The town's charity shop but with a large bargain secondhand book section.

Old Schoolroom Bookshop Joss ✆ 01539 620169 ⊙ Mon–Sat. A small secondhand book corner in the Farfield Clothing shop. All the garments are made locally, from Yorkshire fabrics.

Sedbergh Information & Book Centre 72 Main St ✆ 01539 620125. Local interest and guidebooks, plus a wide range of subjects from over 20 dealers. The place doubles as the tourist information centre.

Sleepy Elephant 41 Main St ✆ 01539 621770 ⌂ thesleepyelephant.co.uk. A wide range of vintage and collectible books.

Westwood Books Leisure Hse, Long Ln ✆ 01539 621233 ⌂ westwoodbooks.co.uk. Spacious shop over two floors with a very large stock of new, secondhand and antiquarian books on all subjects. Sofas, coffee machine and toilets.

The award-winning Slow Travel series from Bradt Guides

Over 20 regional guides across Britain.
See the full list at bradtguides.com/slowtravel.

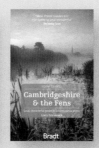

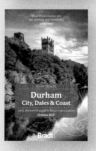

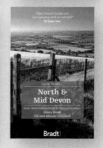

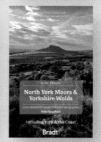

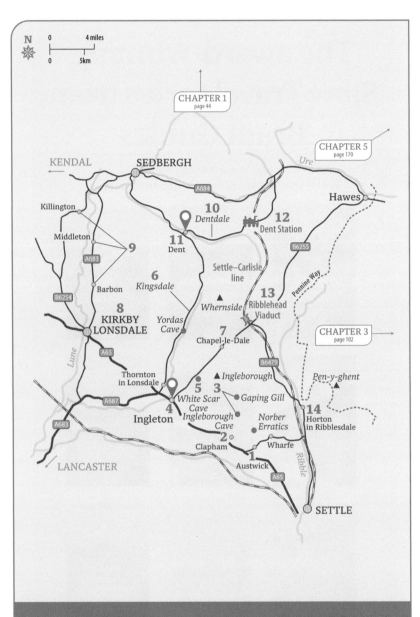

THREE PEAKS COUNTRY

2

THREE PEAKS COUNTRY

Some of the highest land in Yorkshire lies on the western side of the Yorkshire Dales (which actually stray into Cumbria), where the rivers Dee, Skirfare, Greta and Ribble bubble into life. It is an area dominated by three great, brooding hills – **Whernside**, **Ingleborough** and **Pen-y-ghent** – that collectively give this area its unofficial name. Ironically, none of these flat-topped heights could remotely be called a peak but a much-tramped long-distance challenge walk linking the three coined the name and it has stuck.

The legendary walking-book author Alfred Wainwright (1907–91), in his 1970 guide *Walks in Limestone Country*, said of the area: 'This is a region unique, without a counterpart, but its charms are shyly hidden. Those who seek and find them are often enslaved, yet few visitors come looking.' He would probably be astonished and appalled at the numbers of visitors that do come now, but his observation that a little bit of searching can reveal enchanting hidden places still holds true. Some of my first real exploring as a schoolboy was done here, and the hidden places that I discovered then have left indelible marks, and remain very special to me.

This is not as uniform a region as the eastern Dales, but an area of borders, watersheds and transformations. Even before the 1974 county boundary changes bit off a huge chunk of the North Riding and called it Cumbria, Lancashire was never far away, and the local Yorkshire accent has a distinct 'lanky' twang to it. Most of the rivers flow west, to join the Lune, and eventually Morecambe Bay; and where the limestone runs out, the hills develop a distinctly Lake District feel to them.

SELF-POWERED TRAVEL

CYCLING

Two long-distance **road routes** find themselves skirting the Three Peaks. The tough 130-mile **Yorkshire Dales Cycleway** ($\mathring{o}$ cyclethedales.

TOURIST INFORMATION

Ingleton Main St ✆ 01524 241701
Kirkby Lonsdale Main St ✆ 01524 297177

org.uk/route/yorkshire_dales_cycleway) and even tougher 355-mile **Pennine Cycleway** (✆ cycle.travel/route/pennine_cycleway) join forces to creep up Kingsdale and plummet down Deepdale. When they reach the bottom of Dentdale they part company, the former heading down the dale to Sedbergh and the latter up the dale towards Hawes.

It is no surprise that official routes are well represented in **Dentdale**, because its network of relatively flat and quiet lanes just beg to be biked around. The national park's **Cycle the Dales** people have recognised this with 'family ride' circuits of 13 or 19 miles, each going up one side of this picturesque dale and back down the other (✆ cyclethedales.org.uk/route/into_dentdale). You can start anywhere en route but Dent village or Sedbergh would make sense, or of course Dent Station if you arrive by train. (You'll have a stiff climb back up to the station, though.) If you want more of a workout, their 25-mile route linking Sedbergh, Kirkby Lonsdale and Dentdale takes in an uphill leg traversing the hidden valley of Barbondale – hard work, but worth it for the dramatic scenery.

Off-road options are not as extensive here as in other parts of the Dales: there are no big forests or networks of old mine tracks and, sadly, many of the green lanes that should be ideal for biking have been irreparably damaged by 4×4 vehicles and trail bikes. However, some rewarding rides of varying difficulty are described in many guidebooks as well as on the Cycle the Dales website. The latter features a good, testing 19-mile circumnavigation of Pen-y-ghent, but the one they call Tunnels and Bridges suits me best. It is a fairly forgiving 12-mile tour of the bridleways around Clapham and Austwick. For those with a competitive edge, the 38-mile **Three Peaks Cyclocross** race takes place every September (✆ threepeakschallenge.uk). The event enjoys special permission to cycle all three peaks; otherwise, the only summit you can regularly access with a bike is that of Ingleborough, reached with frequent pushing up an often rocky and steep bridleway from Ingleton.

Finally, the **upper reaches of Garsdale and Dentdale** have some quiet and really enjoyable rides that are a mixture of track and tarmac, with the advantage that they are accessible by rail. You could arrive by train at either Garsdale or Dent Station and finish your ride at the other, saving a slog over the Coal Road at the end of the day.

HORSERIDING

There are no trekking or riding stables in the region but riders with their own horses can follow the route of the Pennine Bridleway which skirts the top of Dentdale and Garsdale en route to Kirkby Stephen.

WALKING

The scope for exploring on foot here is extensive, from the three official long-distance paths that pass through the region, the **Ribble Way**, **Pennine Way** and **Dales Way**, (ldwa.org.uk), to the scores of shorter rambles and ambles you'll find described in leaflets which you can pick up at national park and tourist information centres.

The best-known route to traverse is the **Three Peaks**, an unofficial 24-mile challenge of Whernside (2,415ft), Ingleborough (2,372ft) and Pen-y-ghent (2,277ft). Horton in Ribblesdale is the traditional start point, especially if you wish to be registered in the 'club' (threepeakschallenge. uk) by finishing within the allotted 12 hours, but you could start and finish anywhere along the route. If, like me, your preferred walks avoid other people then this is not the route for you as the Three Peaks, both individually and collectively, are extremely popular. The footpaths along the route hold the dubious distinction of suffering the worst erosion of any in the country, requiring thousands of hours of repair work by willing national park volunteers.

One solution to the crowd problem could be to reach the summits individually and by different routes to the 'challenge', because these are three magnificent eminences that each deserve a visit. **Whernside**, to my mind, is best tackled from Whernside Manor in Dentdale, up the bridleway to 'Boot of the Wold' then over open fellside to the summit via the tarns. This is the highest and quietest of the peaks – relish the solitude. A direct descent west takes you into Deepdale where you can hitch down the road or follow beck-side footpaths to your start. **Pen-y-ghent** is the peakiest of the three, neat and well defined. My choice would always be to ascend its precipitous southern nose, from Horton if I've arrived by train, but preferably from Silverdale Road if I have my own transport. This latter option allows a horseshoe walk taking in Plover Hill and returning to the road via Lockley Beck. **Ingleborough** is a hill that's packed with interest from top to bottom. Limestone pavements, disappearing rivers, potholes, an Iron Age fort on the top – and you don't even have to make a round walk of it. Just start at Ingleton, walk the direct path to the summit, then down via Gaping Gill and Ingleborough Cave to descend into the oasis of Clapham village, where a surprisingly regular bus service gets you back to Ingleton.

For those that like someone else to do their navigating for them, **self-guided walks** are available free from the Friends of the Settle–Carlisle line (⊘ settle-carlisle.co.uk/walks) and Dalesbus (page 210). The national park website (⊘ yorkshiredales.org.uk) also suggests some **linear walks** incorporating a bus or train to return you to your start point.

Two of my favourites are **Flinter Gill and Dentdale** (a five-mile, not-too-strenuous circuit; page 94) and **Crummack Dale** (a gentle historical potter from Austwick; see below).

THE SOUTHERN FRINGE

Ingleborough's flanks mark the southwestern boundary of the Yorkshire Dales National Park and it is here that the villages of **Austwick** and **Clapham** nestle beneath limestone crags by the centuries-old coach route from Skipton to Kendal, now the A65.

A few miles further west, this road crosses the River Greta where the small town of **Ingleton** clings to the valley side. Once a busy quarrying and mining community, Ingleton is now the caving capital of Britain and largest 'town' in the locality.

1 AUSTWICK & AROUND

Like many place names in North Yorkshire, this one is Viking in origin, but unusually it was not given by the Danes colonising from the east. The Lancashire coast Vikings were Norwegian, and the furthest they settled up this valley was here, hence Austwick, or 'East Farmstead'. With their pervading sense of solid antiquity, the buildings in and around the village green look as if they've been standing in the Pennine drizzle for centuries. Many structures date from the 1600s, including the fine restored medieval cross on the green. There's a village shop-cum-bakery with a post office here for picking up snacks.

For me, Austwick's best feature is the glorious walking country just to the north, in the tiny valley of Crummack Dale and the gentle hills that encircle it. **Norber** barely qualifies as a hill in its own right; it is really just an extended spur from the Ingleborough massif, but geologists get particularly excited about it because of a group of scattered boulders on its eastern slope. The **Norber Erratics**, as they are known because they don't really belong here, are blocks of a hard, dark rock called greywacke, some the size of small buildings, that were carried up the hill by a wayward glacier 10,000 years ago, and marooned when the ice melted. Some blocks the size of a car settled on softer stone that has now eroded, leaving them precariously balanced on slender, table-leg-like supports. Explore the middle regions to find the best examples.

The summit plateau of Norber is dotted with cairns, probably placed here by shepherds in years past as landmarks. They did not, however, do their job for one 18th-century farmer, Robin Proctor, whose horse was trained to take him home after a skinful in the Gamecock. At the end of a particularly heavy night he mounted the wrong horse, which didn't know the route and promptly walked him off the top of the crag, which bears his name in memorial. **Robin Proctor's Scar** marks the precipitous southern end of the Norber.

"The beck provides a couple of inviting swimming holes and a waterfall or two, before dwindling to a trickle."

If Farmer Proctor's fate does not entice you up to the top, then the valley bottom is the place for you. This is excellent, short-distance rambling territory with an intricate network of paths and bridleways, a relic from the pre-Tudor monastic sheep estates. Sunken walled lanes weave their way between tiny meadows, and cross Austwick Beck repeatedly on ancient single-stoned 'clapper' bridges. The beck itself is remarkable, as it emerges fully formed from a cave at the dale head, provides a couple of inviting swimming holes and a waterfall or two lower down, before dwindling to a trickle just before the serene and snoozy hamlet of Wharfe.

Before you make your way back to Austwick, it is well worth detouring south to Oxenber and Wharfe woods. These are a double rarity, woodlands on limestone pavement, and very old, a combination that makes them floristically very rich. A large proportion of the woodland is hazel coppice, and local people still have ancient commoners' rights of not just sheep grazing, but also nut gathering. Although privately owned, these woods are open access land and walkers are allowed anywhere within them.

¶¶ FOOD & DRINK

Courtyard Dairy LA2 8AS ℰ 01729 823291 ⌀ thecourtyarddairy.co.uk. Just off the A65 on the way to Settle sits a series of old barns converted into a rural retail centre. One of the units houses this fantastic cheese emporium comprising maturing rooms, museum and shop. There's now also a pizza restaurant with a patio with views, and a small self-serve ice cream and drinks machine.

Elaine's Tearooms Home Barn, Feizor LA2 8DF ℰ 01729 824114. A lively, legendary little farm tea room. Cyclists divert here to call in for a cuppa and locals walk over from Austwick for snacks. The hamlet's name – 'Feizor' – is pronounced 'Phaser' and, appropriately, the scenery is set to stun.

The Traddock Graystonber Ln, Austwick LA2 8BY ℰ 01524 251224 ⌀ thetraddock.co.uk. A hotel serving really high-quality lunches and evening meals. They also do teas, coffees and snacks at other times of day – and accommodation, of course.

2 CLAPHAM

Walk a longish mile west of Austwick, and you will find yourself among the buildings of its more popular sister, Clapham, stretched out along the sides of a chuckling beck. Although about the same size as Austwick, it has far more facilities for visitors; its shops, café, car park, pub and information point all contribute to making Clapham a very busy little village at times.

This tourist drawing-power was boosted significantly by the opening of the Victorian railway station, the trains delivering carriage loads of visitors to the newly discovered **Ingleborough Cave** a mile up the valley of Clapham Beck. The cave lies on the land belonging to the Ingleborough Estate which, in the 18th century, belonged to the Farrer family. They had constructed what is still by far the biggest building in the village, **Ingleborough Hall** (now an outdoor education centre; page 76), but it was a great-grandson, Reginald Farrer, who had the most lasting influence. He was a botanist and plant collector in the early years of the 20th century, who brought back many exotic species from the Himalayas and planted them in the estate grounds. Farrer could be very imaginative in his planting techniques, and once fired alpine rock plant seeds at a cliff face from a shotgun to give a 'natural' spread of flowers later.

"The cave lies on the land belonging to the Ingleborough Estate which, in the 18th century, belonged to the Farrer family."

THE UNDERGROUND EMERGENCY SERVICE

An unassuming, plain, grey building, next door to the New Inn in Clapham, is something of a shrine in caving circles. It was once a pub, then stables for the inn next door, but now is known as the CRO Depot, which stands for Cave Rescue Organisation. It possesses such a generic title because, like the FA Cup, it was the first of its kind, and didn't need a name to distinguish it from other cave rescue teams – there weren't any. Since its formation in 1935, the CRO has rescued nearly 3,000 unfortunate folk, many from underground, but also walkers and climbers on the surface, as the organisation doubles as a mountain rescue team.

The modern CRO is a large and very professional organisation, but amazingly, all 80 team members are volunteers and the whole operation is funded by donations.

The estate charges a nominal fee to follow the **Ingleborough Estate Nature Trail** ($\mathcal{O}$ ingleboroughestatenaturetrail.co.uk) along the main Ingleborough track, although it is more of a landscaped garden stroll, and a free bridleway alternative runs parallel, to the cave and beyond. Farrer's collected rhododendrons are a highlight, and at their best from spring.

Estate connections apart, a good deal else to see in Clapham can easily fill half a day. An excellent guide for pottering around the village is the free map/leaflet produced by the village association ($\mathcal{O}$ claphamyorkshire. co.uk) and found in all the shops and café. It shows where little St James's Church is hidden away in the trees; how to find the village hall that often has displays of local artists; and exactly where the five bridges over the beck are. There are two buildings in the village not featured on the map (as they are not open to visitors), but which locals are very proud of. One is the original offices of the *Dalesman* magazine, bastion of Slow principles, in a small cottage near the village hall, before they moved to Skipton. The other is the headquarters of the **Cave Rescue Organisation**, the building next to the New Inn pub (see below).

¶¶ FOOD & DRINK

Growing with Grace Station Rd, LA2 8ER $\mathcal{O}$ 01524 251723 $\mathcal{O}$ growingwithgrace.org.uk ☉ Tue–Sat. A Quaker co-operative organic farm shop selling a wide variety of vegetables, fruit and whole foods, much of it grown in their own greenhouses. There's also artisan bread and a veg box scheme.

New Inn Hotel Old Rd, LA2 8HH $\mathcal{O}$ 01524 489569 $\mathcal{O}$ newinnhotelclapham.com. A large 18th-century coaching inn opposite the market cross. Two bars with open fires serving

Yorkshire real ales. Main bar has a collection of caving cartoons by Jim Eyre, one of the local early cave explorers. Also has rooms.

The Old Sawmill Café Riverside LA2 8DS ✆ 01524 237788 ⬦ oldsawmillcafe.co.uk. Locally sourced coffee and fresh homemade food in a light and airy restored building with wooden period features, right at the entrance to the Ingleton Estate Nature Trail. Dog- and cyclist-friendly.

ACTIVITIES

Ingleborough Hall LA2 8EF ✆ 01524 251265 ⬦ ingleboro.co.uk. Run by Bradford Metropolitan District Council as an outdoor education centre, primarily for Bradford schoolchildren, but they do offer day and half-day activities for non-residents in expert-led climbing, caving and gorge scrambling.

3 INGLEBOROUGH CAVE & GAPING GILL

✆ 01524 251242 ⬦ ingleboroughcave.co.uk

The entrance to **Ingleborough Cave** is a very obvious large hole in the side of the Clapham Beck valley, just over a mile upstream from Clapham village, so to say the cavern was discovered in 1837 would be stretching the truth. The cave's existence had been known to locals for hundreds of years, but the 19th century's upsurge in both scientific exploration and commercial development prompted the estate to blast away a natural dam a short way into the chamber. What they found beyond turned out to be a link to one of the most extensive cave systems in Britain, and a goldmine for their fledgling tourist industry.

Thousands of visitors have enjoyed it in the subsequent centuries. They flocked to Ingleborough Cave in the 1960s when the health and safety culture was not quite as obsessive as today. The cave is now fully lit throughout and hard hats are compulsory, but 50 or so years ago visitors were advised to 'mind their heads' and were given individual candles to light their way. Alan, one of the cave guides, was telling me of an entertaining visit from a deceptively harmless-seeming elderly couple. 'We've actually been here once before,' the old gentleman said. 'Back in 1961 or '62 when we were both teenagers. I'm afraid we didn't behave particularly well. I wrote my initials on the cave ceiling

1 A cheese emporium at the Courtyard Dairy, near Austwick. 2 The Norber Erratics, Austwick. 3 The village of Austwick. 4 The Ingleborough Estate Nature Trail. 5 The extraordinary interior of Gaping Gill. 6 Ingleborough Cave. ▶

MY DESCENT INTO GAPING GILL

The karabiner clicked. 'Sit right back and keep your feet in,' my minder instructed, then he looked me in the eye: 'OK, you ready? Away you go.' With that, a trapdoor opened and my chair disappeared down into absolute blackness with me in it, clutching to my midriff the items on Chester's list.

I'd been talking to Chester the night before in the bar of the New Inn in Clapham about my morning descent into Gaping Gill. 'You'll love it, it's a great experience but take something warm and waterproof,' he said. 'Too many people turn up at the winch in shorts, and bikinis even, not realising just where they are going. They treat it as a funfair ride – but it's a bit more than that. A head torch will be useful and a bit of food if you're planning on staying down a while. A roll-up keeps me warm enough but some folk like to have a small flask of coffee.' About ten seconds into the descent was the first of the several times that I was glad of Chester's advice. The pot-holing club members above had temporarily diverted the beck that created the main shaft, away from it, but there was still a fair amount of water around and I got well sprayed. Gaping Gill is a little like an inverted funnel in shape, so after the initial narrow entrance, although I couldn't see it, I could feel I was in a huge space – large enough to contain York Minster, it turns out. It was a vulnerable feeling to be suspended in the middle of that with just tiny lights visible on the floor below and the roar of the waterfall echoing around the chamber. Almost before I knew it the chair came to a halt at the cave floor and I was helped out and moved to somewhere slightly drier to watch Kevin, the next descender, join us. 'God, did I just do that?' I thought as the chair hurtled out of the dark spray and into the dim pool of light where his welcoming party awaited.

The two of us had a brief tour from another club member and were then let loose to explore with head torches (cheers, Chester). Twenty minutes later, with more and more people arriving, and queuing for the chair out becoming a possibility, I went back up. Chester had said that the ascent would be different and it was. 'You'll see more 'cos your eyes are acclimatised to the dark; look out for Colley's ledge.' This is as far as Colley, the first caver to brave the descent, reached. He looked down into the black, couldn't see the floor and declared Gaping Gill bottomless. What Chester didn't tell me was that for some reason it's a lot wetter going back up.

I stepped out of the chair at the top, completely drenched and in a daze, handed in my numbered wristband (it's handy for them to know how many people are down there at any given time) and went to the checking-in tent to thank the team. I had, and still have, a real feeling of gratitude towards everyone in the Craven Pothole Club (cravenpotholeclub. org) for enabling me to have such a privileged experience. It took the direct involvement of eight people to get me down and back: two doing the checking in, a winch man, a top chair man, two bottom chair men, a guide and an overseer. All were volunteers giving up their holiday time, and what does it cost? About as much as a pub meal – an absolute bargain. Long may it continue.

in candle soot, and my wife set fire to the person in front of her with her candle. It was an accident I think.' Alan pointed out the offending graffiti, still there over 50 years later.

Regular entry is by self-guided tour; other tours can be organised by arrangement. It takes about 40 minutes to travel a third of a mile in and return the same way. The cave is dry, the paths level-ish and the only discomfort a bit of stooping here and there; not at all the claustrophobic experience you might expect.

If you do want a truly adrenaline-charged underground experience, you need not look much further. A mile uphill from Ingleborough Cave, following the dry valley of Trow Gill, you come to an area, described on the OS map as 'pot holes' and 'shake holes', one of which warrants a safety fence around it. This is **Gaping Gill**, a slightly ominous name for something genuinely awe-inspiring.

Fell Beck, tumbling down the eastern side of Ingleborough thousands of years ago, found itself a crack in the soluble limestone to disappear down. Over the millennia this crack has widened into the largest and deepest single vertical drop cave chamber in Britain, and Fell Beck's freefall descent into it forms the highest waterfall in the country, albeit not seen by many people. Sadly more than a few careless people eager for a closer look have made a quick and fatal descent, 365ft to the floor of Gaping Gill, so take care near the edge.

The great news is that a much slower descent of Gaping Gill is possible, but only on two weeks of the year, the week of Whitsun Bank Holiday and the week leading up to August Bank Holiday. Local caving clubs set up a winch to lower willing members of the public down to the bottom of the cave and back for a nominal fee (see opposite). Bradford Potholing Club run it in May (bpc-cave.org.uk) and Craven Pothole Club in August (cravenpotholeclub.org). There must be a catch, I hear you say, and there is. So popular is this service that the wait for your turn at the top can be five hours at busy times. What you can do is put your name down then walk up nearby Ingleborough until it's time for your turn.

4 INGLETON

Ingleton is most definitely a town, albeit a small and friendly one, and it has very successfully reinvented itself after the collapse of a busy industrial past. The last of the coal mines closed in the 1930s, limestone

Ingleton Waterfalls Trail

✳ S Explorer map OL2; start: Falls Café ♥ SD693732; 4½ miles; moderate, well signed but some steep and slippery sections ⟋ ingletonwaterfallstrail.co.uk

This walk is a little classic. The walkers' oracle Alfred Wainwright himself declared: 'Surely, of its kind, this is the most delightful walk in the country. And not only delightful; it is interesting, exciting, captivating and, in places, awesome.' The trail is well signposted in Ingleton and starts down in the valley bottom, where the Thornton road crosses two small rivers just above their confluence to form the embryonic River Greta. If you are driving it is worth coming down here to the car park rather than finding a place up in town, as your walk entrance fee includes parking. Those who arrive by public transport or by bicycle may therefore feel they are subsidising drivers.

Traditionally the route is clockwise, ascending the valley of the River Twiss first; do not be tempted to go maverick, starting with the River Doe and travelling anticlockwise. You may think that you are avoiding the crowds (and the fee) but in reality you will meet everybody else travelling in the opposite direction at some point, probably on all the steep and narrow staircase sections! For solitude, and that would always be my choice on a walk as beautiful as this, the advice is go early. Last time I visited, the nice man in the ticket office said, 'We officially open at 09.00 and I couldn't possibly condone anyone setting off before then as they would not be covered by the owner's insurance [said with a twinkle in his eye]. In any case, it never gets busy until about 11.00. Lazy lot, these trippers.' Another alternative recommended by Wainwright, who was a confirmed sociopath, is to do the walk in winter when there are no crowds and the falls are either roaring with flood water or festooned with ice sculptures.

quarrying stopped ten years later and the town lost its rail link courtesy of Dr Beeching in 1967. Most folk would agree that Ingleton has benefited from the first two changes, but not the last one: a locomotive in full steam, crossing the town viaduct on its way westwards towards Kirkby Lonsdale, would be an inspiring sight today.

Ingleton is thriving now because of tourists, many of whom come for its annual 1940s weekend in July (⟋ ingleton40s.co.uk). The rest of the year, most visitors use it as a service base to explore the scenic delights of its hinterland. It boasts shops, cafés, pubs, a microbar (in the old post office), restaurants and take-aways, supermarket, pharmacy, bakery... even a heated outdoor pool. Ingleton Gala (⟋ ingleton.co.uk) is held annually on the third Saturday of July, and has a villagey, family feel.

As soon as you enter the limestone gorge of Swilla Glen, near the start of the walk, it becomes obvious why this area is deemed so special, Natural England designating it as a Site of Special Scientific Interest (SSSI) for its geology alone. The fenced path clings to the valley side which passes through a tunnel of overhanging ash and hazel boughs on its way to Manor Bridge and the first of the cascades, **Pecca Falls**, which leaps over a hard band of greywacke rock. In the next 500yds the river tumbles over seven rock steps at **Pecca Twin Falls**, **Hollybush Spout**, other nameless rapids and, finally, **Thornton Force**, at 46ft the highest of them all. This time the hard ledge is limestone and the soft rock beneath is vertically folded slate.

For the laid-back and sedate, this is the ideal spot for a laze and/or picnic, while the bold and restless members of the party brave the slippery walk behind the falls or swim in the plunge pool itself. Not far above Thornton Force, the route leaves the Twiss Valley to contour around the hill on the very old Twisleton Lane track and reaches a high point of 934ft above sea level before joining the valley of the **River Doe** for the descent.

Beezley Falls marks the start of the most dramatic section of the whole walk, and is closely followed by **Rival Falls** and the dark depths of **Baxenghyll Gorge**. The inaccessible nature of this place has left the woods relatively undisturbed to form one of the best remnants of ancient semi-natural forest in the area. The giant mature oaks, rare mosses and liverworts, and nesting pied flycatchers and redstarts are in the care of the Woodland Trust, which owns and manages this part of the valley.

Snow Falls is one of the last spectacular diversions on view, before the path passes through an old limestone quarry and back into Ingleton.

The nearest sample of its beautiful countryside is right on the doorstep: the **Ingleton Waterfalls Trail** (see opposite). This is one of two walks (the Ingleborough Estate Nature Trail being the other; page 75), where a fee is charged by the landowner for the privilege. I'm not madly keen on the principle of paying to walk, but I'll bite the bullet, since it's such a spectacular path. If you have found yourself here on a lousy weather day, or you're just feeling lazy, indoor diversions in Ingleton – a smattering of art and craft shops, the pottery being the best, a few tea shops and four pubs – could be your option.

Ingleton's indoor climbing wall (Main St ✆ 0330 113 1154 ✆ ingletonwall.co.uk ☺ Mon–Sat) is available for experienced climbers. If you aren't particularly experienced, but would like to have a go anyway, then ask in the shop about freelance instructors who can coach on the wall, or even take you down a cave.

Ingleton is one of the select places in rural Britain to boast a heated **outdoor pool** (✆ 01524 241147 ⌂ ingletonpool.co.uk ☺ summer daily; winter Sat & Sun), which you can find down by the riverside behind the church. The pool was built by striking coal miners in the 1930s, at the height of the lido boom.

"Sir Arthur Conan Doyle was married in St Oswald's Church here and celebrated afterwards in the Marton Arms opposite."

You could also take a country lane stroll half a mile past the pool to the tiny village of **Thornton in Lonsdale**. Sir Arthur Conan Doyle was married in St Oswald's Church here and celebrated afterwards in the Marton Arms opposite. You would do well to emulate him as it is a great old pub, but mind your behaviour, as the old village stocks are still fully functional nearby.

Ingleton's Tourist Information Centre has a leaflet, 'Westhouse Walks', with three afternoon strolls around Thornton. They also have a free booklet of ten routes called 'Ingleborough Walks', a Yorkshire Dales Millennium Trust project (⌂ ydmt.org); each walk is five to ten miles around the Ingleton area, all reached by public transport.

∜ FOOD & DRINK

Country Harvest A65 ✆ 01524 242223 ⌂ country-harvest.co.uk. Three places in one: gift shop, good café and fantastic food hall. They sell excellent bread from their own bakery, have a proper butcher on-site (already an award-winner despite being in his twenties) and offer a wide range of cheeses from Yorkshire, Lancashire and Cumbria.

Inglesport The Square ✆ 01524 241146 ⌂ inglesport.com/the-cafe ☺ Tue–Sun. Hearty breakfasts and snacks in this café adjoining an outdoor shop. Inglesport also runs the climbing wall (page 81).

Marton Arms Thornton in Lonsdale ✆ 01524 242204 ⌂ martonarms.co.uk. The building dates from the 13th century and retains a lot of its old charm. For drinkers this is an exceptional place with many local cask ales, beers and ciders available, and over 200 malt whiskies to choose from. Food and accommodation are also both highly regarded. Dogs welcome.

Village Kitchen Main St ✆ 01524 241869 ☺ Wed–Mon. Excellent new addition to the town's eating opportunities, with fresh, homemade, great-value specials: try the succulent burgers. Watch the world go by from the forecourt tables.

SHOPPING & ACTIVITIES

Ingleton Pottery Under the viaduct ℘ 01524 241363 ⊘ ingletonpottery.co.uk. An old Unsworth family business. You can see Dan Unsworth, the current potter, hand-throwing a stoneware pot and then buy the results.

5 WHITE SCAR CAVE

Hawes Rd, LA6 3AW ℘ 01524 241244 ⊘ whitescarcave.co.uk ⊙ Feb–Oct daily; Nov–Jan Sat & Sun

North of Ingleton, Twisleton Dale carries the main road to Hawes, past White Scar Cave and through the little hamlet of Chapel-le-Dale. The White Scar experience is very different to that of Ingleborough Cave. It is the longest show cave in Britain so at 80 minutes the tour lasts longer. The beck that created Ingleborough Cave has moved to a lower system, leaving the show cave dry, whereas White Scar is an active cave with the noise and moisture of its creative beck still very much in evidence, meaning there's a real risk of the cave closing in very wet weather.

There is car parking at the cave entrance, a shop and a well-appointed café with outdoor tables. The White Scar experience is convenient, modern and slick, but I have to admit I prefer the 'slower' experience of Ingleborough Cave.

6 KINGSDALE

By car, the way to Kingsdale is a narrow, poorly signposted minor road that sets off from Ingleton in the wrong direction entirely, then doubles back at Thornton in Lonsdale if you follow the sign for 'Dent'. Up a steep hill, down another one, round a bend and suddenly there it is: a hidden valley, tiny and tucked away. This is one of Wainwright's 'shyly hidden places' where 'life here is as it should be; two farmsteads the only habitation, animals graze undisturbed and birds enjoy sanctuary.'

Kingsdale is just a great place to be, an almost guaranteed deserted oasis for those that need solitude to wander, which was why I was surprised on a visit in May 2009 to see what looked like an impromptu campsite near the head of the valley. I assumed that it was a meet of the caving fraternity but on closer investigation found myself in the middle of an archaeological excavation. The group conducting the dig were from the local Ingleborough Archaeology Group and their chair at the time, David Johnson, kindly showed me around the site.

'In 2006 we were excavating a known medieval building when we found remains of a fire pit which was dated to between 6960 and 6660 BC, putting it within the Mesolithic (or Middle Stone Age) period,' he explained. 'What we're doing now is concentrating on features to the side of the fire pit that may be remains of post-holes for a temporary shelter used maybe by hunters, foragers or chert-knappers.' (Chert is the limestone equivalent of flints in chalk, I learnt from David.) The group offers the opportunity for volunteers to join their number, be trained up in a variety of techniques and assist on digs. Contact them if you are interested in future projects (⊘ ingleborougharchaeologygroup.org.uk).

When I chanced upon the archaeologists, I was on my way to a place in Kingsdale that, in Victorian times, was quite a tourist draw. **Yordas Cave** was once a show cave with an admission fee but is now a little-visited hole in the hillside. An inscribed date of 1653 on one of the internal walls testifies to how long this place has been known about, indeed the name indicates an even older heritage. Yordas was a legendary Norse giant who would lure boys into the depths and devour them. Putting aside

"The name indicates an even older heritage. Yordas was a Norse giant who would lure boys into the depths and devour them."

the dangers of being eaten by Vikings, Yordas is considered one of the safer caves to enter without a guide or specialist equipment, although in today's paranoid health-and-safety culture the British Caving Association would probably never put that in writing. Although not signposted, it is marked on the OS map (♀ SD705791) and is relatively easy to find. Just before the last building in the dale where the road is gated is a wooded dry valley. Beyond the low entrance, a torch is all that is needed, and the bigger the better, to see your footing and the details of the roof formations 60ft above. At the back of the cave, 30yds from the entrance, Yordas Gill flows across the floor from right to left, having fallen in through the roof as an elegant waterfall. This is a great place for sensible freelance exploration but not after very wet weather when the cave floor can flood and be very muddy afterwards.

On the fellside above Yordas Wood, just below the summit of Gragareth, lies an area referred to on the map as Turbary Pasture.

◀ **1** St Leonard's Church, Chapel-le-Dale. **2** Yordas Cave, Kingsdale. **3** Thornton Force on the Ingleton Waterfalls Trail.

Turbary is the ancient commoners' right to collect turf or peat, and the fuel was transported via the Turbary Road which is present as a track and makes an excellent terrace walk or cycle along the side of Kingsdale.

7 CHAPEL-LE-DALE

🏠 **Broadrake Bunkbarn**

A church, a pub (if it's open) and some caves; that is just about it for Chapel-le-Dale, but the church is delightful and the caves have intriguingly weird names.

This hamlet is named after 'the church in the valley', **St Leonard's**, a tiny 17th-century building with a history intrinsically linked to the railway that crosses the head of the dale. The church is made of local limestone. On the west wall of the nave is a black Dent marble memorial which reads:

> To the memory of those who through accidents, lost their lives, in constructing the railway works, between Settle and Dent Head. This tablet was erected at the joint expense, of their fellow workmen and the Midland Railway Company 1869 to 1876.

The railway company obviously felt some small responsibility for these accidental deaths as it paid for an extension to the graveyard (hardly a gesture that would have earned them an 'Investors in People' logo today) – but not for the many more that perished from smallpox or fights between workers; some of those victims lie in unmarked graves here.

The once-thriving and legendary pub, the Old Hill Inn, is more of a B&B and glamping-pod place now ($\mathscr{P}$ 01524 241256 $\mathring{\mathcal{O}}$ oldhillinningleton.co.uk). It's only infrequently open to the public, most likely on Saturdays (when there may be food) and occasional evenings. If it is open, drop in and see why it was so fondly regarded, featuring in many a caver's and walker's tale of boozy weekends away.

"It is a pleasant drive and an even better cycle, quiet and relatively flat until Meal Bank at Ingleton."

My recommended slow route linking Chapel-le-Dale with Ingleton is not the busy main road but the old Roman road on the other side of Twisleton Dale. It is a pleasant drive and an even better cycle, quiet and relatively flat until Meal Bank at Ingleton. This route can be extended into a circular easy walk, or a more testing bike ride, on the bridleway over Twisleton Fell. Big pluses are that you get to pass the wonderfully named **Hurtle Pot** and **Jingle**

Pot caves near the church, and cross the fantastic limestone pavement on the fell top. The only minus, except for pushing your bike up or down the steep bits, are the unrestricted views of the still-operating Ingleton quarry – a real eyesore.

SPECIAL STAYS

Broadrake Bunkbarn LA6 3AX ⬧ broadrake.co.uk. Within sight of Ribblehead Viaduct on rustic sheep-farm flats, this excellent modern bunkbarn – which welcomes individuals as well as groups – is a great base for cavers, cyclists and hikers doing the Three Peaks. Whernside and Ingleborough are walkable, while Pen-y-ghent is a short drive away. Ribblehead (on the same level) or Ingleton (down below in the vale) are the nearest stations, cyclable but too far to walk. Various craft courses take place here: you might be sharing the large, light common room with blacksmiths, basket-weavers, spoon carvers or painters.

THE LUNE VALLEY

8 KIRKBY LONSDALE

'I do not know in all my country, still less in France or Italy, a place more naturally divine.' Such was the opinion of 19th-century poet, art critic and bohemian John Ruskin when he first visited Kirkby Lonsdale, and it has to be said that this small market town is still relatively unspoiled and very picturesque. The specific part of town that Ruskin was referring to was the view from the back of St Mary's churchyard over the River Lune towards Barbon Fell and into what is now part of the Yorkshire Dales National Park. J M W Turner, Ruskin's contemporary and friend, immortalised this vista in a watercolour painting, which sold for over £200,000 in 2012. Sadly, the view itself is currently inaccessible following a 2021 landslip, until fundraising can finance repair works; you can get close, though.

Kirkby Lonsdale almost certainly owes its existence to the River Lune, or more particularly, a convenient crossing point over the fast-flowing water, where the town's other big draw now sits – the magnificent 14th-century **Devil's Bridge**. A delightful and very popular walk links St Mary's and the bridge via the riverbank and the steep paved path known as the Radical Steps. The return takes you through Kirkby's attractive **marketplace** and main street.

Have a poke around down nearby side streets and alleyways as well though, where you may find the town's ancient **market cross** in old

Swinemarket, the medieval **Abbot's Hall** and Victorian **courthouse**. My favourite hidden corner is **Salt Pie Lane**, renamed after an enterprising resident who sold hot, salted-mutton pies to traders at the adjacent Horsemarket, some think to deliberately give them a raging thirst which then had to be quenched at her family's nearby pub. Modern Kirkby Lonsdale town centre is far removed from the old days of beast markets and smelly tanneries. In recent years it has become a refined and trendy place, with the main shopping street awash with ladies' fashion outlets and fine art shops, and a book and jigsaw lounge. The town looks especially atmospheric during the annual Christmas fair at the beginning of December.

Devil's Bridge

When the monks of St Mary's Abbey in York built this bridge around 1322 they hadn't figured on the width of 21st-century motor vehicles (a bit shortsighted if you ask me). Consequently, at less than 12ft wide, it was closed to traffic in 1932 and the adjacent Stanley Bridge was built to take the busy A65. Despite its 'narrow-comings', at 45ft above the water and with two 55-foot-diameter arches, this is a staggeringly impressive piece of engineering for its time. Subsequent generations either forgot who built it, or didn't believe that monks were capable of such a feat, and a legend developed that it was the devil himself who was the architect – hence the name. Apparently he agreed to the construction in exchange for ownership of the first soul to cross but was outwitted by a local woman who threw a few tempting pieces of bread across the bridge which her pet dog chased, thus saving her own soul.

▌▌ FOOD & DRINK

Gastronomically, Kirkby Lonsdale punches way above its weight. It has seven pubs, three cafés, several places to eat and a brewery, with quality high across the board. I have tried to narrow down my favourites in each genre below.

Chocolat New Rd ✆ 01524 272830 ⊘ chocolatinkl.co.uk. A shop selling mainly luxury, handmade Belgian chocolates but also speciality teas, coffees and spirits, and ice cream. Children will love the 'faery chocolate mine' in the cellar.
Elodie's Café and Wine Merchant Market Sq ✆ 01524 298050 ⊘ elodies.co.uk ⊙ Wed– Mon. A traditional English café where everything is done well – the welcome, the service

and the food. Provision for special diets is particularly good and the range of fancy teas is astonishing. Small but packed wine shop in the back.

Kings Arms Hotel Market St ✆ 01524 271220. The town's oldest pub with an enormous inglenook fireplace seen at its best on cold, winter evenings. Food served and accommodation available. Local cask ales and a sunny beer garden.

Kitridding Farm Shop LA6 2QA ✆ 01524 567484 ⌖ kitriddingfarmshop.co.uk ○ Thu–Sun. A source of top-quality meats from the on-site butcher, four miles northeast of Kirkby on the old Kendal road. There's also a nice little tea room serving home baking.

Plato's Restaurant Mill Brow ✆ 01524 274180 ⌖ platoskirkbylonsdale.co.uk. If you wish to indulge yourself then this is the place. Plato's prides itself on offering 'the good things in life' which includes sumptuous lunches and evening dining, extravagant cocktails, fine art décor and boutique accommodation. It's not cheap but their off-peak offers are good.

9 THE LUNE VALLEY VILLAGES

The River Lune upstream from Kirkby Lonsdale is a beautiful stretch of wooded waterway meandering for ten miles between here and the outskirts of Sedbergh. Unfortunately, unless you have access to a canoe or kayak, it is almost completely inaccessible as both banks are devoid of public rights-of-way for most of their length. Only two small road bridges span the river along this stretch, and one of them (at Rigmaden) is closed long-term for repairs. As a result, the village communities on either bank have developed in isolation from each other.

"The Romans chose to build a road on the eastern side of the river and an inscribed Roman milepost can still be seen."

The Romans chose to build a road on the eastern side of the river and an inscribed **Roman milepost** (*▥* pounds.rehearsed. yard) can still be seen at Middleton. (Not where the OS map claims, though: it was moved in 2016 to the nearby churchyard of the Holy Ghost, because the cows kept knocking it over.) This ancient route is followed by the busy A683, through Casterton and close to Barbon. Both villages have excellent pubs and Barbon boasts a very popular cheese-shop-cum-café. There was a private girls' school in **Casterton** which was taken over by its more affluent neighbour in Sedbergh and now serves as its preparatory school; the golf club in the village has a café open to all. Set back from the main road, **Barbon** is much more peaceful and the dale to the east that bears its name even more so. A trip up Barbondale makes a very pleasant diversion, whether it's as a scenic route by car to Dent, a rewarding

THE RETURN OF THE PEREGRINE FALCON

Back in the late 1970s, when I was still in my teens, I read a book called *The Peregrine* by J A Baker, a man obsessed by these most magnificent of birds. For this passionate and poetic naturalist, peregrines didn't just fly, they sliced a parabola in a smooth outpouring, like water gliding over stone, or fell as a black bill-hook does into splinters of white wood. What's more, his meticulously observed winter's diary wasn't only inspirational prose, but damned good scientific recording too.

Some of his passion rubbed off on me and I dreamt of seeing peregrine falcons flying in the wild. Those were dark days for birds of prey generally; organochlorine pesticides added to crop seeds had found their way into the food chain via seed-eating birds and had ended up in such concentrations in the bodies of top predators that the poisoning proved fatal. Where it did not actually kill the birds, it weakened eggshells to the point where they smashed easily in the nest and breeding failed. By the 1970s the peregrine was on the brink of extinction in England. Those few pairs that did nest on isolated crags in the north and west of the country were guarded 24 hours a day by dedicated volunteers to prevent the theft of their rare eggs or chicks. Thirty years ago egg collecting was far more widely practised than today, and the hatched young birds could be sold to unscrupulous falconers for thousands of pounds.

I was introduced to my first pair of wild peregrines by an inspirational schoolteacher, Alan Stoddart, who, when on holiday from teaching me and my peers in industrial Lancashire, lived in a caravan in Dentdale. The nest, or eyrie, was on a crag called Combe Scar near the village of Dent, and one Easter I and a few other equally excited schoolboys were sworn to secrecy and taken up to meet the 'guard' in a derelict barn below the crag.

For the following hour or two we watched entranced through binoculars as the male (tiercel) screamed into view at a speed scarcely believable, to deliver food to the female (falcon) who sat incubating eggs on the nest, their staccato calls echoing around the combe. I have seen peregrines many times since, but nothing has ever matched that first electric experience.

Thankfully, those poisonous pesticides have long since been banned, and wildlife crime is now very well policed. Consequently, peregrine falcons have made a remarkable recovery all over the country, recolonising all their old haunts and even spreading on to the artificial cliffs (tall buildings) in many towns and cities. The Yorkshire Dales now boasts about 20 pairs nesting on crags dotted across the national park, including, I am happy to note, the descendants of 'my' pair, still on Combe Scar.

You could come across them anywhere in the Dales, usually given away by their distinctive anchor shape in flight, like a squat kestrel, or their phenomenal hunting speed of over 100mph, if you are fortunate enough to see it. For an almost guaranteed viewing though, go to Malham Cove where the RSPB has a telescope set up on the resident peregrine nest between Easter and August.

there-and-back bike ride on its single-track road or a beckside stroll on the bridleway past Barbon Manor.

The western side of the valley is much less frequented – an area of rolling hills and ridiculously narrow country lanes. One of these minor roads is of great antiquity and was used for hundreds of years for droving sheep down from Scotland to the markets further south – and this drove road is still known locally as the Old Scots Road. All the countryside that the Old Scots Road passes through is rich in wildlife but one small patch of bog right by the roadside near Killington is particularly good: Burns Beck Moss is a nature reserve in the care of the Cumbria Wildlife Trust and very good for bog plants and dragonflies.

Nothing here quite makes it to village status but **Old Town** and **Killington** are the largest hamlets. Ironically, there are no really old buildings in Old Town but Killington has two. The most venerable parts of Killington Hall date from the 15th century but the adjacent All Saints Church is at least a century older and was originally a chapel serving a previous incarnation of the hall. Nowadays Killington is most famous for its annual traditional sports meeting, which includes the ancient art of Cumberland and Westmorland wrestling.

¶ FOOD & DRINK

The Barbon Inn Barbon ⌀ 01524 276233 🖰 barbon-inn.co.uk. This fine village pub serves good beer from the Kirkby Lonsdale Brewery but what draws the crowds are its excellent meals. Dog-friendly accommodation is also available.

The Churchmouse at Barbon ⌀ 01524 276224 🖰 churchmousecheeses.com ☺ Tue–Sun. This is a village store, café and delicatessen all rolled into one with cheese a common theme throughout. A popular cyclist stop, thanks to barista coffee, bike wash, and perhaps the guitar and piano.

The Pheasant Casterton ⌀ 01524 271230 🖰 pheasantinn.co.uk. The Pheasant modestly describes itself as 'bar, restaurant and rooms' but it is much more. This is a very good hotel with luxurious accommodation, top-quality traditional English dining and attentive service.

The Swan Inn Middleton ⌀ 01524 276223 🖰 theswanatmiddleton.co.uk. A 16th-century roadside coaching inn, although it no longer does accommodation. Particularly notable for its large, lovely beer garden.

10 DENTDALE

Whenever I arrive in Dentdale, and the sturdy little village that gives the valley its name, I always feel as if I'm coming home. This is no

fanciful imagining brought on by the homely feel of the place, but because I did spend a fair proportion of my formative years here. Some inspired soul in my secondary school, in industrial Lancashire, decided that we 12-year-old 'townies' should experience country life, so the school bought a cottage in **Dent** for us to stay in. My weekend visits to White Hart House in the 1970s were a revelation; I discovered proper hills (Great Coum was my first summit), swam in clean rivers and saw the Milky Way in a clear, black, non-street-lit sky for the first time.

Times have changed, Dent is much busier now than it ever was in my youth, and sadly White Hart House was sold, but the village still retains its character and the dale remains many people's favourite.

The fact that it is a mere ten miles from Dent Head to Sedbergh, where it meets the Rawthey Valley, makes this quite a small dale, but one packed with fascinating detail. The River Dee is at the heart of much of it, especially in the upper dale, tumbling over limestone ledges, squeezing through narrow 'strids', and on numerous occasions playing hide and seek by disappearing underground, only to reappear hundreds of yards further downstream. The Dales Way footpath hugs the riverbank most of the way down, allowing views of the caves which, unusually, abound down at valley-bottom level, and the rich and enchanting wildlife. You will probably see more dippers per mile of river here than anywhere else in Yorkshire.

"The Dales Way footpath hugs the riverbank most of the way down, allowing views of the caves."

The Settle–Carlisle line calls in at Dent Station, four miles uphill from the village at Dent Head. The view down the valley from here is commanding, and the station's historic snow huts have been refurbished as holiday accommodation (dentsnowhuts.co.uk).

11 Dent & around

The fact that many locals still refer to the village as Dent Town gives us an inkling as to its importance in the past. In its heyday two centuries ago Dent had a market (where the George and Dragon now stands), a racecourse and managed to support 12 pubs and inns – venues of

◀ **1** The Lune Valley. **2** Peregrine falcons have made a noticeable comeback across the Yorkshire Dales. **3** Dent village. **4** The 14th-century Devil's Bridge in Kirkby Lonsdale.

A Dent walk

❄ OS Explorer map OL2; start: The Green ♥ SD704869; 4 miles; moderate, some steep slopes and potentially muddy sections

M ost of Dent's visitors don't stray far from the main street, which isn't surprising as the cobbled surface and whitewashed cottage frontage give it a very attractive, almost Cornish fishing port, look. Also, this is where its two pubs, both cafés, the heritage centre and most of the shops are. I do, however, strongly recommend wandering a bit further afield, namely up the hillside at the back of the village along a lane called Flintergill. This route takes you past a stately Victorian building, formerly the Zion Chapel and now a meditation centre, open to all to just pop in for a moment's peace or join a more formal how-to-do-it course (⌂ meditationcentre.co.uk ☉ Apr–Oct).

Where the tarmac lane becomes a bridleway (♥ SD703867), you enter a Tolkienesque ravine – the real **Flintergill** that the road is named after. You may choose just to explore this enchanting place, or you can extend the walk in a variety of directions, and range of distances, on the maze of paths and bridleways on the valley side. My choice would be to continue up to join **Green Lane**, turn left and skirt the slopes of **Great Coum** for a mile (maybe detouring up the open access slopes to the summit), then descend **Nun House Outrake**. Back in the valley bottom, **Deepdale Beck** and the **River Dee** banks are the most entertaining routes back to Dent.

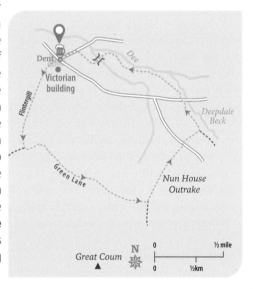

'drunken riots, blasphemy, gambling quarrels and other bygone vices and follies' by all accounts. Hand knitting fuelled its economy, and was practised by just about everyone in the village – man, woman and child (page 96).

Dent's most famous son is undoubtedly **Adam Sedgwick**, who put his education in Dent Grammar School to good use by becoming professor of geology at Cambridge University, and was a personal friend of Queen Victoria and Prince Albert. His radical thinking led him to being dubbed the father of English geology and prompted a water fountain enclosed in a block of Shap granite to be erected in his honour opposite the George and Dragon. It's probably Dent's most-photographed object.

Behind Sedgwick's fountain and down a short alley is the old, squat, sand-coloured stone **church of St Andrew**, surrounded by clipped yews and gravestones. As a boy I remember being morbidly fascinated by stories of a vampire's tomb here. In reality, George Hodgson was a farmer who drank sheep's blood as a tonic – it can't have done him much harm as he lived to 94. His 'vampire' grave is in the church porch.

As a youngster I remember an old filling station as you arrived at Dent village. It's been donkey's years since any petrol was sold here but the old garage building now houses the **Dent Village Heritage Centre**. For a small fee you can learn about rural life in the dale in times gone by and have a brew in the café afterwards. Margaret and Jim Taylor, who own and run the centre, have lived over the road at High Laning Farm for as long as I've been coming here. They're the unofficial Mr and Mrs Dent. Bike hire is available at the farm. The bus shelter opposite the centre offers a pleasant place to sit out a rain shower, and there are free toilets.

FOOD & DRINK

The George and Dragon Main St ✆ 01539 625256 ⚲ georgeanddragondent.co.uk. Most notable as being the brewery tap for Dent Brewery further up the dale – the manager is also the brewer there. Other regional ales are also on offer. Food and accommodation are both very acceptable and excellent value.

Stone Close Tea Room and B&B Main St ✆ 01539 625231 ⚲ stoneclose.com. In a 17th-century listed building, this well-established tea room prides itself on the fresh, local, seasonal, organic, and fair-trade credentials of its food and drink. Wine and beer are available. All the baking is done by Alison on the premises and evening meals are available for residents.

SHOPPING

Dent Stores Main St ✆ 01539 625209 ⊖ closed Wed afternoons. A general store and post office for the village. Also offers B&B.

THE TERRIBLE KNITTERS OF DENT

Peering through a Dent cottage window on an 18th-century winter's evening could reveal an eerie and disturbing sight. Ten or twelve adults, men and women, sit around the outside of the room, swaying their bodies in a circular motion in unison, and singing a rhythmic chant.

In the flickering candlelight, the shadows of their rapidly moving hands dance on the walls. Is this the meeting of a sinister religious cult? No, it's that of the Terrible Knitters of Dent.

'Terrible' referred not to the quality of their work but to the incredible speed with which they moved the wool and needles. They were paid on completed garments and a good knitter could start and finish a whole smock in a day. Every week, a cart would arrive from Farfield Mill in Sedbergh loaded with wool, and would return full of completed garments – miner's jerseys, army stockings and caps, bump-caps for the slave colonies and high-quality woollens bound for the stores of London; they were all made in the parlours of Dentdale.

12 Dent Station

Dentdale, like neighbouring Garsdale, displays a typically Viking pattern of settlement – a scattering of farmsteads, with few if any villages. A cluster of buildings near the top end of the dale, that don't quite manage to form a hamlet, are sometimes lumped together as Cowgill, but more often than not nowadays this corner is named after its most illustrious building.

Dent's railway station sets some kind of record for being further away from the place after which it is named than anywhere else in Britain – the village is a whopping four miles away.

Many people have been caught out, stepped off the train and then been faced with a yomp into town, but it's much worse the other way around. Walking from the village to the station is up a killer hill, as Dent Station holds another record: at 1,150ft above sea level, it is the highest mainline station in England.

Most of the other buildings at this end of the dale are lower down, snuggled along the banks of the Dee, which is at its photogenic and playful best here. The whitewashed Sportsman's Inn sits in an enviable spot with the chapel not far away, and a short mile upstream, a favourite spot of mine, is the old YHA building. Unfortunately, it's closed as a hostel now, but you can still stay there by hiring it as a private self-catering house (deesidehouse.co.uk). Not far from it, at Stonehouse, the highly sought-after **Dent black marble** was quarried and polished. You can see it used decoratively in St Andrew's Church, Dent, and the railway memorial in St Leonard's in Chapel-le-Dale.

Two **walks** here that I always enjoy are a stroll down the river to Ibbeth Peril waterfall and back, and an ascent of Great Knoutberry Hill (possibly the best view in the Dales from the top) via Arten Gill.

RIBBLESDALE

The River Ribble does not spend much time in Yorkshire before it defects to Lancashire. A good way to see every inch of the valley is to follow the Ribble Way footpath which starts at the official source of the river, four miles northeast of the railway. Consequently, the place **Ribblehead**, where the much-photographed railway viaduct of the Settle–Carlisle line straddles Batty Moss, isn't actually the head of the valley, but let's not split hairs. The gloriously lazy way to see most of Upper Ribblesdale is to board the train at Ribblehead and rattle away south, with Ingleborough filling the window on the starboard side and Pen-y-ghent likewise to port. They both come closest to the train and each other at **Horton in Ribblesdale**, the official start and finish of the Three Peaks Challenge. Six miles down the line at Settle, the railway and river both leave the national park and go their separate ways.

13 RIBBLEHEAD VIADUCT

To Network Rail, this is the site of 'Bridge 66 and station'; to everyone else it is one of the most iconic railway landmarks in the world – the Ribblehead Viaduct. Over 400yds long, 104ft high and with 24 arches, it took 6,000 men to build, with 200 losing their lives in the process. To learn about the drama of the viaduct construction and its subsequent history you can visit the Ribblehead visitor centre in the station or get hold of a copy of *Thunder in the Mountains: The Men Who Built Ribblehead* by W R Mitchell. Now in his eighties, Bill, a former editor of the *Dalesman* magazine and self-confessed sufferer of the incurable disease of 'Settle and Carlisle-itis', has produced a riveting account of the soap-opera goings-on at Ribblehead. Life in the shanty towns of Jerusalem and Jericho, rat infestations in Belgravia, the doings of

"To learn about the drama of the viaduct construction and its subsequent history you can visit the visitor centre."

Welsh Jack and Nobby Scandalous, earthquakes, floods and murders – it's all covered in satisfying detail.

Next to the railway line north of the viaduct is a candidate for 'England's remotest house', No. 3 Blea Moor Cottages, at least a mile from any motor vehicle access. The only other building at Ribblehead is its pub, **The Station Inn**, but scattered farmsteads appear as the Chapel-le-Dale and Horton roads drop down to less exposed climes. A short way down this latter route, and accessible on foot from the station, is **Ribblehead Quarry**, disused since 1999 and now being recolonised by wildlife. The quarry is part of **Ingleborough National Nature Reserve** and a 1½-mile walking trail leads you around its waterfalls, ponds and rock gardens. You can pick up a leaflet from the station or download one from ⊘ naturalengland. org.uk. Look out for ravens, oystercatchers and ringed plovers that breed here, but especially Yorkshire sandwort, a small plant that has colonised the wetter areas of the quarry. The bird's-eye primrose is arguably the most attractive member of its family and is a national rarity.

Just beyond the quarry nature trail, **Colt Park Wood** is one tiny but exceptional part of the reserve. It has been described as the best example of an aboriginal scar limestone ash wood in the country, and the variety of exotic and scarce plants is astonishing. Visit in early summer and you could see globe flower, baneberry, alpine cinquefoil, yellow star of Bethlehem and the eccentrically named angular Solomon's seal.

⑪ FOOD & DRINK

The Station Inn Ribblehead LA6 3AS ⊘ 01524 241274 ⊘ thestationinnribblehead.com. This has always been a heart-warming sight for Three Peakers but on cold, wet days, when the fire is roaring, it can be a lifesaver. The best of the food is the traditional English dishes of pies, mash and sausages, and the range of Yorkshire beers is impressive. Bunk barn and camping available; if not occupied by a group, the former may accommodate individual travellers on spec, if you ask nicely in the bar.

14 HORTON IN RIBBLESDALE

Adding an address to a place name, like Skipton on Swale or Thornton in Craven, makes sense when there is another place nearby to confuse it with. Horton's 'in Ribblesdale' makes no sense, as it is the only one for miles, and the nearest is deep in Lancashire – and also in Ribblesdale!

1 The Ribblehead Viaduct. 2 Horton in Ribblesdale. ▶

FELL RUNNING

One question that has always intrigued me about fell runners is not where they do it, how they go so fast, or even what the best technique is – but why do they do it?

Peter Pozman, a 60-year-old teacher from near Wetherby, put me right. 'You know', he said, 'that's a question I ask myself every race, not long after the start, on the first uphill bit when me lungs are starting to scream. I'd always enjoyed walking up the fells, but the older I got the more I realised that I was running out of time to do them all, so I thought I'd better speed up a bit.'

'By jogging, I found I was doing a whole afternoon's walks in less than an hour and seeing loads of countryside in the process. I was doing this once from Nidderdale, up a fell called Great Whernside, when I met someone near the top who looked at me and my tracksuit and trainers and said, "You must be a fell runner." Jokingly I said, "In my dreams I am", but then I thought, "Yeah, I like the sound of that, I am actually fell running here", and I started to take myself a bit more seriously, eventually actually entering some races.

'One of my finest moments was finishing first in the Male 55 and Over class, in a race in the North York Moors, run by a bloke called Dave Parry from Commondale. I love Dave's races – they're really informal. There'd be 80 to 100 of us stood at the start and Dave would shout, "Right, well, it's been snowin' out there and it's startin' to melt, so it'll be real slippy. Last year someone in too much of a hurry took a bit of a tumble, so you might want to go bit easy – go!" And off we went. It was really horrible but I think the conditions suited me; my hill craft as a walker, and understanding of rough ground kept me out of the freezing water, and my feet stayed relatively dry, while the elite athletes couldn't get going. Later in the Eskdale Inn at Castleton, I was watching other people get prizes, when Dave said, "M 55, winner Pete Pozman", and I thought, "Wey hey! Fantastic! Three bottles of wine and my name in print!"

'I had my feet plonked firmly on the ground last week, as I was struggling up a steep slope, and a fella was keeping up with me walking. "So this is fell running", he said. "Is it hard?" "Yes", I gasped. "Especially when I have to talk to people like you at the same time."'

Strange names apart, Horton has much in common with many Dales villages: two pubs, an old arched bridge over the river, a Norman church dedicated to the ubiquitous St Oswald, monastic rule in medieval times and, later, a bad dose of the plague. What singles Horton out today is the influence of outdoor pursuits such as caving (at nearby Alum, Hall and Hunt pots and the Long Churn system), cycling and, overwhelmingly, long-distance walking. The Pennine Way and Ribble Way converge here, but the Three Peaks Challenge is by far the most popular. This route was never really invented, it just sort of evolved and then was popularised by Alfred Wainwright's description of it in *Walks in Limestone Country*, and by the Pen-y-ghent café's 'Three Peaks of Yorkshire club'.

Alas, the café is now closed, with two unfortunate consequences. First, there's nowhere to eat in the village during the day, unless either the Crown or Golden Lion pub happens to be open. Second, there's nowhere to get your Three Peaks stamp: the only way to get official recognition of walking the set now is as part of an organised tour.

For cheap and cheerful bunkhouse accommodation – and decent real ale – you could do worse than head for the Helwith Bridge Inn (⌖ 01729 860220), less than two miles south of Horton.

The annual fell race over the Three Peaks, run over much the same route taken by walkers, has a more definite history. It was first run in 1954 with six runners starting and only three finishing. In April 2023, the 68th race had over 900 starters, with the fastest time an impressive 2 hours and 53 minutes.

FOOD & DRINK

Middle Studfold Farm Tea Room Studfold BD24 0ER ⌖ 01729 860401
⌖ middlestudfoldfarm.co.uk ⊙ Mar–Nov Wed–Sun. A mile south of Horton, just away from the road, is this simple café with terrace tables and a track pump for cyclists.

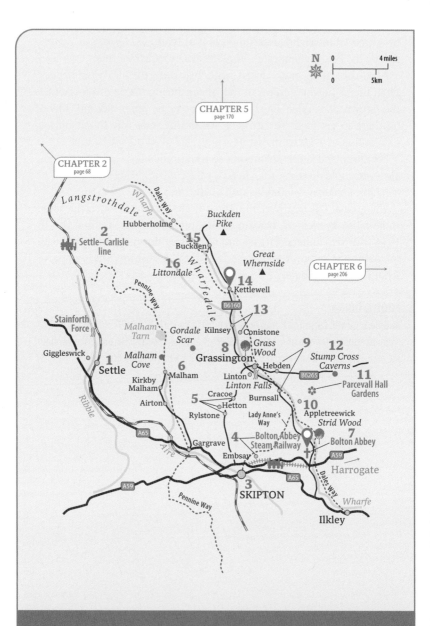

CHAPTER 5
page 170

CHAPTER 2
page 68

Langstrothdale

Wharfe

Dales Way

Hubberholme

2 Settle–Carlisle line

15 Buckden

Buckden Pike ▲

Great Whernside ▲

CHAPTER 6
page 206

16 *Littondale*

Wharfedale

Pennine Way

14 Kettlewell

B6160

13

Kilnsey

Conistone

Stainforth Force

Malham Tarn

Gordale Scar

Grass Wood

9

12 *Stump Cross Caverns*

Giggleswick

1 Settle

Malham Cove

8 Grassington

Hebden

11 *Parcevall Hall Gardens*

6 Malham

Linton

B6265

Kirkby Malham

Linton Falls

Cracoe

Burnsall

10 Appletreewick

Strid Wood

Airton

5 Hetton

Rylstone

Lady Anne's Way

Ribble

7 Bolton Abbey

A65

Gargrave

4 Bolton Abbey Steam Railway

Embsay

A59

Harrogate

Aire

3 SKIPTON

A59

A65

Pennine Way

Dales Way

Wharfe

Ilkley

CRAVEN & WHARFEDALE

3
CRAVEN & WHARFEDALE

This southernmost part of the Yorkshire Dales only just makes it into North Yorkshire, and its closeness to the big cities of Leeds and Bradford makes it probably the most visited region in the national park.

Three rivers drain south here: the Ribble, which then escapes westwards into Lancashire; the Aire; and the longest of the Dales watercourses, the Wharfe. Wharfedale's corridor-like nature sets it apart from the other Yorkshire Dales, that and the river that created it. If forced into a choice, I would have to plump for the **Wharfe** as my favourite Yorkshire river. Its deep, clear pools, strids, riffles and cascades provide an unsurpassed variety of watery landscapes, and arguably the richest wildlife in all of the national park.

Craven, the wild acres of high land to the west of Wharfedale, is a geological wonderland of all things limestone: potholes, 'clint and grike' pavements, disappearing rivers, collapsed caverns and amphitheatres – it's all here, and at its most spectacular around Malham.

SELF-POWERED TRAVEL
CYCLING
Road biking is biased towards the fit and experienced rider here purely because the only roads small and quiet enough to be pleasant on a bike tend to have really steep hills on them at some point. The Yorkshire Dales National Park's **Cycle the Dales** website ($\mathcal{O}$ cyclethedales.org.uk) only suggests three 'family-friendly' routes, each around five flattish miles: a circuit of Malham Tarn, a short loop north of Gargrave, and the back lane between Skipton and Bolton Abbey. Mildly adventurous families might enjoy one of my favourites: a circuit taking in Grassington, Conistone, Kettlewell and Arncliffe, mostly off the main Wharfedale road. You can start or finish anywhere along the route.

Cycle the Dales offers five additional road circuits from Grassington. Of these, the Etape du Dales (109 miles, 10,300ft of climb) and the Tour

TOURIST INFORMATION

Grassington National Park Centre ✆ 01756 751690 ☉ Apr–Oct daily; Nov–Mar Sat & Sun, closed Jan

Malham National Park Centre ✆ 01729 833200 ☉ daily Apr–Oct; weekends Nov–Mar, closed Jan

Settle Market Pl ✆ 01729 825192 ☉ Mon, Tue & Thu–Sat

Skipton High St ✆ 01756 706397 ☉ Mon–Sat

de France in the Dales, emulating the race's route in 2014 (77 miles, 7,110ft) are strenuous but very rewarding. For dedicated tourers, part of the Pennine Cycleway passes through here, and a fair chunk of the 130-mile Yorkshire Dales Cycleway, which starts and finishes in Skipton. It's designed to be done clockwise but there's nothing stopping you going the other way just for the hell of it.

Off-road cycling is even less forgiving to the more leisurely rider than the local roads. No big forests with gentle tracks, or those nice, flat disused railway lines here. It's mainly fellside tracks with serious inclines more suited to two-wheeled athletes. On the plus side, because this is well-drained limestone country, mud isn't generally a problem and many of the bridleways double as green lanes, so are fairly substantial. Cycle the Dales suggests four routes in Craven and Wharfedale, with a ten-mile Settle Loop being the least testing, and therefore the one for me. It crosses Langcliffe Scar and Ewe Moor, taking in the impressive Scaleber Force waterfall, and with only two short difficult sections punctuating a moderate ride.

Off-road biking doesn't get any flatter than canal towpaths, though they can become tedious after a while. The four-mile stretch of the Leeds and Liverpool Canal between Gargrave and Skipton is smooth gravel, and family- (but not wheelchair-) friendly.

HORSERIDING

If availability of trekking is a good measure, then this is the epicentre of horseriding in the whole of the Dales, with two centres.

If you bring your own horse with you, then you, along with the mountain bikers, have access to the area's enormous mileage of bridleways, plus a national trail primarily aimed at horseriders, the **Pennine Bridleway**, which includes the Settle Loop. Accommodation for horses is available at **Craven Country Ride** (Pot Haw Farm, Coniston Cold ✆ 01756 749300 ✆ pothawfarm.co.uk).

RIDING CENTRES

Draughton Riding Centre Draughton, Skipton ✆ 01756 710242
✆ draughtonridingcentre.com.
Kilnsey Trekking and Riding Centre Conistone ✆ 01756 752861 ✆ kilnseyriding.com.

WALKING

Two long-distance trails cross this region on a north–south line: the **Pennine Way** following the River Aire, and the **Dales Way** along the banks of the River Wharfe. Unless you are actually following either of these classic routes they are best avoided. More than enough **alternative day and half-day routes** exist with fewer people to share them with. My preferred strategy is to spread out the OS map (Explorer OL2 *Yorkshire Dales Southern & Western areas*) and plan my own, but there are many walking guides to do it for you if you prefer. The Harvey *8 Walks Centred On* series has three maps for this area, all excellent: Settle, Skipton and Grassington. Two walks that don't make it on to any of these maps but are definitely in my hall of fame are **Great Whernside** from Kettlewell (page 136) and a five-mile/three-pub crawl from **Buckden**, taking in Cray, Yockenthwaite, and the verdant hillside meadows above Hubberholme, getting grandstand views down Wharfedale.

CRAVEN

While for the most part the individual dales of the Yorkshire Dales fit into easily identifiable chunks of scenery, the Craven district is a strangely nebulous idea with no neatly defined edges. I am taking it as stretching from the River Ribble in the west, handy as 'Ribble' means 'boundary' in Anglo-Saxon, to the catchment of the Wharfe in the east. The small town of **Settle** sits along the east bank of the Ribble with the frivolously named **Giggleswick** on the opposite side.

Behind Settle the land rises steeply at the start of well over 100 square miles of wild upland dominated by carboniferous limestone. Geographers name this sort of landscape after the Karst region of old Yugoslavia, and Craven is absolutely classic karst scenery. The hills are not so rugged as to be inaccessible to four wheels, and small roads criss-cross the area, calling in on **Malham** from where it's a stroll to the huge cliff of **Malham Cove**, an extraordinary limestone pavement, and the gorge and waterfall in **Gordale Scar**. **Malham Tarn** is the source of the River Aire which, after a spell underground, winds southwards to **Gargrave** where it picks up the Leeds and Liverpool Canal as a travelling partner for the remaining five miles to **Skipton**. A market town of fair size, Skipton is unquestionably the capital of the Craven district and one that, although not in the national park, proudly labels itself 'Gateway to the Dales'.

1 SETTLE & AROUND

Settle grew as a small market town at the crossing of two important trade routes. It still has its market but passing trade is much less now, since the A65 bypassed the town. Settle really would have been a sleepy backwater if its other transport link had deserted it, as it very nearly did in the 1980s, but the **Settle–Carlisle railway line** remains open, and attracts many of the town's visitors. Settle itself is unassuming with nothing really exceptional to crow about but I like it for all that, especially the maze of old streets creeping up the hillside towards Upper Settle and Castlebergh, the wooded crag that peers over everything.

A short stroll over the river via a small footbridge will bring you to the photogenic village of **Giggleswick** with two notable places of worship: a private boarding school chapel with a striking copper dome and the parish church with a very unusual name. Only two St Alkelda's churches are to be found in the country – this one and one at Middleham in Wensleydale where she lived, died and was sainted. If her name is obscure, what about the manner of her death; not many nuns meet their end by being strangled to death by two Viking women using a napkin!

Settle's biggest attribute is the river and fell scenery around it and one six-mile loop walk gives a taste of both. The outward leg, upstream on the Giggleswick bank, is actually on the route of the Ribble Way, which takes in the hamlet of Stackhouse on the way to **Stainforth**. Here is an old packhorse bridge to cross and the impressive waterfall of **Stainforth Force** to admire; keep an eye open for leaping salmon in late autumn. For half-way refreshment, try the pub in Stainforth. On leaving the Craven Heifer, the footpath back first scales **Stainforth Scar** before contouring the hillside along to Settle via Langcliffe, giving a bird's-eye view of your outward journey all the way.

Settle may be sober and sensible for most of the year, but during July and August its populace seems to go a bit daft as this is the time of the Settle Flowerpot Festival. Most of the town joins in, contributing one or more of the hundred-plus sculptures made predominantly from flowerpots. Not exactly 'Slow' with its use of thousands of plastic pots, but fun all the same.

¶¶ FOOD & DRINK

For such a small town Settle is rich in good places to eat. The pick of the restaurants for me are **Ruchee** (Commercial Courtyard ✆ 01729 823393 ⌕ rucheesettle.com – a warm welcome and delicious Indian cuisine), **The Fisherman** (Church St ✆ 01729 823297 ☺ Mon–Sat – top-quality fish and chips to eat in or take away) and **Bar Thirteen** (Duke St ✆ 01729 824356 – officially a café-bar but almost a pub. Lots of craft beers and gins but no food).

For a brew and a snack, the best two cafés are **Ye Olde Naked Man** (Market Pl ✆ 01729 823230) and **The Folly Coffee House** (Victoria St ✆ 07932 825185 ⌕ thefolly.org.uk ☺ Mon–Sat), in an amazing Grade I-listed 17th-century building which also houses a museum and craft shop. My cycling friends rate the cheap and cheerful **Singing Kettle** (High St ✆ 01729 823125) while busy local bike shop **3 Peaks Cycles** (Market Pl ✆ 01729 824232) has a good café.

The best pub options are across the river in Giggleswick. **The Black Horse Inn** (Church St ✆ 01729 821303 ⌕ blackhorsegiggleswick.co.uk) is an old and very traditional pub next to the church. Food is good-quality pub grub and beers are from Yorkshire. Accommodation is available. Just outside the village by the railway station, the **Craven Arms** (Brackenber Ln ✆ 01729 825627 ⌕ craven-arms.co.uk) has exceptional food and a range of local draught beers, as well as rooms. There are some great-value midweek dinner, bed and breakfast deals.

2 THE SETTLE–CARLISLE LINE

⌕ settle-carlisle.co.uk

Some who have heard of this famous line assume that it is one of those privately run steam railways reopened and kept going by volunteers at weekends. In fact it is part of the National Rail network, with a regular scheduled service, although steam excursions do happen occasionally (see ⌕ uksteam.info). The line never did quite close but it came to within a hair's breadth of it in the 1980s and its present fame owes more than a little to the vociferous and successful campaign for its salvation. The Settle–Carlisle line was, and is, so well loved because of its spectacularly scenic qualities and – from an engineering perspective – daft route.

In the 1860s, the Midland Railway Company relied on goodwill from the owners of the two existing lines to Scotland, the London and North Eastern Railway and the London and North Western Railway, to transport its freight and passengers north. When the companies fell out, the Midland had no alternative but to build its own line along the only route left available; not the flat land to the east or west of the Pennines, but straight up the middle and over them.

This resulted in an incredible 72 miles of line possessing 14 tunnels and 20 viaducts; arguably the most stunning route in the country, providing an ever-changing catalogue of panoramas. Scarcely a moment passes when you are not crossing a towering viaduct over a hillside beck or emerging from the darkness of a tunnel to be presented with another valley and another vista. Marvellous!

Although the line is busier now than ever in its history, those 1980s campaigners and their 21st-century counterparts are not complacent. Various interested charities and trusts have teamed up to form the Settle–Carlisle partnership and their joint website is the definitive reference point for anything to do with this iconic railway line. For the most spectacular section, ride from Settle as far as Appleby-in-Westmorland. You can join free guided walks along the line on Saturdays; see ⬦ friendsofdalesrail.org for details.

3 SKIPTON

By Yorkshire Dales standards, Skipton is a large town. It owes its origins to those white, woolly grass-eaters in the surrounding fields – hence the 'sheep-town' label. Its commercial and industrial prominence owes more to its rail and canal links with the bigger towns of West Yorkshire.

All the wool and cotton mills are closed now, but the railways are always busy, taking commuters out to Keighley, Bradford and Leeds, and bringing tourists in. Many of these visitors do use Skipton as a gateway to the rest of the Dales, but lots don't get any further, as there

1 Settle in the snow. 2 Skipton Castle. 3 The Leeds and Liverpool Canal passes through Skipton. 4 The Settle to Carlisle steam railway at Armathwaite. 5 Visit Stainforth Force in autumn for a chance to see salmon leaping. ▶

is a wealth of diversions to occupy them in and around the town. The **Leeds and Liverpool Canal** is a big draw, whether you're chugging along it on a narrowboat, strolling beside it on the towpath or just sitting in a waterside café or pub watching other people chug or stroll. I think that the most attractive bit of the canal is a small dead-end offshoot called the Spring Branch that curls around the back of **Skipton Castle** giving walking access to Skipton Woods – well worth a potter, especially in May when the carpets of wild garlic and bluebells beneath the trees are at their peak.

"Skipton Woods are worth a potter, especially in May when the carpets of wild garlic and bluebells are at their peak."

If you fancy more than a short stroll along the canal towpath – perhaps after admiring the lively statue of legendary Yorkshire fast bowler Fred Trueman in the main basin – the walks up the main canal in either direction are pleasant enough. Eastwards to **Low Bradley**, a return riverside footpath completes a six-mile circuit. This can be extended slightly to visit the village of **Cononley**, if only for half-way refreshment in its cracking little pub. The western route, ten miles there and back to **Gargrave**, has an alternative return on footpaths following the railway line. For an easy, flat bike ride, the canal towpath between Gargrave and Skipton is now well surfaced with smooth gravel, but with short steep steps halfway.

Skipton Town Hall (High St ✆ 01756 706397 ⏾ skiptontownhall. co.uk) has been well refurbished with good wheelchair access and a bright, appealing (free) museum. There are regular events here, and it offers plenty of useful tourist information. The town's annual 'Skipton Now' Festival runs in August, and there's a biennial Puppet Festival (⏾ welcometoskipton.com) in the same month, running in even-numbered years.

Skipton Castle

✆ 01756 792442 ⏾ skiptoncastle.co.uk

I'm a bit fussy about castles. All too often I find them, and abbeys for that matter, a little samey – a set of ruins given the standard English Heritage treatment – but Skipton Castle is definitely not in that category. What makes it different is its completeness: it is a fully roofed and remarkably well-preserved medieval building, a fact for which we have one woman to thank – Lady Anne Clifford. She was the incumbent owner at the time of the Civil War when Skipton Castle, a Royalist stronghold, held out under siege for three years before finally falling to Parliamentarian forces in 1645. On Oliver Cromwell's personal instructions the castle was 'Puld downe and demolisht allmost to the foundacon', and that could have been it – another ruin. However, in 1658, with the monarchy restored, and that bounder Cromwell gone, Lady Anne set to rebuilding the castle, finally, personally planting a yew tree in the central courtyard to celebrate the completion in 1659. Ironically, Lady Anne was the last Clifford to live in Skipton Castle as she died without heir and the estate was sold.

I am a little embarrassed at how many trips to Skipton it took me to finally visit the castle. I suspect many visitors like me admire the magnificent gatehouse but, because the main building is only two storeys high and all hidden behind trees, assume that there's not much else to see, but there is, with over 20 rooms to visit (and children's activities too). There's a tea room, a bookshop, and a picnic area on the chapel terrace. Check for special events because these can really make your visit memorable; I was lucky enough to be there in May during the War of the Roses re-enactment, which the children watching got really excited about, and so did I, if I'm honest. The boy next to me said, 'I liked the sword fight best when they were really going at it and clanging their swords. It's a good job they were wearing armour 'cos they could easily have chopped each other's arms off. I wish I could have had a go with my brother.'

FOOD & DRINK

J Stanforth – Celebrated Pork Pie Establishment Mill Bridge ✆ 01756 793477 ◷ stanforthbutchers.co.uk. Their pork pies are so delicious that customers write poetry about them. They also sell other locally sourced meat products.

The Narrowboat Victoria St ✆ 01756 797992 ◷ markettowntaverns.co.uk. A refreshing change this, a wine bar that has reverted to a pub, and a good one at that. Wide range of local cask ales and European brands, reasonable wine list, and the food all fresh and home-cooked. Intimate feel, particularly the upstairs gallery area which sports a unique canal mural.

The Railway Cavendish St ✆ 01756 228307 ◷ therailwayskipton.co.uk. This ex-backstreet-boozer has been tastefully refurbished and is now a popular eatery and B&B.

Tempest Arms Elslack BD23 3AY ✆ 01282 842450 ◷ tempestarms.co.uk. A 16th-century inn regarded equally highly by connoisseurs of food, beer, wine and comfort. The atmosphere is friendly and relaxed and the food traditional English, all sourced locally. Accommodation also very good.

The Three Sheep Tea House High St ✆ 01756 709988 ☺ Mon–Sat. Good coffee and fresh homemade cakes, with outside tables out back on a cobbled side street.

4 EMBSAY & BOLTON ABBEY STEAM RAILWAY

✆ 01756 710614 ⬧ embsayboltonabbeyrailway.org.uk ☺ summer daily; spring & autumn Sat & Sun; various seasonal specials

Oh, Dr Beeching, what have you done? Only five miles of the original Skipton–Ilkley railway remain and three of those are managed by the volunteers of the Yorkshire Dales Railway Museum Trust. They operate trains, mainly steam, between Embsay and Bolton Abbey. While this is a fun 15-minute nostalgic experience it is not a particularly useful mode of transport from A to B. Both stations have a shop and café, and you may be tempted by occasional special events like a Thomas the Tank Engine day for the little ones or afternoon teas and footplate experiences for the big ones.

5 HETTON, RYLSTONE & CRACOE

Some visitors head north on a minor road, a welcome respite from the A65, and find themselves in **Hetton**, a sleepy hamlet with an exceptional pub, the Angel Inn, and a farm-based brewer. The Dark Horse Brewery (⬧ darkhorsebrewery.co.uk) is a breath of fresh air in the craft brewery industry. It's small and has no pretensions of grandeur, yet it has earned itself a reputation for brewing consistently high-quality beers during the ten years it's been producing. Its brewer, Richard Eyton-Jones, has steered the business along a true Slow, community-based path by sponsoring the Grassington Festival (now defunct) and local transport (such as the Wharfedale Packhorse minibus), supplying farm shops with fine beer and even recycling spent brewing grains into dog food.

Nearby, **Rylstone** (pronounced 'Rill-stun') is a humble hamlet that no-one would have heard of had it not been for the exploits of its Women's Institute. It was they that famously took their clothes off for a calendar photo shoot to raise money for leukaemia research, a story told in the film *Calendar Girls*. Many of the photos were taken down the road in the Devonshire Arms, the village pub of **Cracoe** (pronounced 'Cray-coh'). The village postman (long since retired) was one of the few people to appear in the film as themselves.

A choice of two enchanting walks links these three villages: a two-mile low-level potter along Chapel Lane or a five-mile circuit including the war memorial on the summit of Cracoe Fell.

⏸ FOOD & DRINK

The Angel Inn Hetton BD23 6LT ✆ 01756 730263 ⏚ angelhetton.co.uk. No longer a pub, but a stylish and fashionable Michelin-starred restaurant with upscale accommodation packages. Booking ahead essential.

Devonshire Arms Inn Cracoe ✆ 01756 699191 ⏚ devonshirearmsinncracoe.co.uk. Everything a village pub should be – very welcoming, proper beer, excellent food and good-value B&B. Pet- and cyclist-friendly.

Jacksons of Cracoe Cracoe BD23 6LB ✆ 01756 730269 ⏚ jacksonsofcracoe.co.uk. This is basically a butcher's shop with a twist. Not only can you buy top-quality local meat, including limestone beef and Dales lamb, but also they have some of the best sausages in Yorkshire, homemade cakes and preserves, and Brymor Farm ice cream (page 201). The in-house tea shop allows you to sit in and sample the local produce.

6 MALHAM & AROUND

🏠 **Malham Youth Hostel**

The first time that I visited Malham I was astonished at how small it was. How could such an insignificant hamlet be so well known? The truth is that it's not the buildings of Malham itself that are famous but the surrounding countryside: primarily **Malham Cove**, **Gordale Scar** and **Malham Tarn**. Hundreds of thousands of people come to see these natural wonders and they need somewhere to stay, park, eat and drink, so a service machine has developed, including two pubs, three cafés, around a dozen places to stay, and the National Park Centre to tell you about it all. There's even a working forge, where you can watch blacksmith Annabel Bradley at work (⏚ malhamsmithyonline.co.uk ☺ by appointment, or drop in on spec).

"The first time I visited I was astonished at how small it was. How could such an insignificant hamlet be so well known?"

Ironically, some visitors don't make it any further than the village; they see a picture of Gordale Scar in the visitor centre, buy a postcard of the cove, have a cup of tea and drive to the next place without seeing anything real – which is such a shame because the real things here are magnificent. Malham has two big events during the year, an

animal-themed activity week called the **Malham Safari** during spring bank holiday week, and the much more traditional **Malham Show** (⌇ malhamshow.co.uk) on August Bank Holiday Saturday.

Upper Airedale has two other villages, **Kirkby Malham** a mile downstream from Malham, and **Airton** the same distance again. Both are peaceful modest places with unusual buildings used as hostels. For groups, Kirkby Malham's is the Parish Hall (⌇ 01729 830740) while Airton's (for 'walkers, cyclists, climbers, family groups') is the Friends' Meeting House (⌇ airtonbarn.org.uk). Kirkby – for many years the home of author Bill Bryson – also has the parish church for the whole dale, a 15th-century building on a much older site, and the best pub in the dale, the Victoria Hotel. Airton boasts a farm shop selling all sorts of local produce, and cups of tea, at Town End Farm.

Malham Cove

I am not sure which experience of Malham Cove has left the biggest impression on me: the first time I stood below it gazing at the breathtaking scale of the curved wall in front maybe, or later that same day lying at the top with just my face over the overhang lip and 260ft of dizzying space below. Wherever it is viewed from, this is an awe-inspiring place that well deserves its ranking in any list of the Seven Natural Wonders of Britain.

The geology of the area seems simple; a beck flows out of Malham Tarn just over a mile north of the cove, but very quickly disappears underground as limestone rivers often do. The dry valley continues southwards, finishing as a notch at the top of the cove, and a river appears from the foot of the cliff. The obvious assumption is that it is the same water top and bottom and the river used to flow over the top of the cliff, creating the cove by erosion – but not so. The reality is a lot more deceptive: the cliff was formed millions of years ago by an upthrust of the mid-Craven fault. Much later, at the end of the last ice age, meltwater from a glacier formed a monstrous waterfall that eroded the cove four miles back into the hillside and sculpted it into its present curving shape. When the ice melted, the waterfall disappeared. Just to make it even more confusing, water-dye experiments have shown that the water

◀ **1** The limestone pavement at Malham Cove. **2** The village of Malham.
3 The breathtaking curved wall of Malham Cove.

from Malham Tarn does not reappear at the cove but travels at a lower level, reaching the surface south of the village at Aire Head Spring. The beck that bubbles out at the base of the cove is a different river entirely.

You really need to get close up to Malham Cove to experience the full effect; fortunately it is easily accessible for everyone, wheelchair users included. An easy mile from the main car park/bus stop brings you to the bottom of the cove from where you can marvel at the scenery, admire climbers scaling the crag or visit the RSPB base and watch the nesting peregrine falcons. Other birds to look out for here are little owls, green woodpeckers and one of the few natural-site nesting colonies of house martins. The steep slog up the Pennine Way to the top of the cove is worth the effort because the **limestone pavement** behind the cliff edge is a lush arctic/alpine rock garden in summer. Rarities like alpine bartsia, mountain pansy, bird's-eye primrose and mountain avens all thrive here in the sheltered crevices, or grykes.

Gordale Scar

When the 19th-century romantic artists and writers went in search of wild nature in Britain some of them discovered Gordale Scar and were suitably impressed. Wordsworth attempted to persuade others to visit: 'Let thy feet repair to Gordale-chasm, terrific as the lair where the young lions crouch.' Not modern-day brochure-speak, but he obviously liked it here. Thomas Gray the poet was a little more delicate; he declared that he could only bear to stay for a quarter of an hour, and even then 'not without shuddering'. All agreed that no painting could do justice to the scale of the ravine, except James Ward who solved the problem by producing one of the largest canvases ever attempted. His 14-foot by 12-foot painting is regarded as one of the most important 'sublime landscapes' of its time; it hangs in London's Tate Britain – it's so big it has a whole wall to itself.

So, does it merit all the hype? Yes, is the answer. Gordale Scar is impressive enough as a deep and fairly dry canyon now, but it must have been a terrifying place when the glacial meltwater river that excavated it was still raging. Despite its drama, Gordale is remarkably accessible along its flat lower section, about a third of a mile of wheelchair-negotiable track to the foot of the dual waterfall. If you do arrive on foot,

1 The view back from Gordale Scar. 2 Malham Tarn at sunrise. ▶

a convenient alternative return route to Malham is to follow Gordale Beck downstream as it leaps over Janet's Foss, and babbles through Wedber Wood en route to join the newly emerged River Aire. It is possible to escape out of the top end of Gordale Scar, but it does require a serious scramble alongside the waterfalls. It is worth doing just for the fun of it, but it will also lead you towards Malham Tarn and make a fantastic full-day walk possible, linking all of Malham's celebrity venues – the cove, the foss, the scar and the tarn.

Malham Tarn

The Malham Tarn estate is now under the stewardship of the National Trust but a clue to one of its earliest owners lies in the name of the highest fell in the region. At 2,169ft above sea level, Fountains Fell rises over nearly 12 square miles of prime limestone sheep country, and reminds us of the huge power and influence the monks of Fountains Abbey had, from a good 25 miles away near Ripon. After the dissolution of the monasteries the estate passed through many hands and finished up in the possession of the Morrison family. In the 1850s James Morrison converted what was a Georgian hunting lodge into Tarn House, then promptly died, leaving the estate and an awful lot of money to his son Walter. As a very rich socialite, Walter invited all and sundry up to Malham with celebrity guests including influential thinkers John Ruskin, Charles Darwin and John Stuart Mill. Writer Charles Kingsley was a regular visitor and much of his children's novel *Water Babies* was inspired by Malham Tarn.

In 1946 the last private owner of the estate bequeathed it to the National Trust and so it remains. The tarn itself is a National Nature Reserve, ecologically important through being one of only eight upland alkaline lakes in Europe. The lake has breeding great crested and little grebes, with winter bringing more waterfowl like pochard, wigeon, teal and goosanders. Alongside the open water are rich floral fen and bog areas. Access to all of the nature reserve is free of charge except for a wheelchair-accessible boardwalk across the bog that has a token entrance fee.

The National Trust also produces informative leaflets for a range of waymarked walks around the estate, from an eight-mile yomp up Fountains Fell to an easy, flat 4½-mile stroll around the tarn. The latter makes for a lovely family bike ride on surfaced tracks. The leaflets can be obtained from the NT's visitor centre in Malham village or are downloadable from its website.

SPECIAL STAYS

Malham Youth Hostel Malham BD23 4DV ✆ 0345 371 9529 ⌂ yha.org.uk. Malham's hostel still offers individual dorm beds (as well as en-suite private rooms and group accommodation) and is very well situated for the backpack-toting Slow Dales traveller. Pubs, cafés and a shop are on your doorstep, while Malham Cove, Gordale Scar and Janet's Foss are walkable directly from the hostel. Cyclists, whether on road or mountain bikes, have lots of options for circular routes, with all the tick-box sights easily visitable in a day on two wheels. Camping and cabins are available, and there's a good self-catering kitchen-diner.

FOOD & DRINK

Lister Arms Malham BD23 4DB ✆ 01729 830444 ⌂ listerarms.co.uk. A very good all-round pub. Traditional pub meals are hearty and high quality, a wide range of local beers are available; and accommodation is comfortable and dog-friendly.
Old Barn Tea Room Malham BD23 4DA ✆ 01729 830486 ⌂ oldbarnmalham.co.uk ☺ summer daily, otherwise variable: check website. A nice, small, unfussy café (muddy boots welcome) in the village centre. The all-day breakfast is recommended.
Town End Farm Tea Room Scosthrop, Airton BD23 4BE ✆ 01729 830902 ⌂ townendfarmshop.co.uk ☺ Tue–Sun. Part of a farm shop on a working farm, selling snacks and drinks.
Victoria Hotel Kirkby Malham BD23 4BS ✆ 01729 830499. A peaceful, welcoming village pub and easily my favourite in the dale. Changing list of mainly Yorkshire cask ales and good pub meals.

MID WHARFEDALE

Most of the River Wharfe's length is downstream of the Yorkshire Dales, and into the county of West Yorkshire, but our interest lies upstream in its midsection. **Bolton Abbey** sits at the border, just in North Yorkshire and the national park, and Mid Wharfedale continues nearly ten miles northwards from here to the small town of **Grassington**, with much to please in between.

7 BOLTON ABBEY

The ecclesiastical remains at the tiny village of Bolton so dominate that the whole place is now called Bolton Abbey (⌂ boltonabbey.com;

A walk from Bolton Abbey

✻ OS Explorer map OL2; start: Bolton Abbey ⚲ SE075541; 8½ miles; moderate, one or two steep sections and care needed navigating on the moor in bad weather

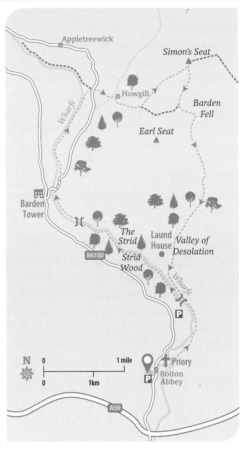

My favourite walk from Bolton Abbey is a longer one that includes Strid Wood but continues upriver following the route of the Dales Way to Howgill. Here a permissive path climbs through the woods to open fellside and ultimately to the summit of Simon's Seat. The return journey takes in Barden Fell and descends the spectacular Valley of Desolation, again on a permissive path. At the end of this walk, if your legs are up to it, detour a couple of hundred yards up the road to Laund House to pay your respects to a venerable old-timer. The Laund Oak, by the roadside, is one of the oldest oak trees in the country, a peer of the Sherwood Forest Major Oak, and over 800 years old.

free entry). Ironically, for a building that was never completed, it is one of the most intact priories in the country with the original nave still used as the **priory church of St Mary and St Cuthbert**. You can wander freely around the 12th-century ruins and remains, with easy cycle access, enjoying the tranquil riverside setting. This riverside site ranks with Rievaulx and Fountains (page 240) as one of the most awe-inspiring positions for an abbey anywhere. No wonder the Augustinians moved here from their original priory in Embsay. After the Dissolution, the priory church's nave remarkably survived as a place for local worship. Meanwhile, the abbey lands passed through various noble hands until arriving into those of the Duke of Devonshire in the 18th century; the Cavendish family still own and operate the estate.

Their lands extend upstream to include **Strid Wood** and **Barden Tower**, **Barden Moor** and, on the other side of the river, the wide tracts of **Barden Fell**. These are the places to head for if you are seeking solitude because most visitors stay around the priory or on the riverbanks between Bolton Bridge and a charismatic Victorian building, the **Cavendish Pavilion**. This is still doing what it was designed for in 1898, serving tea, sandwiches and cakes to thousands of visitors from the north of England. Children won't be interested in that though; once they have had their ice cream they will be drawn like magnets to the river to paddle, fish for minnows and **swim** in the deeper pools, and it is safe to do so here unless the river is running high and fast. The estate doesn't actively encourage swimming but they don't discourage it either. **Fly fishing** is also possible in the river; trout or grayling day tickets are best purchased online in advance, and it's obviously best where the swimmers and paddlers aren't.

If you have children who are not interested in the river, or it is too cold or flooded, there are other things to keep them entertained, including the Welly Walk for instance, or nature bingo in Strid Wood (all the instructions and game cards are downloadable from the website before you visit). For really enquiring youngsters or mature learners, the estate produces a teachers' pack, designed for school groups but just as interesting for adults and families. Alternatively, if there are enough of you, it is possible to hire a guide from the estate to run workshops on a wide range of topics from outdoor poetry and art to wildlife and bushcraft activities.

Strid Wood

This area of woodland, though not very big or containing any especially rare or spectacular species, is a delight. The trees, mainly oak, cling to the deep sides of Strid Gorge and support a rich population of birds in the spring and fungi in the autumn. The dawn chorus here in June features all the signature woodland birds of Yorkshire: redstarts, pied and spotted flycatchers and wood warblers. Dead wood is drummed on and excavated into by green and great spotted woodpeckers, and nuthatches and treecreepers scuttle around on the wrinkled trunks. The woods are special, but it is the River Wharfe that makes this place exceptional, and gives it the name.

Strid is local dialect for stride and refers to one place where the river narrows to a step's width across. In reality it is more like a leap, and a brave one at that, because the whole river thunders through the gap below. The Strid is even more dangerous than it seems because both banks are actually suspended ledges of gritstone covering deep undercuts on both sides. Numerous swimmers over the years have been taken under them by wayward currents and drowned. On less vigorous stretches of the river, dippers bob on the rocks, grey wagtails leap for flies in sunny spots and, if you're lucky, a common sandpiper will trill its alarm as it disappears upstream.

"The woods are special, but it is the River Wharfe that makes this place exceptional, and gives it the name."

Six waymarked trails can be found in Strid Wood, some very short and wheelchair accessible and all less than two miles long. They can get very crowded on summer weekends, especially on the car park side of the river.

Barden Tower

This imposing building has lots going for it, not least the fact that wandering around it is free of charge. Despite its name, it is more than just a tower, but not quite a castle, and has had a few changes of role in its long life. Originally a Norman hunting lodge, it was later extended into a fortified house by Sir Henry Clifford, who fancied living in the country rather than Skipton Castle. That accomplished renovator, Lady Anne Clifford, got her twopenny-worth in during the 1650s but on her death the tower passed to the Earls of Cork and fell into decline. After a spell as a farmhouse in the late 18th century it was abandoned.

---

1 View over the spectacular Bolton Abbey. **2** Strid Wood supports a rich population of birds. **3** A circular walk from Grassington takes in wonderful Grass Wood. **4** The village – or town! – of Grassington. ▶

The building next door to the tower was never abandoned: the Priest's House was built by Sir Henry Clifford for his personal chaplain and is now what must be one of the most atmospheric wedding venues in the country. The old stables next door have been converted into a very convenient self-catering bunkhouse (Barden Bunkbarn) for large parties.

🍴 FOOD & DRINK

Back o' th' Hill Farm Storiths BD23 6HU 🖉 07702 415772 🖉 backothhillfarm.co.uk ⊙ Summer Sat & Sun. Stylish drinks, light meals and bakes on a cyclists'-favourite back lane, just over the river from Bolton Abbey. Cosy, small-scale bunkhouse accommodation too.
The Cavendish Pavilion BD23 6EX 🖉 01756 710245 🖉 cavendishpavilion.co.uk. For location, the pick of Bolton Abbey's cafés, especially if you sit outside by the river, nestled underneath the hills on either side. Only sandwiches and small snacks in the way of eats, though.
The Tea Cottage 🖉 01756 710495 🖉 teacottageboltonabbey.co.uk. In the 'village centre', with terrace tables overlooking the priory and riverside. Home-cooked light meals, cream teas, gin and prosecco.

Pubs

The Devonshire is the only hostelry in Bolton Abbey but three miles down the road (and into West Yorkshire) Addingham has two proper pubs worth calling in on.

The Devonshire Arms Hotel & Spa BD23 6AJ 🖉 01756 718100 🖉 thedevonshirearms. co.uk. When a place adds 'and Spa' to its name you know what you're likely to get: opulence at a price, and that's the case here. This isn't a pub as such, but the bar is a comfortable place to sample a range of Theakston beers and upmarket bar meals. For really fine dining there is the sumptuous Burlington Restaurant. Accommodation, with a newly refurbished spa, is luxurious but expensive.
The Fleece Main St, Addingham 🖉 01943 830397 🖉 the-fleece.com. A large pub with a welcoming taproom and posh restaurant. Exceptional seafood, good beer.
The Swan Main St, Addingham 🖉 01943 430003 🖉 swan-addingham.co.uk. A friendly village local with real fires and regular live music. Superb beer, good food.

8 GRASSINGTON

🏠 Grassington House

'Now that's a good question and I wish you had asked someone else,' said the welcoming lady at the Devonshire Institute reception. 'I could flannel on for ten minutes trying to answer it but, to be honest, I don't know. If you do find out come back and tell me.'

My question was a simple one, or so I thought. 'Is Grassington a town or a village?' I had been given a variety of conflicting answers by other locals up to this point. 'Village of course, it's too small for a town' (barmaid). 'Town I think. Isn't that what the "ton" means?' (local artist). 'No, this is a village, Skipton's the town' (farmer).

The definitive answer is that it is a town; the official reason being it was granted a charter for a market and fair in 1282. Grassington has played a few roles in its time, originally as the name suggests as a place for grazing cattle, then a market for selling them. The town was very involved with both the long-gone lead-mining and textile booms, and the railway made a fleeting visit then left again. Now this is the administrative centre for Upper Wharfedale in the background but its public face, especially from Easter to October, is tourism. Grassington is one of the best-loved and most-visited places in the Dales. It has a National Park Centre, a small folk museum, a clutch of pubs and cafés as well as numerous art and craft shops, mostly clustered around the Market Square.

Grassington's popular music and arts festival ran for over 40 years, but unfortunately no longer operates.

If the crowds in town get too much, two nearby rural diversions are within easy walking distance: **Grass Wood** upstream and **Linton Falls** in the opposite direction. If you continue downstream on the Dales Way footpath, or back roads, there are a series of very photogenic and individual villages to visit: **Burnsall** right on the river and **Hebden** and **Appletreewick** just above it.

Grass Wood

As I'm a naturalist, this is one of my favourite places in the Dales – no, not just in the Dales, anywhere. A circular walk from Grassington of not much more than three miles takes in one of the most beautiful stretches of the River Wharfe, a Woodland Trust Reserve, a Yorkshire Wildlife Trust Nature Reserve and one of the most important archaeological sites in Yorkshire. Doing the route clockwise the river comes first and, if it is warm enough, you may be tempted to have a swim in one of the deep pools. The Wharfe is probably the best Yorkshire river for wild swimming (page 26) and this mile-long section is one of its best but take care near Ghaistrill's Strid – it is another powerful 'narrows' with dangerous undercuts like its Bolton Abbey namesake.

If you are lucky enough to be here in early summer, the floral display once you enter the wood will blow you away if you are that way inclined. This is an ancient woodland designated as a Site of Special Scientific Interest and especially rich in flower species: carpets of bluebells in May give way to betony, St John's wort, basil, marjoram, lily of the valley and herb paris to name but a few. Keep an eye out for orchids as some rare ones have a foothold here.

Higher up on the hillside as the trees thin to meadow on the limestone pavement, butterflies are everywhere: fritillaries, peacocks, blues and heaths, and the rare northern brown argus if you are lucky. Another scarce insect lives here – the yellow ant; you may well not see them but the distinctive grassy humps of their anthills testify to the antiquity of the meadows.

The return route to Grassington is on the Dales Way footpath, passing extensive archaeological remains of old settlements. For 2,000 years the inhabitants of the Dales have been gradually moving their homes down towards the river, leaving faint footprints behind – Bronze Age at the top, Iron Age and medieval in sequence lower down.

Linton & Linton Falls

The dramatic natural cataract of Linton Falls on the River Wharfe is nearer to Grassington than the village of Linton, so the choice of name is a little odd. It possibly has something to do with the church on the riverbank a quarter of a mile downstream. This is Linton's parish **church of St Michael and All Angels**, a long name for a tiny medieval building but in a magical setting. The church is even further from the village than the falls, probably because it re-uses the site of an earlier pagan shrine, so it is perhaps apt that the Green Man, a pagan symbol, should be carved into the church roof timbers. Despite there being no footpath from the river to Linton village it is still worth strolling up the road for half a mile to see the pretty village green and packhorse bridge and have a meal or drink in the Fountaine Inn. If water levels are low enough you can recross the river via stepping stones to return to Grassington along the north bank.

 SPECIAL STAYS

Grassington House Grassington BD23 5AQ ✆ 01756 752406 ⬦ grassingtonhouse.co.uk. This elegant Georgian house, tastefully restored by owners Sue and John Rudden, is right on the marketplace cobbles in the centre of town. It offers unapologetic luxury in a five-star hotel with a top-class restaurant. You can watch the world go by from the restaurant's outside tables, enjoying a five-course gourmet dinner, or perhaps the special Sunday roast featuring 14-hour slow-cooked beef. After a bracing day outdoors, the large bath tubs and king-size beds provide the ideal way to wind down. You don't even need a car to get here, or get around: the hotel is five minutes' walk from the bus station, with routes to many places in and around the Dales. Day walks and bike rides start right from the hotel door, and enable you to explore Wharfedale in the authentic Slow way, but also in style.

¶¶ FOOD & DRINK

Grassington has lots of cafés close together, a sign of healthy competition and good quality all round.

Corner House Café Garrs Lane ✆ 01756 752414 🖉 cornerhousegrassington.co.uk. Offers substantial locally sourced meals as well as coffee and snacks in a friendly atmosphere. Interesting specials, with tables inside and on the forecourt.

Forester's Arms Main St ✆ 01756 752349 🖉 forestersarmsgrassington.co.uk. My favourite pub in Grassington, this is a friendly and welcoming place with well-kept cask Yorkshire beers and good food. I enjoyed the tenderest Dales lamb that I have ever had here. Great fish and chips, too.

Fountaine Inn Linton BD23 5HJ ✆ 01756 752210 🖉 fountaineinnatlinton.co.uk. A welcoming pub with accommodation, and in a great setting, overlooking the village green on the beck-side. Named after a local man who made his fortune in London at the time of the Black Death – burying bodies! Range of local cask ales on tap, including their own-brand Fountaine Inn ale.

Grassington House The Square ✆ 01756 752406 🖉 grassingtonhouse.co.uk. Very good food in a lovely Georgian building. Meals are designed to be eaten as multi-courses, so portions aren't huge. Afternoon tea particularly recommended, as is their accommodation.

9 HEBDEN & BURNSALL

Hebden is a solid little village with a decent café and pub and a very obvious lead-mining past. Lots of small miners' cottages line Mill and Back lanes as they creep down the hill to the river. Stepping stones and a footbridge here allow the Dales Way path to cross the Wharfe on its way to **Burnsall**. Between the two places is a dramatic half mile of watercourse as the river eats into high limestone banks to form the precipitous crags of Loup Scar and Wilfrid Scar, popular 'leaping' rocks into the deep river pools. St Wilfrid also gives his name to the very old church close by.

THE FITTON FAMILY FLAG

Burnsall Feast Sports are rife with tradition, none more closely followed than the fixing of the flag on race day. The Fitton family did it for decades before the role passed to the Stockdales: Jim and his son now organise the fell race. Former flagmaster Chris Fitton recalls:

'I don't know how old I was when I first climbed the fell on Sports Day, possibly four or five. My father had been doing it for many years prior to the war and established it as a family ritual. The object of the exercise was to carry the flag up and put it securely into the cairn which still stands proud at the top of Burnsall Fell. Then, as now, it represented blessed relief to aching legs as the halfway point that all competitors in the Classic Fell Race must pass prior to the heart-stopping descent.

'Since that first time around 1948, I and assorted family members have climbed the fell faithfully every year. The group of between five and ten has included pregnant mothers, newly born toddlers, grandchildren, children, adults up to their late seventies together with boyfriends, girlfriends and occasionally somewhat reluctant strangers who, full of ale in the Red Lion the night before, having heard of the annual pilgrimage, swore they would join us and, more often than not, did. This motley group would always assemble around 07.00 outside the car park, hopefully with the flag. The flag is, and always was, the great problem. No-one can ever find it.

'Committee members provide storage space for the various accoutrements of the Sports Day, and the night before it is all brought down to the green. As often as not, the flag is missing. Over the years it has taken the shape of an old cream bed-sheet, a St George's flag, and once, bizarrely, a National Benzole flag.

'Sometimes there is a pole but no flag, and sometimes a flag but no pole.

'The route taken never varies, and we have a breather at the top of the field before reaching the summit around 7.30, to drain a celebratory flask of whisky once the flag is securely installed. Finally, the view is admired and we stick out our chests and say to each other that we should do this more regularly. We never do.

'On our return home, a vast and well-earned breakfast is consumed and I offer up a prayer that whoever brings down that flag gives it to someone who can remember, 12 months later, what he did with it.'

Burnsall's most striking landmark is its graceful five-arched stone bridge spanning the river. Right by it is a splendid green, ideal for picnics, and overlooked by pubs and cafés. The village's most famous event is its annual fell race which was first run in the 1870s, making it the oldest of its kind in the world, a fact that the villagers are fiercely proud of. Evidence that sporting events have been part of the Feast of St Wilfrid since before Elizabethan times gives it an even more impressive claim of antiquity. For labyrinthine historical reasons, Burnsall Feast (⌂ burnsallsports.co.uk) takes place in August, with the races being run on the Saturday following the 12th of that month.

The 'Classic' fell race, as it is called, starts from the bridge with competitors aiming for a flagged cairn on Burnsall Fell about 1½ miles away and 1,000ft above the village. The best runners make the flag in just over ten minutes, which is quick, but nowhere near their suicidal descent speed, as some of them manage the return in less than three minutes.

⫲ FOOD & DRINK

Devonshire Fell Hotel Burnsall BD23 6BT ✆ 01756 729000 ⌂ devonshirefell.co.uk. Just out of the village and overlooking the river, this country hotel offers very highly regarded lunches, afternoon teas and evening meals. Prices are high but you are paying for real quality. Pet-friendly accommodation also available.

The Red Lion Burnsall BD23 6BU ✆ 01756 634542 ⌂ redlion.co.uk. An ancient building with 900-year-old cellars that have a resident ghost who allegedly turns the beer pumps off and causes people to trip down stairs. Food features game in season and locally sourced meats and cheeses. A range of cask beers, mostly from Yorkshire. Highly regarded accommodation.

Wharfe View Tea Room The Green, Burnsall YO23 6BS ✆ 01756 720237 ⌂ wharfeviewtearoom.com ◔ Sat–Wed. Fresh homemade sandwiches, light meals and cream teas in this welcoming café overlooking the riverside green, very popular with walkers and bikers.

10 APPLETREEWICK

If ever a name conjures up pastoral loveliness it's this one, but over the years locals have tired of the full tongue-twisting mouthful and shortened it to 'Aptrick'. Sunday name or not, this is a very agreeable place, especially down in the valley bottom where the river bounces and swirls its *"Down in the valley bottom,* way through a series of rapids, beloved *the river bounces and* of slalom kayakers. Not many villages of *swirls its way through* this size manage to support a pub these *a series of rapids."* days, but Appletreewick keeps two going comfortably. One of them, the Craven Arms, incorporates the village's most remarkable building: not the pub itself but a cruck barn behind it. This is modern but made to a very old design and with a heather-thatched roof, the first of its kind built for 400 years in the Dales.

I'm sure Aptrick has produced many remarkable people over the centuries, but for the one that made the biggest impact on the world stage we have to go back to the early 1600s. **William Craven**, a humble village lad, was sent off to London to apprentice as a draper and, to cut a long story short, did quite well for himself. By the time he returned he had made his fortune, earned himself a knighthood, spent a term as Mayor of London and married the king's sister. I can imagine his reception on returning to the snug of the Craven Arms: 'Na then Billy. Tha's not done badly. Tha round, methinks.' It's thought that William was the inspiration for the well-known story of Dick Whittington.

You can take a stroll downstream to the stepping stones near **Howgill**. This is another inviting, swimmable section of river and quiet enough to offer a really good chance of seeing the local wildlife. I know that there are otters and crayfish here, even though I haven't seen either of them alive. On my last swimming visit here I landed on a mid-river rock that held the chewed-up remains of a native white-clawed crayfish, its one remaining claw bearing its furry killer's teeth marks.

FOOD & DRINK

Craven Arms Inn BD23 6DA ✆ 01756 720270 🖱 craven-cruckbarn.co.uk. A wonderfully atmospheric building restored to its original state of oak beams, flagstone floor, gas lights and open fires. Traditional pub games, good food and a range of Yorkshire cask beers.
The New Inn West End BD23 6DA ✆ 01756 720252. Unspoilt village local, for many years ahead of its time as the only non-smoking pub in the country. Serves a wide range of Yorkshire real ales and good food. Comfortable B&B.

11 PARCEVALL HALL GARDENS

BD23 6DE ✆ 01756 720311 🖱 parcevallhallgardens.co.uk ⊙ Apr–Oct

'Serene' was the word that sprang to mind when I first set foot over the threshold here, which is no surprise, as that is the feeling its creator was trying to achieve. I say 'creator' although Sir William Milner did not build the hall from scratch, but renovated a derelict Elizabethan building in the late 1920s. He definitely did create the garden though, skilfully laying out borders, terraces and woodland – transforming what was previously open agricultural fellside. Sir William came from

◄ **1** The village of Burnsall. **2** Linton Falls, near Grassington. **3** Parcevall Hall Gardens.
4 Exploring Stump Cross Caverns.

a wealthy socialite family, a world that he did not fit into easily. He was quiet and retiring, writing once of his delight in 'sitting with a friend in front of a roaring log fire, in companionable quiet over coffee'. He was a deeply religious man so it is apt that his legacy, the hall, is now leased to the church to be used as a retreat, and the rest of us can use the tea room and gardens for the same purpose. Slightly at odds with this genteel ambience but testimony to the huge changes Sir William managed here, the hillside above Parcevall Hall is so wild and intimidating that the Anglo-Saxons named one ravine the Troll's Arse, now Trollers Ghyll, and there are still tales of the ghostly dog with giant shining eyes called the Barquest, whose appearance foretold a death.

12 STUMP CROSS CAVERNS

HG3 5JL 01756 752780 stumpcrosscaverns.co.uk Wed–Sun

The name suggests that there was once an old way-cross near here, on the Grassington to Pateley Bridge packhorse route, but no evidence of it can be found on the ground now. What there are in abundance are telltale signs of a lead-mining past: disused levels, tips and literally hundreds of old shafts pockmarking the surface of the moor. It was lead miners searching for more rich seams of metal who discovered the natural fissure at Stump Cross in 1860, but it was worthless to them as a source of ore.

"Most cavers visit just for the thrills, but some important scientific discoveries have also been made along the way."

But one local man had his finger on the pulse of the burgeoning Victorian tourist industry and realised that there was more than one way to make money underground. William Newbould bought the cave and opened it to the public, charging one shilling per person per visit – at the time, roughly the price of six pints in a pub. In the subsequent 150 years, the Stump Cross cavern system has been extensively explored and found to extend over four miles.

Most cavers visit just for the thrills, but some important scientific discoveries have also been made along the way. We know, for instance, that the cave was open to the outside about 90,000 years ago, because animal bones dating from this time have been found inside. The Yorkshire Dales must have been a very cold place then, as these remains are from animals that all live in today's Arctic regions. Fragments of skeletons from bison and reindeer have turned up, but the prize find was the well-preserved skull of a wolverine, one of the few ever to be found in Britain. Entry into the cave (with a 20-minute film show) is reasonable value – less than six pints of beer today, certainly – but if going underground doesn't appeal, then the modern information centre, gift shop and recently refurbished café at ground level are all free of charge to visit.

Grimwith Reservoir, a mile or two west of the caverns on the main road, is Yorkshire's largest, and more beautiful than the name might suggest. There's car parking and wheelchair-accessible paths round the water's edge.

UPPER WHARFEDALE

Further upstream, Wharfedale heads between the high fells beyond the twin villages of **Kilnsey** and **Conistone**, splitting into the two arms of **Littondale** and **Langstrothdale**, which then wrap around the top of Craven in a cosy embrace. Usually, as you head up a hill-country valley, settlements become sparser and smaller; Wharfedale does not deviate from this norm, and beyond Grassington there is nothing even remotely resembling a town.

Kettlewell justly claims to be the largest of the Upper Wharfedale villages, and will be familiar if you have seen the film *Calendar Girls*, as this was the location used for much of the action. The valley's only road winds its way through **Starbotton**, and reaches another parting of the ways at **Buckden**. If you are using wheeled transport you have a choice here; right takes you to **Cray** and then over to Bishopdale and Aysgarth and, at 1,400ft, it is the highest bus route in the Dales – a spectacular run on the number 875 but only once a week in summer

EXTREME CLIMBING IN WHARFEDALE

At 170ft high, Kilnsey Crag is not huge, but the glacier that scraped away its bottom section thousands of years ago has left a bizarrely suspended lump of rock that doesn't look as if it should stay up. The 40-foot overhang is a magnet for extreme climbers and there are numerous described routes on Kilnsey Crag. The first person to complete a new route has the honour of naming it; 'Sticky Wicket' I can see the logic of, but 'Let Them Eat Jellybeans'? The most difficult climb, Northern Lights, was climbed in the year 2000 by S McClure and graded 9a – that's 'virtually impossible' to you and me.

(Sunday, noon from Kettlewell, returning 16.00 from Hawes). A left turn at Buckden follows the River Wharfe through **Hubberholme** and then a much higher pass over the flank of Dodd Fell direct to Hawes – much too high and steep for a bus unfortunately, but an enjoyable drive in a car. If you can manage it on a bike, you deserve a medal: it's Yorkshire's highest tarmac road, reaching 1,932ft. It's well known to cyclists as 'Fleet Moss', with stretches of 1 in 5.

13 KILNSEY & CONISTONE

These two villages, though they have half a mile of clear valley and a river separating them, have been tied since the 14th century when they were known as Conyston cum Kylnesey. They still have a joint church and village hall (and one of the biggest agricultural shows in the Dales in early September) but Kilnsey has the lion's share of the visitors. This must be partly down to the attention-grabbing cliff that looms over the village.

Kilnsey Park & Trout Farm

✆ 01756 752150 ⌂ kilnseypark.co.uk ⊙ Easter–Oct daily; Nov–Easter Tue–Sun

Kilnsey's other big draw is this, a business unashamedly aimed at families with fun fishing, an adventure playground and trails, and cuddly animals to pet. There's also a red squirrel enclosure. For adults this is a working trout farm where you can learn to fly fish, hire rods, and buy smoked, frozen or fresh fish. Or just eat it in the farm-shop café: this is the only place I have ever heard of that does battered trout, chips and peas.

Kilnsey Park is also serious about its environmental impact, generating its own hydro-electric power, running a red squirrel breeding programme and a reintroduction scheme for lady's slipper orchids.

🍴 FOOD & DRINK

The Tennant's Arms Kilnsey BD23 5PS ✆ 01756 753946. A big place with a large central stone-floored bar and smaller opulently decorated rooms. Nothing super-luxurious, but a range of beers and very good-value food, especially the Sunday carvery. Accommodation available.

---

1 Kilnsey village and the looming cliff behind it, Kilnsey Crag. 2 Arncliffe is in Littondale.
3 Hiking Great Whernside. 4 Kettlewell has become a centre for hikers. ▶

ALBINONI/S

SS

PETE STUART/S

ANDREW ROLAND/S

14 KETTLEWELL

Transport on foot, whether two or four, has long been a theme here. Kettlewell grew up at the meeting place of packhorse and drovers' routes and is now quite a centre for walkers, using many of those old bridleways of course. I'm sure our ancestors would find our habit of walking for leisure very odd though, especially our penchant for deliberately heading for the highest hilltops. Their walks were everyday practical means of journeying from village to village and valley to valley via the lowest and easiest route. They wouldn't dream of aiming for the summit of **Great Whernside**, which is my favourite destination from Kettlewell.

Another thing our ancestors might find weird is Kettlewell's August **Scarecrow Festival** (⊘ kettlewellscarecrowfestival.co.uk), when the village is invaded by inventive and humorous homemade effigies ranging from the scary to the satirical. It claims to be 'Britain's best'!

¶¶ FOOD & DRINK

All three pubs in Kettlewell are worth visiting. In my view **The King's Head** on The Green (⌀ 01756 761600 ⊘ thekingsheadkettlewell.co.uk) is the best for food (check out their

The ascent of Great Whernside

❉ OS Explorer map OL30; start: Blue Bell Inn ♀ SD968723; 7 miles; moderate–difficult, with steep slopes near the summit and care needed with navigation

This impressive fell (not to be confused with Whernside) rivals the Three Peaks for altitude but has far fewer visiting walkers. The outward route from Kettlewell tours the full length of the village to Fold Farm campsite then follows Dowber Gill Beck up the hillside, with birds your only company; meadow pipits and wheatears mainly, but ring ouzels breed in the quiet corners. The public footpath stops after a mile or so, at the remains of Providence Lead Mine, but, as this is all open access land, you can head straight up the slope to the summit. You will have earned the next flat mile of ridge walk north, with glorious views of Nidderdale to your right and Wharfedale to the left (weather permitting). After a steep descent to Tor Dike, the return route is an historic one along ancient bridleways with an optional mile-and-a-bit extension to Starbotton. Back in Kettlewell you can rehydrate in one of its cafés or three pubs – a fairly good choice, but not a patch on the 13 hostelries that existed at the height of the village market's importance a couple of hundred years ago.

large specials menu) and **The Blue Bell Inn** by the bridge (✆ 01756 760230) serves the best range of beers (with eight local cask ales), but don't forget to call in on **The Racehorses** (✆ 01756 760233 ⬦ racehorseshotel.co.uk) as well – they do good pizzas.

Take-away hot drinks and snacks are available from the **village shop** on Middle Lane, and from the **Cottage Tea Rooms** (no inside tables, but tent seating outside) opposite the main car park. For a proper sit-in café, you can enjoy barista coffee, craft beers, imaginative cakes and 'tasting tapas' at the **&then Tasting Deli** (🅕 andthendelikettlewell ☺ Tue– Sun) across from The Racehorses.

15 BUCKDEN

A Bronze Age stone circle at Yockenthwaite provides archaeological evidence of people living in this valley for thousands of years, but Buckden is a relative latecomer. The name gives a clue as to why; Buck-dene, the valley of deer, refers to the Norman hunting forest of Langstrothdale, and the village was created as their forest keeper's headquarters. Only later when the forests were cleared and the last deer had been killed did Buckden become a market town dealing in sheep and wool. The market is long gone but there is a village store open every day, a local artists' gallery that doubles as a national park information point, and a farm

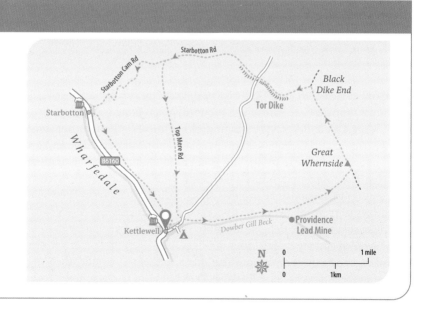

THE SOLE SURVIVOR

'That plane is too low,' thought 12-year-old Norman Parrington, as he stared up into the snowy sky from his school playground in Kettlewell on 31 January 1942.

The all-Polish, six-man crew of the Wellington bomber that Norman had seen were oblivious to the danger that they were in because of the blizzard, so did not see the summit ridge of Buckden Pike looming up until it was too late. The plane clipped a stone wall at 200mph and hit the mountain, slithering several hundred feet before stopping. The rear gunner's turret, with Joe Fusniak in it, was completely knocked off the aircraft on the initial impact, a fact which probably saved his life.

Concussed, and with a broken ankle, he crawled to the remains of the rest of the plane to find only one companion still alive, but seriously injured. With the blizzard still raging, Joe realised that he needed to get off the mountain to save both their lives.

He crawled nearly a mile through the snow, hopelessly lost, until he chanced upon a set of fox tracks which eventually led him down to the White Lion Inn at Cray, and safety. Sadly, the Parker family living in the pub couldn't understand Joe's broken English as he tried to explain the plight of his crewmate. By the time he managed to convince them that he wasn't a German pilot, and that a rescue was needed, the weather was too bad to send out a search party. The following day the plane was found, but too late; Joe's friend Jan Sadowski had died in the night.

In 1942 in recognition of his bravery, Sergeant Joseph Fusniak was awarded the British Empire medal by George VI, but was haunted for years afterwards by memories of his lost companions. In 1973 he personally erected a stone cross near the site of the crash, with fragments of the aircraft embedded in its base, and a small sculpture of a fox attached, in thanks to the animal that saved his life.

shop stocked with local Heber Farm lamb and beef. Like Kettlewell it is now a tourist centre with a high proportion of visiting walkers.

Most stick to the gentle pastoral strolls in the valley bottom, but some are tempted up the hill behind the village and **Buckden Pike** can be a tremendous little excursion. This is not a long walk, less than two miles from pub to summit, but it is steep and exciting. Normally, a circular route is just as good done in either direction, but this is one walk I would always start by following the direct route up alongside Buckden Beck. This way the scenic delights are more visible, a tricky, slippery descent is avoided and my dodgy knees don't get such a hammering. If you can manage to be there on a sunny day after a spell of wet weather then you are in for a treat because Buckden Beck's descent is precipitous to say the least. The OS map shows three waterfalls, but there are at least four times that number, of various sizes. High up the hill, the beck emerges from the remains of Buckden lead mine, a peaceful place away from the roar of water, to rest and contemplate. A direct line uphill across open access land will bring you to the summit ridge; turn left and it's a short stroll to the trig point at 2,303ft. Turn right on a short detour of a couple of hundred yards or so and you will arrive at a cross marked on the map as 'Memorial Cross', the site of dramatic and tragic wartime events (see opposite).

There's also a terrific lower-level four-mile circular walk linking up Buckden, Cray and Hubberholme. Follow the track rising north from Buckden – you can later drop to Cray and find a path above the pub heading west along a glorious natural terrace, with exquisite views right down Wharfedale. When you reach **Hubberholme**, pop into the church – a beauty, with a rare rood-loft dating back to 1558. The writer J B Priestley's ashes are buried somewhere here, but the exact location is kept secret. From here you can follow the Dales Way back, along the lane and then along the river to Buckden, where you can buy a hot pie and drink from the village shop and enjoy them on the green.

A good time to come is mid-June, when you can enjoy Buckden Gala (⊘ buckdengala.co.uk).

⫶⫶ FOOD & DRINK

The Buck Inn Buckden BD23 5JA ⊘ 01756 761933 ⊘ thebuckinn-buckden.co.uk. After a period of closure, the Buck has been refurbished and is back in business as the hub of village life. The beer is as good as ever and food is traditional and affordable pub fare. Dog-friendly B&B available.

The George Inn Hubberholme BD23 5JE ⊘ 01756 760223 ⊘ thegeorge-inn.co.uk. This Grade II-listed, 17th-century building was first a farm and later a vicarage, but is now a cracking little pub. All of the food is good but their pies have won awards (Monday is pie night) and Sunday dinners are very popular. Local beers, including the own-brand George Inn ale from Wensleydale Brewery, and a heated, covered courtyard. Good-value, dog-friendly rooms.

16 LITTONDALE

This tributary valley of the Wharfe shares with Wensleydale the unusual feature of taking its name from a small village in the dale and not the river. The River Skirfare begins its life at the head of the valley where Foxup Beck and Cosh Beck meet, after which it flows serenely down the middle of a typical small Yorkshire dale past the hamlets of Halton Gill, Litton, Arncliffe and Hawkswick. Remnants of the ancient hunting forest cling to the steep valley sides and support rich mixtures of limestone flowers. Herb paris is one of them and is known as a primary woodland indicator species, one that only grows in very old and undisturbed woodland, so its presence in Hawkswick and Scoska Woods in particular testify to their age.

Arncliffe, with its characterful green, is the largest of the dale's hamlets and takes its name from the days when eagles were found in Yorkshire, 'erne' being the old English name for the white-tailed eagle. Two minor roads link Littondale with neighbouring valleys, Halton Gill to Stainforth in Ribblesdale and Arncliffe to Malham in Airedale. Both routes are spectacular and only suitable for healthy cars or very fit and healthy cyclists. It's a shame that they're too steep for buses as they would make superb scenic routes.

FOOD & DRINK

The Falcon Inn Arncliffe BD23 5QE ✐ 01756 770205. A time-warp gem that served as the original 'Woolpack' in early episodes of the TV soap *Emmerdale*. Serves Timothy Taylor's beer straight from the cask in a jug and lunchtime snacks including legendary pie and peas. B&B is on offer and free permits for wild brown trout fishing on the nearby River Skirfare are available to residents.

Queen's Arms Litton BD23 5QJ ✐ 01756 770096 ⌂ queensarmslitton.co.uk. Friendly rustic pub with generous portions of locally sourced food and beers from down the dale in Ilkley. Good value and comfortable rooms too.

Adventures in Britain

LIZZIE CARR

PADDLING BRITAIN

50 BEST PLACES TO EXPLORE BY SUP, KAYAK & CANOE

Bradt

CAROLINE MILLS

CAMPING ROAD TRIPS UK

30 ADVENTURES WITH YOUR CAMPERVAN, MOTORHOME OR TENT

Bradt

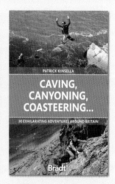

PATRICK KINSELLA

CAVING, CANYONING, COASTEERING...

30 EXHILARATING ADVENTURES AROUND BRITAIN

Bradt

LOTTIE GROSS

DOG-FRIENDLY WEEKENDS

50 BREAKS IN BRITAIN FOR YOU AND YOUR DOG

Bradt

"Bradt Travel Guides are *gorgeous and wonderful*" *The Sunday Times*

Perfect escapes in Britain's special places

Slow Travel Family Breaks

Jane Anderson · Holly Tuppen

Bradt

WILLIAM GRAY

FAMILY WILDLIFE ADVENTURES

50 BREAKS IN SEARCH OF BRITAIN'S WILDLIFE

Bradt

Bradt GUIDES

TRAVEL TAKEN SERIOUSLY

bradtguides.com/shop

 BradtGuides @BradtGuides @bradtguides

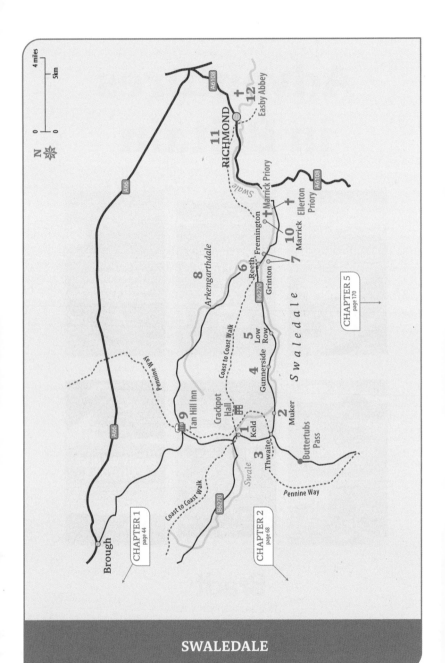

SWALEDALE

4
SWALEDALE

The Yorkshire Dales vary in character, with each valley possessing its own unique quirks, but Swaledale always seems to me more different than the others. It is a dale apart, with much more of a northern feel to it: place names are almost all unadulterated Norse, woods are few and far between, and people almost as thin on the ground. Swaledale is the least populated of the Dales, with no towns at all above Richmond, and no main roads. It is quiet and wild, and for those reasons alone is many people's favourite.

For the past thousand years Swaledale's economy and landscape has been shaped by two things: sheep and lead. The lack of trees is down to historical forest clearance for grazing but doesn't come close to the devastation wrought by the huge lead-mining industry of the 18th and 19th centuries. Most of the Yorkshire Dales still bear the scars of this former activity, but Swaledale more than most.

The dale takes its name from the **River Swale** which bubbles into life high on the flanks of High Pike Hill, but only earns its name down in the valley, just above the village of Keld. It careers downhill, leaping over waterfalls at every opportunity, past the villages of **Muker** and **Gunnerside** and catching its breath a little at **Reeth**. This is the largest village and unofficial capital of Upper Swaledale and Arkengarthdale, sitting as it does at the point where the two valleys meet.

During the next nine miles, the river gets its second wind, speeding up and racing on through the rapids at Marrick Priory to arrive in style at Town Falls in Richmond, below the walls of the castle.

SELF-POWERED TRAVEL
CYCLING
I have two measuring scales for the bike-friendliness of an area. Swaledale scores highly on one, absence of traffic, but not on the other: absence of nasty gradients. However, anyone hale and hearty enough

TOURIST INFORMATION

Reeth Hudson House, The Green ✆ 01748 884059 ⏱ Mon–Sat
Richmond Market Hall ✆ 01748 826468 ⏚ richmondinfo.net

to consider riding the **Yorkshire Dales Cycleway** will laugh in the face of hills, and this route visits Swaledale. It arrives at Gunnerside via the Oxnop Beck road from Askrigg and returns to Wensleydale from Grinton on the Greets Moss road. Both are much quieter than, and at least as scenic as, the more celebrated Buttertubs Pass (page 151).

For **road cycling** here, Cycle the Dales (⏚ cyclethedales.org.uk), the cycling arm of the Yorkshire Dales National Park, features the 27-mile Swaledale Circular and 41-mile Tour de France Two Cols (the two 'cols' being Buttertubs Pass and the moortop Reeth–Leyburn road).

I have another favourite road circuit, not official because of one short section off tarmac, but an exhilarating eight miles starting and finishing at one of the best pubs in the dale. From the Punchbowl at Low Row, go over Isles Bridge to Crackpot (get off and push by the waterfalls). Continue uphill to Summer Lodge where the road gives way to half a mile of stony farm track. When you reach tarmac again turn left and enjoy four miles of gentle downhill freewheeling to the main road, then back to the Punchbowl for a well-earned pint overlooking the valley.

For **off-road biking**, I reckon that this is the best to be had in the whole of the Dales, because of the huge choice of bridleways and green lanes. Most are remnants from the lead-mining days so are substantial tracks rather than those irritating spectral bridleways – bold green lines on the map that turn out to be imaginary trails in real life, buried under waist-deep heather. There are some good suggested routes on the website of the Dales Bike Centre (⏚ dalesbikecentre.co.uk), just outside Reeth. Each route is about 20 to 30 miles, with plenty of strenuous uphills and majestic ridgetop views; GPX downloads are available for each.

The **Swale Trail** is the most popular route in the dale: a well-signposted 13-miler from Reeth to Keld. There's a lot of often bumpy bridleway and stony farm track, plus narrow tarmac lanes. The eastern half between Reeth and Gunnerside is fairly flat and OK for family riding. The western half between Gunnerside and Keld is hilly and more challenging and needs some experience of mountain biking, especially in the dramatic, fjord-like curve outside Keld. Those with robust bikes, a sense of mild adventure, and patience with opening gates, will love it though: the views are not bettered by any similar leisure route in England. To return, either retrace your steps or come back along the road – it's not that busy.

Bike hire is available from the Dales Bike Centre (page 156). A day's rental costs as much as a dinner for two, but you will get stories to dine out on. And for your money you get high-quality road, mountain or e-bikes, whose discreet motors will push you easily up the steepest climbs.

WALKING

The **Pennine Way** long-distance National Trail briefly enters Swaledale at the western end, calling on Thwaite, Keld and Tan Hill.

A much more popular route these days is the **Coast to Coast Walk**, not originally an official trail but an invention in the 1960s by the inspirational walker and writer Alfred Wainwright. AW, as he is often affectionately known, claimed modestly that he laid a ruler on the map from St Bees in Cumbria to Robin Hood's Bay in the east, and the route almost chose itself. Don't believe a word of it; it could easily have followed Teesdale just to the north or Wensleydale to the south but he deliberately picked Swaledale as the most rewarding walking hereabouts. The route has at last received the establishment recognition it deserves: in 2025 the 197-mile odyssey is due to become a National Trail.

Unless you are on the full sea-to-sea challenge you're unlikely to want to complete the 30-mile traverse of the dale from Nine Standards Rigg to Richmond, although I do like the idea of following a river from its source. A more practical challenge is perhaps to catch the number 30 **Little White Bus** (℘ 01969 667400 ⊘ littlewhitebus.co.uk) up the dale and walk back along a section or sections of AW's route. There are a variety of choices: **Keld to Reeth**, 11 miles across the lead-spoil desert of Melbecks Moor; **Keld to Gunnerside**, 6 miles of some of the best riverside walking in the country; **Gunnerside to Reeth**, another lovely 6 miles, this time along the hillside and through one of Swaledale's few forested areas, Rowleth Wood, an early-summer sylvan paradise, with rare lime-loving plants in bloom and warbler song in the air; and **Reeth to Richmond**, 10 to 11 miles – AW gives a choice of riverside or hillside walking, but both routes take in the ruins of Marrick Priory.

An easy and popular walk follows the **Swale Trail** bike route (see opposite). The Little White Bus stops at various points along the 13 miles between Reeth to Keld, enabling easy one-way or partial trips.

UPPER SWALEDALE

Keld, **Muker** and **Thwaite** form a triumvirate of tiny grey-stone hamlets at the three corners of a triangle, with the isolated hill of Kisdon in the centre. Kisdon is almost an island in fact, being practically surrounded by water; Straw Beck to the south flowing through Muker, and the embryonic River Swale hugging its north and east flanks from Keld downstream. Finally, on the western side, a small stream, with the odd name of Skeb Skeugh, wriggles its way through tiny fields and under dry stone walls to Thwaite. Because of its splendid isolation Kisdon is good walking country, and, weather permitting, you'll always have a panoramic view in one direction or another. Strange then, for such an obvious vantage point, not to have a path to its 1,637ft summit; last time I was up here, with a walking partner, we both bemoaned the slog through deep heather to reach the cairn (with particularly colourful language on her part). Once there, though, we revelled in its inaccessibility, sharing a big sky of scudding clouds with no-one but soaring buzzards and passing ravens.

1 KELD

For such a small place, the number of buildings barely making double figures, Keld boasts unexpected fame. Its strategic position at the crossing point of the Pennine Way and Coast to Coast Walk helps, but these trails were both deliberately routed here for good reason – the scenic delights of **Keld Gorge** (if you want to make a round walk of it, use the bridleway that rises over Kisdon Hill for the return leg). The River Swale tumbles over a series of waterfalls – Wain Wath Force, Catrake Force and Kisdon Force among others – beloved of adrenaline kayakers when in spate and wild swimmers at gentler times. Many of these swimmers and paddlers stay in Keld, on the lovely riverside campsite or in the bunkhouse run by the Rukin family at Park Lodge Campsite (see opposite).

From the 1950s Keld was known as a 'dry' village, with the old Cat Hole Inn bought by the Temperance Society and closed – spoilsports! Further bad news in 2006 was the closure of the youth hostel, but this was tempered by its reopening as a pub/hotel, Keld Lodge: the village is no longer dry.

One building just outside Keld, in a stupendous position gazing down Kisdon Gorge, is **Crackpot Hall**. Originally a shooting lodge, then gamekeeper's house and finally farm, it ended its occupied life in the 1950s and is now a forlorn but atmospheric ruin. Somewhat ironically, you can find out about Crackpot Hall and many other local historic buildings in a building whose fortunes have headed in the opposite direction. The derelict Keld Literary Institute was refurbished in 2016 and reopened as the excellent **Keld Resource Centre** (⊘ keld.org.uk).

¶¶ FOOD & DRINK

Keld Green Café DL11 6LL ⊘ 01748 898778 ⊙ summer Thu–Tue, winter Thu–Sun. Almost next to the lodge, this welcoming place has a 1930s-Dales-house-front-room vibe, period furniture, stone floors and all. Live-in owners Quinn and Sally do deservedly popular full breakfasts and homemade meals.

Keld Lodge DL11 6LL ⊘ 01748 886259 ⊘ keldlodge.com. On the top road just out of the village, this former youth hostel is now a hotel with restaurant and bar – the nearest thing to a village pub. Dinner but no lunches.

Rukin's Park Lodge Campsite DL11 6LJ ⊘ 01748 886274 ⊘ rukins-keld.co.uk. A village-centre farm providing a-bit-of-everything service, with a riverside campsite (gloriously cheap and simple), basic groceries and tea shop.

2 MUKER

Muker is the largest of the three villages, with one of my favourite Dales pubs, the Farmers Arms, and a couple of shops. The old vicarage, built in 1680, is a characterful building housing the general store, which also doubles as the village tea shop. Muker's church, dedicated to St Mary the Virgin, was a welcome arrival, relatively late in the day; until 1580, locals had to carry their dead ten miles along the 'Corpse Road' to Grinton, the nearest consecrated graveyard. In the old school (⊘ theoldschoolmuker. co.uk ⊙ variable) is a two-storey craft centre and gallery displaying the work of over fifty artists, many local, and an area to relax with machine drinks and snacks.

Brass-band music has often been a traditional leisure activity in mining communities, and the lead miners of Swaledale were no exception. The miners are long gone but two bands remain in the dale, one in Reeth and the other based here in tiny Muker. All the players in Muker Silver band, aged between ten and 70, live in the vicinity of the village, and the community is fiercely proud of its musical ensemble. Look out for them at shows and fêtes in the summer, and Christmas carol events as far away as Richmond. They are always high on the bill at the Muker Show, on the first Wednesday of September, where you will also be entertained by local produce and craft judging, sheepdog trials and fell races.

FOOD & DRINK

Farmers Arms DL11 6QG ✆ 07951 016155 ⏚ farmersarmsmuker.co.uk. A really welcoming village local serving good local beers and traditional bar snacks. For sale at time of going to press.

Muker Village Tea Shop and Stores DL11 6QG ✆ 01748 886409 ☺ summer Thu–Tue, winter Fri–Sun. Sells local beers and jams, cakes and lunches, and a range of teas and coffees.

SHOPPING

Swaledale Woollens DL11 6QG ✆ 01748 886251 ⏚ swaledalewoollens.co.uk. Swaledale and Wensleydale sheep provide the wool to keep the hand-knitting tradition alive, and the garments and rugs created by thirty-odd local makers are sold here, under the name of the knitter.

3 THWAITE

The tiny hamlet's renown lies in its situation rather than its buildings, and in two celebrity old boys. John Kearton, a 19th-century sheep farmer, had two sons – Richard and the unusually named Cherry – whose phenomenal knowledge of natural history from an early age was their passport out of their humble-born lives. While 'beating' on a grouse shoot, the young Richard called in a grouse to one of the shooters, and so impressed was the gentleman with the farmer's lad's abilities that he offered him a job where he worked, at Cassell's publishing house in London.

"The patchwork of fields around Thwaite encompasses some of the most unspoilt, traditional hay meadows in the Dales."

Cherry later joined his brother, and the two of them went on to have illustrious careers as writers, broadcasters and nature photographers, befriending royalty and American presidents, and inspiring a youthful Sir David Attenborough. Richard was a noted lecturer, so in demand that he could flout normal after-dinner dress codes; I think I would have liked a man who refused to wear any suit he would not feel comfortable climbing a tree in. The brothers are remembered in various local plaques and inscriptions, on their old

EVERY COW 'US TELLS A STORY: SWALEDALE'S BARNS

Almost every first-time visitor to Upper Swaledale asks the same question – 'What are all those buildings dotted around the fields?' – and the answer they receive depends on who they asked in the first place. If the enquiry was put to a knowledgeable tourist or national park employee they are likely to be informed that these buildings are field barns. If they asked a local farmer, on the other hand, they will probably have been told that they are cow 'usses – local dialect for cow houses, which tells you far more about their past function.

The valley bottom up here is rich cattle pasture and an idyllic place for cows to graze in summer, but winters this far up the dale can be ferocious. Back in medieval times, cattle often shared the living space with farmers in winter, the shared body heat keeping everyone alive and relatively comfortable. In the 16th century, when dairy farming really took off here, the residents of Upper Swaledale developed another system whereby each field of cattle had its own barn where the animals lived during the winter.

Inside, the building was divided into two by a wooden screen called a skelboose (from the Viking word 'skel' meaning 'divided') with the cows tethered on the 'boose' side and the other end, the hay mew, full of hay to sustain the beasts until springtime. The farmers' children often had the twice-daily job of letting the cows out for water, clearing manure and replenishing the hay in the stalls. 'I wasn't very old,' remembers Margaret Fawcett, 'I'd mebbe be 12 when I started doing this. There was four barns I used to go down the fields to. I'd let them out then put the hay up at the front there for them t'eat and they went to water and always came back by t'time you'd mucked out.'

Sadly, this traditional system doesn't sit well with modern dairy farming, so most of the old cow houses have fallen into disuse. In 2015 though, the Yorkshire Dales National Park set up the **Every Barn Tells a Story** project (everybarn.yorkshiredales.org.uk) to halt this decline. They have been surveying and renovating barns, recording memories of farming families that used them in the past, producing education packages for local schools, and supporting art projects inspired by these iconic old buildings.

A **walk** booklet detailing a circular route between Muker and Keld, and including some of the more interesting barns, can be picked up from national park visitor centres, or found online (yorkshiredales.org.uk).

school in Muker and cottage in Thwaite, and in the name of the Kearton Country Hotel in the village.

The patchwork of fields around Thwaite encompasses some of the most unspoilt, traditional hay meadows in the whole of the Dales. The national park rightly prizes them, and the field barns, or 'cow 'usses', that dot the pastoral landscape (see above). They encourage farmers to

keep the old ways going, like late hay-cutting (rather than the modern practice of silaging), which encourages a wonderful floral display in June and July, and is a joy to walk around for all but hay-fever sufferers.

Thwaite is on one of Swaledale's few links to the outside world, along the road to **Buttertubs Pass**. This strange name refers to caves near the highest point, that either resemble traditional butter containers, or really were used to keep it cool in transit, depending on which old story you choose to believe. The roadside viewpoint above Thwaite shows Swaledale off to its greatest photographic effect.

¶¶ FOOD & DRINK

Kearton Country Hotel DL11 6DR 🖉 01748 886277 🖄 keartoncountryhotel.co.uk. A fine hotel with a tea shop offering basic snacks, open to non-residents. Temporarily closed and up for sale at time of going to press.

4 GUNNERSIDE

I had one of those it's-hard-to-imagine moments while basking in the sun, sipping a cup of tea on a bench outside the tea room in Gunnerside. The only sounds were the tinkling of water from the nearby beck, and the odd distant clang of a blacksmith's hammer. Enveloped in this rural comfort blanket, it was indeed astonishing to consider the frantic industrial past of 150 years ago, when Gunnerside was nicknamed Klondike. The only rush in Gunnerside now is to the bar in the community-owned village pub, the Kings Head, at closing time.

If you follow Gunnerside Beck for a mile or two upstream from the village, you are not only rewarded with a delightful wooded walk, but will get first-hand experience of the impact of past lead mining in this little valley.

5 LOW ROW

Even smaller and quieter than Gunnerside, Low Row is really just a string of buildings punctuating the main Swaledale Road for a mile or so, three of which are worthy of mention. On the fellside above the hamlet, by the side of the Corpse Road route, sits a little-visited

◀ 1 Crackpot Hall near Kisdon Gorge had many incarnations before being left to ruin. 2 Muker's silver band. 3 The village of Gunnerside.

barn with the uninviting name of the **Dead House**. In medieval times, coffin carriers, on their way to the church at Grinton, would temporarily leave their cadaver and nip downhill to the local ale house for refreshment, before continuing their solemn journey. We don't know where Low Row's pub was, or what it was called, before the 1600s, but from that time it has been the Punch Bowl Inn, next to the church in an area called Feetham.

¶¶ FOOD & DRINK

Punch Bowl Inn DL11 6PF ✆ 01748 886233 ⬥ pbinn.co.uk. The beers here are well-kept local brews, but the emphasis is on food. Meat and game from the dale and fish from Hartlepool are served in the restaurant that sports a 'Mouseman of Kilburn' carved bar created in the Robert Thompson workshops in North Yorkshire – look out for the trademark carved mice. B&B available.

MID SWALEDALE: AROUND REETH

6 REETH

🏠 **The Burgoyne**

Reeth is a Saxon name meaning 'by the stream' which is odd, because it isn't. Two watercourses are not far away though, the River Swale to the south and Arkle Beck to the north draining the valley of Arkengarthdale. Reeth sits strategically between the two valleys, raised safely out of flood range of both boisterous rivers. I like Reeth but it doesn't have the cosy atmosphere of some villages: the village green is disproportionately large, giving the place a spread-out feel.

Reeth was, and still is, the capital of Swaledale, and site of the only market above Richmond, hence the size of the green. The days when the market would fill this space are long gone but one is still held every Friday. All of Reeth's pubs face on to the green and it does well to support three today, but this is nothing compared with the early 1800s at the height of Swaledale's lead-mining boom. Reeth was the centre of the industry and had a staggering ten pubs at the time. The spiritual needs of the miners were met by three chapels, two of which are still open for worship. Reeth has never had its own church, being part of the parish of Grinton with the church a mile away.

Tourism is by far the biggest employer here now, and virtually every visitor to Swaledale calls in on Reeth. That couldn't stop the loss of all the main cafés post-lockdown – however, the reopening of the Copper Kettle in late 2023 may be an encouraging sign of recovery. And the Tourist Office on the southwest corner of the green seems to be surviving, on volunteer staff. There are still gift shops, a general store and (hurrah!) a village post office here too.

If you appreciate arts and crafts then carry on up Silver Street from the green and find the **Dales Centre**, a modern set of industrial units which is home to a range of small craft businesses such as sculptors and shoemakers. They produce wonderful work; it's just a shame that the modern centre they are in is so uninspiring. For a little educational entertainment there is the **Swaledale Museum** (✆ 01748 884118 ⬧ swaledalemuseum.org ◷ Jun–Sep Wed–Sat; Oct–May by appointment) in the old Methodist schoolroom on the corner of the green, a quaint and very traditional local history archive with small shop.

If you don't need educating or entertaining, just a bench in a quiet corner to sit and muse or read in the sun, then the **Community Orchard Garden** is the place. It's easily found, at the southwest corner of the green, free and accessible to wheelchairs.

Reeth gets busy over Whitsun, in late May to early June, when the **Swaledale Festival** (⬧ swalefest.org) takes place – a celebration of music and the arts. **Reeth Show**, on August Bank Holiday, is a typically lively Yorkshire agricultural jamboree.

Reeth has a wealth of appealing walks, but if you only have time or energy for one it has to be a circular tour of both rivers. First go south from the green to Back Lane, then over the river via the footbridge. (A temporary, likely permanent, diversion is in place because of a collapsed footpath.) **Watch sand martins** flit in and out of their riverbank burrows in summer as you follow the bridleway downstream to Grinton. Here you can resist the temptation to enter the fine Bridge Inn, or not as the case may be. Return to Reeth across the field footpath, diverting up Arkle Beck for a short explore before re-entering the green at its northern end. A delightful three-mile easy stroll.

 ## SPECIAL STAYS

The Burgoyne Reeth DL11 6SN ✆ 01748 884292 ⬧ theburgoyne.co.uk. This is treat-yourself luxury overlooking the village green, with a price to match, in a grand Georgian house that has been steadily refurbished since 2018. The integral '1783' bar-restaurant serves locally sourced fine dining – sea bream, venison or butternut-squash 'steak', for instance – with ingredients from the Burgoyne's own kitchen garden. Wheelchair access is available in the Eskeleth Room, but phone ahead to discuss requirements – the room can be reconfigured to suit.

¶¶ FOOD & DRINK

There are also two small cafés on Silver Street: **Reeth Bakery** and **Two Dales Bakery**.

Copper Kettle The Green. Reeth's café scene is hopefully back with the reopening of this local favourite. Warm welcome and tasty home-cooked food: try the Grasmere gingerbread and lemon cheesecake.

Ice Cream Parlour The Green ✆ 01748 884929 ⏚ reethicecreamparlour.co.uk. Twelve flavours of Brymor Ice Cream from Jervaulx, or hot drinks for those chilly days.

Lacey's Cheese Dales Centre ✆ 01748 880238 ⏚ laceyscheese.co.uk. They say cheese makes you dream. Simon Lacey learnt the craft of cheesemaking at the Swaledale Cheese Company but dreamt of running his own business, and here it is. The cheeses are all handmade using traditional methods and locally sourced products. This isn't a shop – it's where they run their cheesemaking courses – but you can buy their products in the village gift shop and post office.

Pubs

None of Reeth's three pubs on the Green can really compete with the excellent hostelries in the surrounding villages but it's great that they are all still serving real ale, cooking homemade food (book ahead), offering accommodation, and thriving in such a small place. They are:

Black Bull Hotel High Row ✆ 01748 884213 ⏚ theblackbullreeth.co.uk. Worth a look for its upside-down sign, a gesture of rebellion from a previous landlord to the national park authority over a planning dispute. Beer garden out back.

Buck Hotel DL11 6SW ✆ 01748 884210 ⏚ thebuckreeth.co.uk. Range of real ale and cider and a large pub-classics menu. Regular live music.

The Kings Arms High Row ✆ 01748 884259 ⏚ thekingsarms.com. Deserves a visit on a cold evening for the fireplace alone, as it must be one of the biggest in the country. When the fire is well banked up the bar feels like a sauna.

7 GRINTON & FREMINGTON

⌂ **Grinton Lodge Youth Hostel**

Neither of these neighbouring hamlets has enough to warrant village status today, but an amateur historian will enjoy piecing together jigsaw pieces of a busy and influential past. The bridge linking Grinton and Fremington is at the first point on the River Swale above Richmond where the river could be forded, hence its importance. The oldest evidence is from the Iron Age, with the remains of a fort just east of Grinton by the river, a settlement 1½ miles upstream at Maiden Castle, and boundary earthworks between the two hamlets, blocking the valley bottom completely at one time.

For 400 years St Andrew's Church in **Grinton** was the only one in Upper Swaledale and had the biggest parish in Yorkshire. This accounts for the size of the building; which led to its nickname, 'Cathedral of the Dales'. Although most of the church fabric is now fairly recent, there are fragments of the original Norman church, built by the monks of Bridlington Priory, a long way from home. Bats inhabit the church, both real pipistrelles in the roof space and in the form of striking copper sculptures hanging from the walls, courtesy of Michael Kusz from the Dales Centre in Reeth (page 153).

"For 400 years St Andrew's in Grinton was the only one in Upper Swaledale and had the biggest parish in Yorkshire."

Other buildings to seek out are the fine village pub, the Dales Bike Centre, Fremington corn mill, with its rare wooden waterwheel, and Grinton Lodge. The last was once a Victorian shooting lodge owned by Tory MP and colliery owner John Charlesworth Dodgson-Charlesworth but is now a castle-like youth hostel, where campers can enjoy wonderful views over the valley.

A maze of footpaths and bridleways links all these places, in a choice of pleasant valley-bottom strolls, but two obvious higher-level walks also warrant a try: **Fremington Edge** on the north side of the valley, and **High Harker Hill** on the Grinton side.

 SPECIAL STAYS

Grinton Lodge Youth Hostel Grinton DL11 6HGS ✐ 0345 3719636 ⟁ yha.org.uk. Imposingly situated up a hillside, a short but steep walk from the village pub, this former shooting lodge looks more like a castle – maybe even a fortress. From the terrace tables off the central courtyard you have a mighty view over Mid Swaledale. There are plenty of options for individuals, families and groups: camping, glamping, bunks and private rooms. With two self-catering kitchen-diners, and spacious lounges, there are places to eat, relax and socialise. The hostel serves breakfast and evening meals, with wine and beer available.

THE NOT-SO-FAMOUS GROUSE

It's 05.45 on a cold April morning and I'm not tucked up in bed but huddled in a wall corner of an old sheep-shelter in Arkengarthdale. I'm wearing most of the clothes I possess, a woolly hat down over the ears and sporting a drip on the end of my nose. 'Why?' I hear you ask. Well, following a tip-off from a birdwatching friend, I'm in the right place to wait for dawn to break and witness a unique stage show. Two of the players are already here. I can see them through a convenient hole in the wall, on a stage of short, cropped grass surrounded by tussocky rushes and heather. As the morning brightens, colour washes into the landscape and I can make out detail in the birds. They are the size and shape of small chickens, very dark with intense red eyebrows – they are male black grouse or moorcocks (*Tetrao tetrix*).

The two birds are suddenly joined by a third which struts into the arena and spreads its tail to reveal a white pompom of feathers beneath. He opens his mouth and, in a bubble of warm misty breath, produces a bizarre series of indignant burbles and hisses aimed at the other two males, who reply in a similar fashion. What I was witnessing was a communal courtship display called a 'lek', which is performed by black grouse and only two other species of bird in Britain. By the time I'd seen enough and slunk away downhill out of sight, six males were giving it what for, and an audience of female grey hens was watching from the periphery, selecting their preferred mate – presumably the most impressive strutter and burbler.

What makes this seem doubly special is its increasing rarity. The black grouse is in serious decline nationally: Swaledale's is the most southerly population in England and the only one in Yorkshire. Since 1996 a consortium of interested parties, including the RSPB, Natural England and shooting organisations, have initiated the Black Grouse Recovery Project for the north Pennines. Their main push is on habitat improvement, reducing sheep grazing on moor edges and encouraging traditional hay meadows, and it seems to be working.

Wi-Fi may be sketchy, but you're probably here for the scenery and active travel rather than the internet: the Swale Trail starts here, and there's a good cycle shed.

¶¶ FOOD & DRINK

Bridge Inn Grinton ✆ 01748 884224 ⌖ bridgeinn-grinton.co.uk. A 13th-century coaching inn, well-loved by locals and visitors. Food is high quality with a range of local ales to accompany it. Day fishing licences and rods for hire behind the bar. B&B on offer with some good off-peak deals.

Dales Bike Centre Fremington ✆ 01748 884908 ⌖ dalesbikecentre.co.uk. Full-function bike shop and hire, with a light and spacious new extension for its classy café. Range of teas and coffees, stacks of cakes, all-day breakfasts and light meals: cyclists will particularly enjoy the plum flapjacks. 'Bunk and breakfast' accommodation is also available.

8 ARKENGARTHDALE

If the name of the valley itself isn't eccentric enough, then what about some of the places in it? Booze, Whaw, Raw and Faggergill could easily have been words picked at random for their comedy value. Arkle Town sounds as if it should be the largest settlement here, but there is virtually nothing of it; that title goes to the compact village of **Langthwaite**, straddling Arkle Beck with a graceful, stone, arched bridge that featured in the 1980s BBC TV series *All Creatures Great and Small*.

The lower dale is surprisingly lush and wooded for Swaledale, but if you travel up the valley on the road towards Brough, the landscape turns much less cultivated and more open. Just beyond the head of the dale, and right on top of the moor, where the words wild and bleak usually apply, a most unexpected sight materialises out of the cloud, mist or snow – an inn. The Tan Hill Inn to be precise, at 1,732ft above sea level the highest pub in Britain (and one of the most remote from other habitation, too).

¶¶ FOOD & DRINK

Charles Bathurst Inn Langthwaite DL11 6EN ✐ 0333 700 0779 ⊘ cbinn.co.uk. A large roadside inn named after the local lord of the manor and lead-mine owner. CB Inn, as it's known, is friendly and popular, valued for its cask beer from Black Sheep, Theakston and other local brews, extensive wine cellar and very good food. Meat and game are all sourced from Swaledale. Highly regarded, dog-friendly accommodation.

Red Lion Inn Langthwaite DL11 6RE ✐ 01748 884218 ⊘ langthwaite-redlion.co.uk. A marvellous, atmospheric little village local, almost as different to the CB Inn as you could get. Octogenarian Rowena Hutchinson has been landlady since 1979. Black Sheep beer, hot drinks, local honey and preserves and bar snacks, but nowhere near the emphasis on food of its near neighbour, and no accommodation.

9 TAN HILL INN

DL11 6ED ✐ 01833 533007 ⊘ tanhillinn.com

I'll ask the obvious question. Why would anyone in their right mind build a pub up here, on an extraordinarily remote junction of roads on the moors northwest of Arkengarthdale? Coal, is the short answer. The black stuff has been dug out of the ground on Tan Hill since the

12th century, and remnants of the pits, shafts and quarries still dot the moorland around the inn. The current 17th-century building replaced an earlier one which catered to the miners' needs in this lonely spot, and has been here ever since. At 1,730ft above sea level, this is the highest pub in Britain.

The last mine closed in 1929, but the pub managed to keep going because of its high-altitude fame, and more passing trade began in 1965 on the opening of the Pennine Way footpath, which goes right past the front door. Iconic 1980s television adverts for double glazing, an annual sheep show in May, and regular live folk and rock music have kept people making the pilgrimage up the hill. Is it worth it? Absolutely: this is a place full of character, almost a world apart, and cannily reinvented as a destination place to eat and stay. The menu offers pub classics with a dash of style, and there is a big range of premium and cask beers including own-brand Tan Hill Inn bitter, pilsner, and even Dark Skies Stout – a reminder of the stargazing opportunities here on a clear night, untainted by light pollution.

Often there's live music: typically a guitar-vocalist or two, sometimes with drop-ins and jam sessions. A roaring fire warms the bar, which is a comfort if you can get close to it – access is often blocked by the resident cats and dogs, and sometimes even sheep, toasting themselves by the hearth. If you come in winter, be prepared for a long stay, as the pub can be cut off for weeks on end after heavy snow, and consequently has its own caterpillar-tracked snowmobile.

The wide range of sleeping options on offer includes plush B&B, bunkroom beds, campervan parking and wild camping outside.

10 MARRICK

What is now a favoured haunt for white-water canoeists and kayakers was obviously once likewise for builders of monasteries, because two are here, one on either side of the river. The remains of **Ellerton Priory**, constructed in the late 12th century for Cistercian nuns, were incorporated into a Victorian shooting lodge which is now a private

◀ 1 The Swaledale Festival sees Reeth come alive. 2 If you're looking for a remote pint, try the Tan Hill Inn. 3 Come spring, early risers in Arkengarthdale may be fortunate to see the black grouse lek. 4 Langthwaite featured in the 1980s version of *All Creatures Great and Small*.

house on the south bank of the river. Nearby, but on the opposite side of the river, were the Benedictine nuns at **Marrick Priory**. I like to imagine those medieval ladies dressed in different coloured habits, waving to each other across the rapids. Not surprisingly, considering its position, Marrick Priory is now an outdoor education centre (but still owned by the Church of England). While it caters mainly for groups of schoolchildren, the centre's instructors and equipment can be hired for a day or half day. **Marrick village** lies about half a mile up the hillside, at the top end of a very pleasant walk through Steps Wood.

"Marrick lies about half a mile up the hillside, at the top end of a very pleasant walk through Steps Wood."

LOWER SWALEDALE: INCLUDING RICHMOND

There's yet more exquisite scenery here. **Richmond** itself is handily placed for walks into the dale, with paths along the valley and high up along the level-topped cliff of Whitcliffe Scar.

11 RICHMOND

This isn't just Richmond, this is *the* Richmond – the one that all 56 others worldwide are named after, including its better-known Surrey counterpart and far bigger sister in Virginia, USA. The name is pure French, Riche Mont meaning Strong Hill, and refers to the defensive site the Norman **castle** is built upon, high above a loop in the river and still massively imposing.

The Swale has made no concessions to civilisation; it is still wild and frisky, plunging over the spectacular cascade of **Town Falls**, directly below the castle. Riverside Road follows its northern bank and is a lovely place to walk, cycle, picnic or paddle, but take note of the signs warning of dangerous, fast-rising water levels at times.

In the town centre, all roads seem to lead to the cobbled **marketplace**, and it does take your breath away when you emerge into it because it is enormous – one of the largest marketplaces the country. The then Prince Charles was certainly taken with it on his visit in 2005, likening it to the grand Tuscan piazza of Siena in Italy. On most days this exotic ambience is not obvious as the marketplace doubles as a large free car park. But it is impressive when empty, and at its very best on Wednesdays and Saturdays, when the market displaces the parked cars. The third Saturday of the month is particularly good as it also incorporates a farmers' market.

North of the marketplace modern Richmond begins to intrude, but there are three places to seek out: the **Georgian Theatre Royal**, the **Richmondshire Museum**, and the **Friary Gardens**. Where the green space of the last of these is now, was once the site of an old Franciscan Friary and it still retains the statuesque ruins of an old bell tower, and a monastic sense of peace and serenity. There's also a good deal of conspicuously handsome **Georgian streetscape**, in Newbiggin and elsewhere, and some alluring back alleys, or **wynds**, such as Cornforth Hill, leading steeply down through two of the surviving town gateways.

For some strange reason Richmond town does not venture south of the river at all, the only building of note on this side being the **old railway station**. The rest remains as park or farmland, ideal country for walking, with grandstand views of the castle in the old town. An upstream stroll takes you on to the Round Howe nature trails, a series of scenic woodland loops, linked to make one four-mile walk, or individual shorter circular walks. If you head in the other direction from town, one mile downstream you will find the riverside ruins of Easby Abbey, and a return path on the other side of the river following the old railway line. This route is called the Drummer Boy Walk (page 162). Hudswell and Hag woods, on the south bank of the river, just over a footbridge a mile west of the town, offer a maze of footpaths around 400-year-old woodlands. For exploring the town itself on foot, three very good trails are available free from the tourist information centre or online (richmond.org/Explore/Walks-and-trails). Ask about the free guided town walks held on Thursdays and Saturdays at 11.00.

"All roads seem to lead to the cobbled marketplace, and it does take your breath away when you emerge into it."

It's no surprise that Richmond is the cultural centre of Richmondshire (an old unofficial fiefdom), and it hosts a wealth of regular events throughout the year. If you want peace and quiet you had best avoid them, but if you want lively entertainment then time your visit for two in particular. **The Richmond Meet** is an annual fair, held over the Spring Bank Holiday weekend; and during the last week in September the **Richmond Walking and Book Festival** (booksandboots.org) features guided walks for all abilities during the days, and evening events to celebrate the written word.

Richmond Castle

Riverside Rd 01748 822493 summer daily; winter Sat & Sun; English Heritage

Few towns are more dominated by their castle than Richmond, partly because the town is relatively small but also because this is a genuinely impressive building. The 100-foot-high keep towers over everything and, in my opinion, provides a viewpoint from the top to equal any in Yorkshire. Swaledale snakes away westwards while to the east lies the flat Cleveland plain laid out like a green patchwork quilt, with industrial Teesside hinted at in the distance.

Back in 1066 William the Conqueror had a dilemma. He was now boss of a lot of foreigners in their own country, who didn't like him. His strategy was to delegate – allocate big chunks of land to his trusted earls and barons and let them control the resident Anglo-Saxons. His cousin Alan Rufus was given this corner of North Yorkshire and he must have had a healthy respect for the locals as he immediately set to building a castle on a 'strong hill' to defend himself. Most of the other Norman lords started with a temporary wooden fort, but Alan went for stones straightaway, making Richmond castle the equal-oldest stone Norman castle in England with those in Durham and Colchester. Big as it is, the castle was once even more extensive as it included what is

THE RICHMOND DRUMMER BOY

I can remember being told this story as a child and hoping that it wasn't true, the horror of a solitary underground death filling my young mind with nightmares. It's said that soldiers in Richmond Castle chanced upon a small hole in a cellar wall which seemed to continue as a passage. It was too narrow for an adult to enter so they sent in a young drummer boy, complete with drum, to explore. He was instructed to bang his drum as he walked so the soldiers could track his progress by listening above ground. They followed the faint drumbeats across the marketplace and Frenchgate towards Easby Abbey for half a mile when the sound suddenly stopped. The unfortunate boy was never heard or seen again but a stone was laid at the point where the drumming was last heard, and it can still be seen in a field at the end of Easby Wood. Ghostly subterranean drumming can also be heard on still evenings – in my nightmares at least.

now the marketplace within its walls. During the 14th century, worried about Scottish invasion, the town populace was allowed behind the protective outer bailey which stood where the crescent of market-side Georgian buildings is now. When the Scots danger passed, the bailey was gradually dismantled, leaving the marketplace as part of the town and not the castle. This explains the odd position of the castle chapel, Trinity Church, outside the walls; it now houses the Green Howards Museum.

English Heritage charges a reasonable entry fee into the castle and it is money well spent; you can access walkways around the walls, a small museum and a shop, but the keep alone is worth the fee. It's worth spending time contemplating the impressive exterior of the building too.

Richmondshire Museum

Ryder's Wynd ✆ 01748 825611 ⬦ richmondshiremuseum.org.uk ⊙ Apr–Oct Mon–Sat

This small local history museum tucked away in Ryder's Wynd near the tourist information office covers life as it was in Richmond and Swaledale in a gentle, traditional style. No touch-screen virtual experiences here or even audio-visual presentations, just artefacts, models and reconstructions. Subjects covered include lead mining, a village post office, a town chemist's shop, toys through the ages and a set from the 1980s BBC TV series *All Creatures Great and Small*, based on the life of vet James Herriot, who lived and worked in this area.

Green Howards Museum

Trinity Church Sq ✆ 01748 826561 ⬦ greenhowards.org.uk ⊙ Mon–Sat

The Green Howards Regiment has been in existence since 1688, but has only been based in Richmond since 1873. The unusual name originates from an early Regimental Colonel, Charles Howard of Castle Howard fame, but as another Howards Regiment existed at the time, they had to distinguish between the two. Based on colour of uniforms the Green Howards and the Buff Howards were born.

Many of the Green Howards were killed in World War I, after which a number of their private memorabilia collections were sent to the regiment. The collections of mainly medals and uniforms were housed in barrack rooms, huts and sheds from 1922 until the empty Holy Trinity Church came up for sale in 1970. If you has a military background or Green Howard connections then you will love this place; others may not. The Museum Trust realised this and has worked hard on much-needed modernisation. Popular additions are the Kidzone where children can dress up (always a winner, and entry is free for under-10s) and the Family History Research Centre.

The Georgian Theatre Royal

Victoria St ✆ 01748 825252 🖑 georgiantheatreroyal.co.uk ◷ hourly tours, six days a week during daytime for much of the year

My choice of production was *A Midsummer Night's Dream* by Bill the Bard or *Bouncers and Shakers*, a 1980s-style comedy with a warning about strong language. I suppose I should have gone traditional when visiting the country's oldest surviving Georgian theatre building but I never could resist a John Godber play (and he is from Yorkshire). The show was brilliant, well directed and acted, with the character of the venue adding to the experience. This is a wonderful place, part Grade 1 listed building, part museum, but also a very busy working theatre.

It was built In 1788 at the height of Richmond's heyday by actor/manager Samuel Butler, but, faced with dwindling performances, closed in 1848. Miraculously the buildings were still intact in the 1960s when a group of local campaigners formed a non-profit trust and the theatre reopened. Although the facilities were extended in 2003, the auditorium remains unchanged and still only has a capacity of 214 in a sunken pit, boxes on three sides and a gallery. It is quaint, intimate, authentic and as far removed from a modern concert arena as you could get, and I loved it. So did Cathy and Graham, the couple sitting next to us. 'We come here at least once a month, sometimes twice in the same week. There's all sorts on – comedy club last week, that was good, rock music tribute bands, Shakespeare, lots of jazz evenings next month. We don't really mind what we see; it's the place we love.'

The Old Railway Station

Station Rd ✆ 01748 828259 🖑 thestation.co.uk

Richmond's old railway terminus, or 'The Station' as it is simply known, is probably busier now than it ever was when trains arrived daily from Darlington and beyond.

---

1 Richmond's skyline, dominated by the impressive castle. 2 Town Falls, Richmond.
3 The atmospheric ruins of Easby Abbey. 4 Richmond Castle. ▶

This building has a very special place in the Richmond community's heart; the local people fought tooth and nail to keep the railway open in the 1960s but lost out in the end. Their successors, and maybe some of the original activists, formed the Richmondshire Building Preservation Trust in 2003 and have steered the project that has produced this cultural centre. I like the fact that they have not forgotten the building's roots: over a small display of memorabilia in the main café area, a screen shows evocative images of the steam era.

Hundreds of people pass through the doors daily to visit the cinema, café-restaurant, art gallery with its regular changing exhibitions, and heritage centre. Many, myself included, leave with bags laden with goodies produced on-site by artisan food makers. If you need a place to rest, there are comfy chairs to sit and relax on.

🍴 FOOD & DRINK

I've covered places to eat and drink in town, at the Old Railway Station and out of town separately. For its size, Richmond is a little disappointing on the gastronomic front.

Richmond town

Black Lion Finkle St 🕾 01748 826217 🖱 blacklionhotelrichmond.co.uk. An atmospheric pub with rooms in an ex-Georgian coach house. Yorkshire cask beers and food menu of 'decadent pub classics'.

Little Drummer Boy Tearoom Finkle St 🕾 01748 850706 🖱 thelittledrummerboytearoom.co.uk. Busy local favourite with wide-ranging menu of fresh, Yorkshire-sourced dishes, cakes and cream teas. For meals, their sibling tapas restaurant is round the corner in Newbiggin.

Rustique Chantry Wynd 🕾 01748 821565 🖱 rustiquerichmond.co.uk. A sister restaurant to Rustique in York with the quality just as high. The meals are French-influenced and served in a lively bistro atmosphere.

Wilfred Deli & Pantry Finkle St 🕾 01748 821034 🖱 wilfreddeli.co.uk. Take-away savoury and sweet snacks and locally roasted coffee, and a tempting deli counter. Similar emphasis on locally sourced food and wine at their fine-dining restaurant nearby in Newbiggin: booking/appointments essential (🕾 01748 889869).

Richmond Old Station

The Angel's Share Bakery 🕾 01748 828261 🖱 theangelssharebakery.com ☉ Tue–Sun. Artisan breads and sourdoughs, hand-crafted from local ingredients, plus traybakes, quiches, patisserie, salads and cheeses.

Archers Jersey Dairy Ice Cream 🖉 01748 823367 👌 archersicecream.com ⊙ Wed–Sun.
John and Susan Archer made a bold move when they lost their Friesian dairy herd to foot-and-mouth disease. They replaced it with a herd of Jersey cattle and decided to make ice cream. The rich creamy milk is brought straight from the farm to the parlour in The Station and made into a wide array of flavours.

Out of town

For quieter drinking and food worth travelling for, two pubs stand out.

The George and Dragon Hudswell DL11 8BL 🖉 01748 518373
👌 georgeanddragonhudswell.co.uk. A fabulous community-owned pub. The welcome is genuine, beers are locally sourced and well kept, there are over 60 whiskies to choose from and their pies are legendary. No wonder it's a multiple winner of various CAMRA and 'pub of the year' awards. Most important of all, this place is the heart of the village community, and usually buzzing. It's a couple of miles from Richmond, so just about walkable.

Shoulder of Mutton Kirby Hill DL11 7JH 🖉 01748 905011
👌 shoulderofmuttonkirbyhill.co.uk. Attractive ivy-fronted building in the centre of the village with rooms, and views of Ravensworth Castle. Excellent food and beer. Accommodation available.

12 EASBY ABBEY

DL10 7JU; free access, English Heritage

Easby is a tiny hamlet perched on the banks of the Swale, three-quarters of a mile downstream from Richmond, and home to this substantial and atmospheric ruin. Historians always suspected that Easby had been a Christian site long before the abbey was built, and this was confirmed in 1931 when pieces of ancient stone carvings were found built into the walls of the church. When pieced back together they re-formed a magnificent 8th-century English cross, now in London's Victoria and Albert Museum. The dedication of the church to St Agatha was also a clue as her cult was a very early one, at its peak when Christianity first came to Britain. Poor old St Agatha, by the way, was tortured in life by having her breasts cut off and presented to her on a platter. A superficial similarity in shape led to the ignominy of her becoming the patron saint of bakers and bell makers. Recently, and I think a touch

"Easby is a tiny hamlet perched on the banks of the Swale, and is home to this substantial and atmospheric ruin."

more respectfully, she has been venerated in a more serious way as patron saint of breast cancer patients.

The present church was rebuilt in 1152 at the same time as the abbey by the 'White Canons' of the Premonstratensian order, who decorated it with colourful frescoes. Some of these survived the Reformation by being whitewashed and are now re-exposed in these more liberal times.

The history of the abbey has run along the same lines as many other Yorkshire abbeys: 12th-century founding on land donated by the local Norman lord, 300 years of power and influence followed by an abrupt end with Henry VIII's dissolution of the monasteries. A common practice at this time was for valuable relics in the abbey to be re-used by the, then new, Anglican churches. Easby Abbey's bell and choir stalls found their way into St Mary's Church in Richmond and are still there.

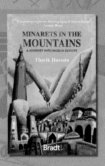
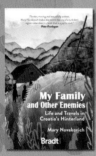

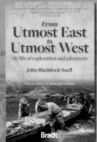

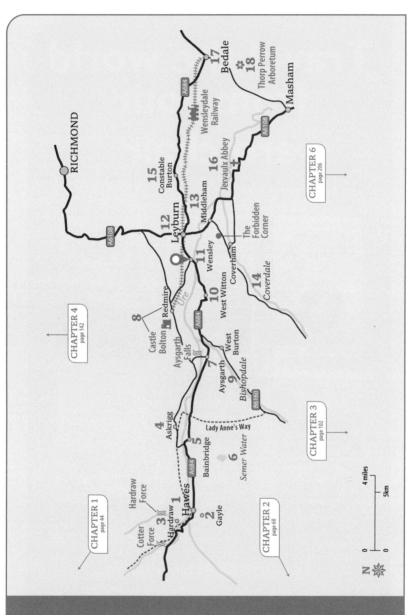

WENSLEYDALE

5
WENSLEYDALE

'This is in most places waste, solitary, unpleasant, unsightly, mute and still.' Poor old William Camden didn't much enjoy his visit to Wensleydale in 1590. We tend to place more value on wilderness today, so much so that this valley is one of the most popular tourist destinations in Yorkshire, and in peak holiday season at least you would have to work hard to find the 'solitary, mute and still' elements. The main valley is the longest of the Yorkshire Dales, and, oddly, named after one of its smaller villages rather than its river, the Ure. The busy A684 runs most of its length, linking the bustling towns of **Hawes**, **Leyburn** and **Bedale**, and the honeypot villages of **Bainbridge** and **Aysgarth**. Wensleydale has a fascinating history and bags of charm; a visit to the museum at Hawes can give you an excellent insight into the area's past, and traditions from quieter times. To escape the crowds, try heading away from the valley-bottom roads, up the fellsides or into one of the tributary side valleys like **Coverdale**, **Bishopdale** or **Raydale**. Alternatively, visit the main valley at off-peak times, especially after heavy rain when its many waterfalls are at their most spectacular.

SELF-POWERED TRAVEL
CYCLING
One long-distance road route, the **Yorkshire Dales Cycleway**, nips into Wensleydale at Hawes and then out again from Askrigg over into Swaledale, returning lower down and running the full length of Coverdale.

The route is featured on the national park's **Cycle the Dales** website (⌂ cyclethedales.org.uk). The site also suggests three-day rides that involve Wensleydale: over Buttertubs to Swaledale and back via Leyburn ('Tour de France Two Cols', 40 miles); over Fleet Moss to Wharfedale and back via Leyburn ('the Hawes toughie', 45 miles); and the Eden Valley to Reeth via Tan Hill (54 miles). These are long and hilly routes for fit and experienced bikers only. The website does not list any **easier rides** for families or less masochistic folk, but I think some perfectly suitable rides exist. The trick is to avoid the main A684 of course, and this can be done almost completely in a 9-mile circuit taking in Askrigg, Thornton Rust, Aysgarth, Carperby and Woodhall, with fine valley views all the way. One or two short, steep sections keep you warm, and the roads are relatively quiet. Other very short but highly scenic circular rides include Lower Coverdale – where you could join up Coverham, West Scrafton and Carlton (6 miles) – and Raydale from Bainbridge via Marsett and Stalling Busk (7 miles).

In Lower Wensleydale where the hills settle down into hummocks, a triangle of land between Leyburn, Bedale and Masham contains a network of very quiet minor roads – excellent gentle biking country. Those lovely people at the Wensleydale Railway allow bikes on the train for free so you could take a one-way rail journey from Bedale to Redmire, then make up your own route back on little roads for 20 miles, or as far as you fancy, and hop on the train further down the line. Aiskew, adjoining Bedale, has a welcoming bike-shop-cum-café, **360 Cycleworx** (360cycleworx.co.uk ⊙ Tue–Sun).

For **mountain bikes**, Wensleydale is as good as anywhere in the Dales. The Cycle the Dales website (page 171) recommends a testing 18-mile circuit of Dodd Fell. Much of this route is on the arrow-straight, stony rollercoaster of Cam High Road, one of Britain's most thrilling Roman Roads. My favourite shorter routes are from West Burton (go east on Morpeth Gate green lane to Witton Steeps, down the road to West Witton and return via Green Gate green lane; 6 miles) and from Bainbridge (up to Stake Allotments via High Lane and Busk Lane tracks; 10 miles, half on tarmac and half on gravel).

HORSERIDING

There are no longer any trekking centres in Wensleydale, but the North Yorkshire Council website (northyorks.gov.uk) lists two circular routes suitable for riders, with access for horseboxes: the relaxing and gentle 9-mile R5 round Thornton Watlass, and the steeper and rougher, but very scenic, 10-mile R4 round Carlton.

WALKING

The **Pennine Way** long-distance **National Trail** crosses the upper reaches of Wensleydale at Hawes on its way from Fountains Fell to Great Shunner

Fell. Hawes is also on the route of an unofficial circular trail of 52 miles, a traverse of both Wensleydale and Swaledale, called the **Herriot Way** (⬧ herriotway.com). Elsewhere, the 24 miles of dale, daleside and side dales offer a plethora of full-and part-day walks to suit almost everyone. I say 'almost' because those of you searching for the high peaks won't find them here. Wensleydale's hills aren't as extrovertly obvious as the Three Peaks or Wharfedale Fells so consequently don't draw the crowds. These are my sort of hills – empty ones.

The best highish-level walks, I think, are **Penhill Beacon** above West Witton, **Wether Fell** from Hawes and a short, sharp pull to the summit of **Addlebrough** near Bainbridge. Upstream of West Burton is the hidden, unnamed valley containing Walden Beck, with two short roads that lead in and suddenly stop. During all my time in this secluded corner I have never seen another visiting walker, just farmers going about their business. **Cotterdale** near Hawes and Hardraw is a similar quiet idyll.

UPPER WENSLEYDALE: HAWES, GAYLE & HARDRAW

1 HAWES

🏠 **Thorney Mire Cabin**

Sitting at the meeting point of at least four ancient packhorse routes, Hawes is undoubtedly the capital of Upper Wensleydale and its position far up the dale makes it the highest-altitude market town in Yorkshire. Its popularity has waxed and waned over the years: booms with the building of the Lancaster–Richmond turnpike road and the coming of the railway in the 1870s, slumps when the mills went quiet, and on the railways closure in the 1960s. Hawes is now busier than it ever has been but the tourists that the town almost completely depends on are visiting to celebrate one of its oldest industries: cheese production.

Visitors generally first head for the old railway station, where the national park has a **visitor centre** with the hugely absorbing (and wheelchair-friendly) **Dales Countryside Museum** attached (⊘ dalescountrysidemuseum.org.uk). You can spend an entertaining and informative couple of hours here, without noticing the passing of time. It's more a celebration of family life in the country than a set of this-is-what-happened-here displays. Cheese- and butter-making, sheep farming, lead mining and hand knitting are all brought to life by an outstanding collection of local bygones and domestic objects gathered from all over the Dales. It amply justifies the entrance fee, especially for children, who get in free and will really enjoy the hands-on displays and dressing-up opportunities.

The shops and businesses of Hawes are a nice mix, with butchers, electrical stores, grocers and hardware shops catering for the locals but also the expected wealth of outdoor gear, gift and craft shops, and numerous cafés of course. If you want to see Hawes at its vibrant best then go on a Tuesday outside of school holidays, the day of the street-stall market. The **Farmers' Auction Mart** is always an entertaining, multisensory experience bustling with livestock. It runs on various days, often Tuesday or Saturday – see ⊘ hawesmart.co.uk for precise dates.

Wensleydale Creamery

Gayle Ln ✏ 01969 667664 ⊘ wensleydale.co.uk

Lovers of real Wensleydale cheese have some unlikely benefactors to thank for Hawes's main attraction: the French, a local farmer called Kit Calvert, and two Plasticine heroes in the form of Wallace and Gromit.

The recipe for this mild, white cow's-milk cheese almost certainly came over from France with the Cistercian monks and was passed down via farmers' wives to the dairy at Hawes. Twice in the last 80 years this sole producer of genuine from-the-dale Wensleydale cheese almost closed. The first time, in the 1930s depression, local farmers rallied around one of their own, Kit Calvert, who called a meeting in the town hall and bullied enough support to keep the dairy running. On the next occasion in 1992 the then owners, Dairy Crest, actually closed the dairy and had the effrontery to move production to Lancashire. A team of ex-managers bought the building and opened it under the

1 The Wensleydale town of Hawes. 2 Cheese for sale at the Wensleydale Creamery. ▶

name of Wensleydale Creamery, but making it a going concern wasn't easy. The breakthrough came when, in *A Close Shave*, one of Nick Park's inimitable Wallace and Gromit animations, Wallace, uttered the immortal words 'Not even Wensleydale?' when he finds his lady friend doesn't like cheese – and the creamery's steady business exploded. The visitor centre now entertains around 300,000 people a year who enjoy the 'cheese experience' tour, explore the museum, eat in the restaurant or just select gifts from the now huge selection of branded cheeses and Wallace and Gromit memorabilia in the shop. Not an especially 'Slow' experience, though!

Hawes boasts another small and little-known cheese producer – the Ribblesdale Cheese Company (⌂ ribblesdalecheese.com) is based on the industrial estate.

The **Yorkshire Dales Cheese Festival** is an annual event that takes place over a week in autumn (⌂ yorkshiredales.co.uk/yorkshire-dales-cheese-festival) and the Wensleydale Creamery is one of its main venues.

Sheepdog demonstrations

Haylands Bridge ⌕ 07593 966271 ⌂ sheepdogdemo.co.uk

One of the Dales' iconic images is the sheepdog at work. The remarkably precise choreography depends on only a handful of commands, some whistled, some shouted – such as 'Away!' (circle the sheep anticlockwise) or 'Come by!' (clockwise). At the auctions down in Skipton, dogs can cost as much as a secondhand car.

The sight of a farmer with a collie or two managing a flock is an absorbing and serendipitous delight. And it's one you're very likely to encounter by chance, almost anywhere in the Dales, especially if you cycle or walk a back lane or path. If you want to learn more, or simply guarantee seeing it in action, Hawes is the place to do it. Working sheepdog demonstrations are run on summer Thursday evenings, and autumn afternoons, by local farmer and former world sheepdog triallist Richard Fawcett. They take place in a picturesque field between Hawes and Hardraw by Haylands Bridge.

 SPECIAL STAYS

Thorney Mire Cabin Appersett DL8 3LU ⌕ 07852 948929 ⌂ thorneymirewoodlandretreat.co.uk/cabin.html. Get away from it all without having to get away from it *all*. This is a hand-built wood cabin in privately owned woodland that mixes creature comforts (central heating, comfy beds, wood-burning stoves) and facilities (USB sockets, 4G) with rustic solitude. There's even a special ceiling window for stargazing. Enjoy supper out on the decking, watching red squirrels at the feeder. Water comes from the site's own borehole – you can test if Yorkshire Tea really does taste best with Yorkshire water. Hawes is a two-mile walk away. You might need a torch for the way back.

¶¶ FOOD & DRINK

Not counting pubs, there are around ten places in Hawes where a brew and a snack can be had and to be honest I could quite happily recommend any of them. Whittling the list down to three, my recommended pub, take-away and café are:

The Board Inn Market Pl ✆ 01969 667223 ✍ theboardinn.co.uk. A family-run pub that is proud of the local provenance of its food. Always at least three Yorkshire beers on offer. Dog-friendly, including some of the accommodation.

Caffe Curva Market Pl ✆ 01969 667209. Everything on the enticing breakfast and lunch menus is homemade, locally sourced and tasty, with lots of vegan options and a supper club on Friday evenings. Watch the world go by from the patio tables out front.

The Chippie Market Pl ✆ 01969 667663 ☉ Tue–Sun. Friendly and good value for eating in or out.

2 GAYLE

This hamlet owes its existence to one building, not a church or castle for a change, but a mill. **Gayle Mill** (✆ 01969 629348 ✍ gaylemill.org. uk) is the oldest virtually unaltered cotton mill in the world. It was built here in 1784 by the Routh brothers, two canny entrepreneurs who saw the business opportunities the new turnpike road would bring to Hawes. They did not really see beyond cotton spinning, but in its long life since, the mill has harnessed water power

"This hamlet owes its existence to one building, not a church or castle for a change, but a mill."

for a bewildering range of functions: flax spinning, wool spinning, woodworking machinery and electricity generation for the village. In 1988 the mill finally closed its doors as a commercial operation, and the building fell into disrepair.

That could have been it had it not been for local volunteers who joined the Gayle Mill Trust and worked tirelessly to return the mill to its former glory. One of the team, Tony Routh, was its last apprentice back in the 1960s. 'It was like coming home,' he said. 'When we started the project,

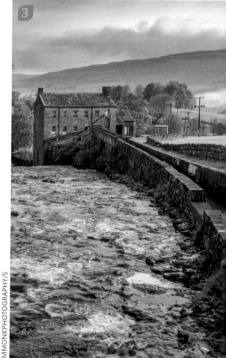

the building was just as it was the day that I walked out and into a new job – a few more cobwebs perhaps, and a bit more lime off the walls. We've come a long way since then though, and it's great to see it now, completely brought back to life.'

Coming third in the national final of the BBC's *Restoration* series in 2004 proved crucial in securing funds and now the turbines are turning again to produce electricity and work timber once more. The mill is open for tours on Thursdays, and a shop sells hand-crafted wood products made on site. If you want to get involved, sign up for one of their two-day working courses.

Gayle has two other aquatic attractions. **Blackburn Farm** (⌀ 01969 667524 ⌀ blackburnfarmhawes.co.uk) has a small lake stocked with rainbow trout available for angling, a lovely low-key campsite, and a footpath to stroll alongside Gayle Beck upstream. A delightful walk in itself, but it has the added bonus of **Aysgill Force** waterfall, about a mile away and especially impressive at high water levels.

3 HARDRAW

This sleepy little hamlet follows a typical Dales formula: an old pub, a new church on an old site, a stone bridge over a small beck and a scattering of other buildings, some farms and some cottages, with one tea room doubling as a felt studio. The pub, the Green Dragon, is worth a visit for its local cask ales and timeless interior – particularly if you're a fan of the Channel 5 series *All Creatures Great and Small*, whose pub scenes were filmed here. But what makes Hardraw really *"It has a steady, timeless air – a feeling of permanence – but appearances can be deceptive."* different is just upstream, in the pub's back garden. A beck leaps off an overhanging 100ft limestone cliff: this is **Hardraw Force** (○ summer 10.00–17.00; winter 10.00–16.00), the highest single-drop waterfall above ground in England. The whole place has a steady, timeless air about it – a feeling of permanence – but appearances can be deceptive.

Hardraw very nearly didn't exist at all beyond 1889. Hardraw Beck is only a small stream, in fact in midsummer it is not usually much more

◀ 1 & 3 The hamlet of Gayle owes its existence to the mill, the oldest virtually unaltered cotton mill in the world. 2 Hardraw Force – the highest single-drop waterfall above ground in England.

than a trickle, and on the morning of 12 July 1889 that is just how things were. By the afternoon though, things were very different, and at the end of the day known ever since as the Great Flood, Hardraw was all but wiped off the map. Around noon, livid black clouds over Shunner Fell burst into ferocious rain with the deafening crack of thunder.

"If Hardraw has whetted your appetite for waterfalls, you'll really enjoy Fossdale's neighbouring valley."

Thousands of tons of water roared down the hillside and funnelled into Hardraw Beck. By the time it reached the village, terrified residents watched a wall of water yards high tear around the corner and slam into buildings; all were flooded and some demolished. The graveyard was torn up and coffins and gravestones washed two miles downstream. A huge tree smashed a hole in the wall of the Green Dragon Inn and all the bridges disappeared completely.

Dales folk are resilient and Hardraw was repaired and rebuilt, but one reconstruction not many people are aware of is the waterfall itself. Such was the power of the surge that the lip of the falls was scoured away and Hardraw Force became a cascade down rock and loose boulders, losing its title of highest single-drop fall in the process. The landowner at the time, Lord Wharncliffe, wasn't having that. On inspecting the damage, he turned to his estate manager and commanded, 'Put it all back.' The very best stonemasons were hired and the lip was rebuilt. Few of today's thousands of visitors to Hardraw Force realise that they are looking at a manmade top to the cliff, still cunningly secured with metal pins.

Not all people visit Hardraw Scar to view the waterfall. The acoustics of the gorge here are perfect for outdoor music apparently, so once a year in early September it is the venue for a prestigious brass band competition. The Force is also a grand place for a bracing dip, but presumably not during the performances.

If Hardraw Force has whetted your appetite for waterfalls, then you will really enjoy Fossdale's neighbouring valley. Cotterdale wraps around the western flank of Great Shunner Fell and is drained by two beautiful becks, East and West Gill, which between them boast nine waterfalls. They join forces to form Cotterdale Beck and produce three more cascades, the final one, **Cotter Force**, being the most impressive. It is also the most accessible, on foot or by wheelchair, being 300yds from the A684 at Holme Heads Bridge. Bring your towel: this is another super secluded place for a quick dip. Unlike Hardraw Force it's open 24/7, and is free.

🍴 FOOD & DRINK

The Cart House Hardraw ✆ 01969 667691. A bridge-side café offering homemade, and mostly organic, food, with a felt studio attached and basic campsite behind.

Green Dragon Inn Hardraw ✆ 01969 667392 ⌂ greendragonhardraw.com. Worth a recommendation for the 13th-century building and well-kept selection of beers alone. Perhaps the only pub in the country with its own waterfall. A wide variety of accommodation is available.

MID WENSLEYDALE: ASKRIGG TO WEST WITTON

4 ASKRIGG

Askrigg is more famous to a certain generation as a film set for a television series rather than as a village of great character and rich history. But it's **James Herriot** country we are in, and this is the fictional village of Darrowby where the 1980s BBC series about a Yorkshire vet, *All Creatures Great and Small*, was filmed. (The 2020s Channel 5 remake of the same title was filmed over in Grassington, page 124.)

Askrigg is very old, with evidence of Iron Age settlement, but the name is younger and pure Norse, describing its position admirably on a ridge of high ground (rigg) where ash trees (ask) grow. The village's heyday was in the 1700s when it had the only market in Upper Wensleydale, a booming textile industry (hand knitting mainly) and a reputation for clock-making. The local lords of the manor were the Metcalfes, who ruled the roost from nearby Nappa Hall, once an impressive 15th-century fortified manor house but now a working farm and a little decrepit. One of many fine short walks from Askrigg takes in the hall and Nappa Mill before returning to the village via the banks of the River Ure.

"The name Askrigg is pure Norse, describing its position on a ridge of high ground (rigg) where ash trees (ask) grow."

Askrigg's market ceased trading long ago when Hawes took over as the local commercial centre, but the **market cross** is still here, as is a reminder of a cruel past. An iron ring is still set into the marketplace cobbles, where bulls would be tied, to be baited with dogs. The **bullring** was also used for another purpose, a sort of heavy gauntlet-throwing challenge, where a man wanting a fight would turn the ring over and another fancying his chances would turn it back. Presumably they would then set to knocking lumps off one another.

Most of Askrigg's interesting old buildings are clustered around or near the marketplace. St Oswald's Church is here, as is the Kings Arms. None of the village textile mills are still in operation but one, Low Mill, is very active in another way, as an outdoor activities centre (see below).

A handy waterside **walk** from the village traces the upstream course of the beck that used to power Low Mill's wheel. Your rewards for following Mill Gill are views of a series of pretty waterfalls wrapped in folds of oak woodland, culminating after a mile or so in the highest, **Whitfield Gill Force**. At this point you can return to Askrigg via an old green lane or carry on uphill to explore the scars, shake holes and swallow holes of Whitfield Fell.

FOOD & DRINK

The Bake-Well Market Pl ✆ 01969 629296 🖉 thebakewellaskrigg.com. A welcoming café with patio tables; a 1944 Austin Ten is usually parked opposite. Enjoy homemade preserves and freshly made sandwiches and rolls using locally sourced ingredients. Wide range of veg/vegan/'free-from' options.

Crown Inn Main St ✆ 01969 650387 🖉 crowninnaskrigg.co.uk. Locals refer to this as the 'Top Pub', the Kings Arms being the 'Bottom Pub', and this is their preferred drinking place. Beer is Black Sheep and Theakston; traditional pub grub.

Kings Arms Main St ✆ 01969 650113 🖉 kingsarmsaskrigg.com ☺ Mon & Wed dinner, Thu–Sun lunch & dinner). This is the Drover's Arms of the 1980s' *All Creatures Great and Small* fame as celebrity photos on the walls testify. It was chosen because it looked so traditional-old-Yorkshire, and it still does. What's more, the welcome is genuinely friendly. Theakston, Black Sheep and house beer brewed by Askrigg's own brewery.

Sykes House Main St ✆ 01969 650535 🖉 sykeshouse.co.uk. You can buy picnic supplies and snacks from this friendly general store and newsagent. A post office operates on Mondays and Wednesdays and there are B&B rooms upstairs.

ACTIVITIES

Low Mill Station Rd ✆ 01969 650432 🖉 lowmill.com. A residential outdoor centre with a wide range of activities: canoeing, climbing, caving and the like, for groups. They cater mainly for school groups, but if you are staying locally you can pre-hire an instructor for up to ten of you for a day's activity of your choice.

5 BAINBRIDGE

Bainbridge is a mere mile from Askrigg as the curlew flies, but a meandering two via the road over Yore Bridge. It is a similar size to its neighbour and probably at least as old; a Bronze Age earthwork sits just to the south, and on top of Brough Hill a Roman fort. The Latin invaders named this place Virosidum. Modern-day Bainbridge is a strangely sprawling settlement which suffers more than a little from having a busy 'A' road cut across the village green.

The village does have one famous old tradition which has sadly lapsed in recent years: that of the blowing of the Forest Horn. Back in the 14th century when much of Upper Wensleydale was hunting forest, a horn was sounded every winter night at 22.00 to guide benighted travellers in the forest safely back to Bainbridge. This custom was continued for hundreds of years but was only documented in the 19th century when the role of hornblower was passed down the Metcalfe family, who still live in the village. An old cow horn dating back to 1611 was replaced in 1864 with the present one, a huge African buffalo horn that resides in the Rose and Crown Hotel. Starting on 27 September, which is the feast of the Holy Rood, for those that don't know, a long, clear blast of the horn echoed around the dale each evening, and continued to brighten the winter nights until Shrovetide the following February. The Rose and Crown's fabulous building is one of the oldest in Wensleydale. They pride themselves on their homemade food and welcome dogs and muddy boots; if you drop in, try and persuade the landlord to restart the 22.00 horn-blowing. If enough of us do, we might get this ancient tradition going again.

¶¶ FOOD & DRINK

Corn Mill Tea Room DL8 3EH ✐ 01969 629405 ✐ cornmilltearoom.co.uk ☺ Easter–Oct. Within earshot of the River Bain. Full breakfasts, lunches, afternoon tea and snacks. Sister café of the Bake-Well in Askrigg (see opposite).

Yorebridge House DL8 3EE ✐ 01969 652060 ✐ yorebridgehouse.co.uk. Country house hotel with excellent restaurant, justifiably popular despite the expense, thanks to high-quality, locally sourced produce. Similarly, accommodation is luxurious but very pricey.

6 SEMER WATER

Natural lakes are in short supply in Yorkshire so consequently the few that exist tend to earn undeserved fame. Semer Water, in little Raydale, is trumpeted as the largest lake in North Yorkshire but at less than half a mile long it is not going to excite anyone who has visited the Lake District. It's pronounced 'Semmer-water', or even 'Semmer-watter' (particularly if you're referring to the beer named after it), and the name comes from the elements 'sea', 'mere' and 'water'. The information board on its pebbly beach calls it 'Lake Semerwater', which therefore means effectively 'Lake Lake-lake-lake', probably Britain's only genuine quadruply-redundant place name.

Semer Water is also alleged to conceal a drowned town under its surface, but with a maximum depth of 30ft it could scarcely hide a solitary two-storey building. Having said all that, Semer Water is a gorgeous place, a haven for winter wildfowl and summer watersports with a rich enough mix of marshland wildlife to prompt the Yorkshire Wildlife Trust to declare it a nature reserve.

The legend of the flooded town, while patently not true, is an entertaining moral homily. The gist of the story is that a wandering saint visited bustling Semer Town disguised as a pauper and begging food and shelter. He was rudely turned away from every house save that of a poor, old couple who treated him like one of the family. The following day he cursed the town with the words:

**Semer Water rise! Semer Town sink!
And bury the place all save the house
Where they gave me meat and drink.**

You can park at the north end of the lake for a small (and enthusiastically enforced) fee in summer, but for peace and quiet head down to the other end. Here, the wetland nature reserve is a glorious place to explore in early summer with the spongy ground festooned with water-loving plants, nothing very rare, but a wide variety including marsh valerian, bog bean, ragged robin, marsh cinquefoil, and marsh and spotted orchids, with yellow waterlilies on the open water. Crooks Beck wriggles its way through the marsh to empty into Semer Water, but when it emerges at the other end of the lake it is now known as the River

---

1 Semer Water – the largest lake in North Yorkshire. 2 Askrigg was the fictional village of Darrowby in the 1980s series of *All Creatures Great and Small*. 3 The Rose & Crown in Bainbridge is one of the oldest buildings in Wensleydale. 4 Yore Mill is located close to Aysgarth Falls. 5 Aysgarth Falls are at their most dramatic after rainfall. ▶

GRAHAMMOORE999/S

PETE STUART/S

SS

DAFYDD AP_W/S

STEPHEN GARNETT PHOTOGRAPHY

Bain. Its 1½-mile journey to the River Ure makes it the shortest river in England, but in that brief distance it does manage to boast a population of native crayfish and some of the finest brown trout fishing in the Dales.

7 AYSGARTH

This is an odd split-site village. The main settlement, presumably the original 'clearing in the oaks', is the place you'll find the petrol station, village shop and area's post office, and is situated on the main road on top of a hill. There's a quaint Edwardian Rock Garden here, by the turnoff to Thornton Rust. It's privately owned but open to the public and worth a nose around.

"There is no single spectacular drop but a series of limestone terraced steps at Upper Force, Middle Force, Lower Force."

The most visited part of Aysgarth however is half a mile east, down by the river: the buildings clustered around the famous Aysgarth Falls. **St Andrew's Church** is here, on the hillside overlooking Yore Mill and the river. The church is the probable original reason for the separation: it is a restored 16th-century building but almost certainly on an older religious site, maybe even pagan, connected with the Falls. It was at its most influential during medieval times when the church was owned by Jervaulx Abbey (page 201). Its present claims to fame are the old abbey rood screen and vicar's stall that were moved here at the time of the Dissolution. This work of art was too valuable to dismantle so was carried the 13 miles in one piece on the shoulders of 20 men.

It is the River Ure that most people come here to see, or more specifically, its 200ft descent in the space of less than half a mile that constitutes the **Aysgarth Falls**. There is no single spectacular drop but a series of limestone terraced steps at Upper Force, Middle Force, Lower Force and a further unnamed waterfall lower down – let's call it Bottom Force. Come here after a dry spell and you will wonder what all the fuss is about but if the river is full the name 'force' (from the Viking word *foss*, meaning waterfall) becomes more appropriate and the roar of the combined drops can be heard a long way away.

However big and brown the Ure is, the **riverside walking** is a delight, and accessible for wheelchairs and pushchairs all the way to Middle Force. The only drawback for me is the crowds; it can get very busy with the adjacent National Park Visitor Centre attracting its quota of visitors. It's not too difficult to find a little solitude though, as most people stroll to the falls and back on the north bank. If you walk through the churchyard and down to the river on the other side you may well find that you have it to yourself. Alternatively, head away from the river into Freeholders' Wood where the national park has reinstated a traditional hazel-coppicing system and is currently encouraging the return of the common dormouse to its preferred habitat. Look out for their nest boxes in the shrubbery.

Beyond the woods, a choice of **footpaths** can take you to the villages north of Aysgarth and the river, Redmire, Castle Bolton and Carperby with its fine pub, the Wheatsheaf, and old market cross. A local nature reserve has been created a couple of miles west of Carperby on the site of an old lead mine. The small roadside car park and picnic site at Ox Close allows easy access to the fantastic flora here. South of the river, the main valley is joined by the tributary Bishopdale and, slightly removed downstream, the village of West Witton.

Close to the falls, **Yore Mill** is an imposing four-storey building built in 1784, the same year as Gayle Mill (page 177). It is not quite so precious to industrial archaeologists, as it was substantially rebuilt in 1852 after a fire, but it still merits Grade II listing. It has changed jobs through its long life, first cotton spinning, then knitting yarn and later corn grinding and flour rolling. For ten years after milling finished in the 1950s Yore Mill was a cattle-food depot before becoming a horse-drawn-carriage museum; it's now flats and holiday lets, with a craft shop and café in the outbuildings.

¶¶ FOOD & DRINK

Fairhurst's at Berry's Farm Shop Swinithwaite DL8 4UH ✆ 01969 624668 🖑 fairhursts.co.uk/fairhursts-at-berrys. A farm shop, café and lots besides. They pride themselves on excellent sustainable credentials throughout.

George and Dragon Inn Main St, Aysgarth DL8 3AD ✆ 01969 663358 🖑 georgeanddragonaysgarth.co.uk. A Grade II-listed 17th-century coaching inn with separate bar and restaurant. The superb food is a mixture of traditional, local and fine cuisine, and all the beer is brewed in the surrounding dales. Accommodation available.

Hamilton's Tea Room Aysgarth DA8 3AE ✆ 01969 663423 🖑 yoredalehouse.com ⊙ Wed–Sun. Very welcoming and comfortable. Part of Yoredale House B&B.

Mill Race Teashop Aysgarth Falls DL8 3SR ✆ 01969 663446 🖑 themillraceteashop.com. Great views of Upper Falls (there can't be many places where dippers are visible from the gents' toilets). Real coffee, great cakes, afternoon and cream teas, plus savoury 'cheese teas'.

Wensleydale Ice Cream Thornton Rust DL8 3AS ✆ 07792 380177
⌂ wensleydale-icecream.co.uk ⊙ 11.30–16.00 Fri–Sun. On the quaint back lane just outside Aysgarth, Hardbank Farm's recent barn conversion houses an ice-cream parlour and coffee shop, with milk sourced from the farm's own Jerseys.
Wheatsheaf Carperby DL8 4DF ✆ 01969 663216 ⌂ wheatsheafinwensleydale.co.uk. The Wheatsheaf describes itself as a 'traditional country inn' and I wouldn't argue with that. The staff are welcoming and helpful, the beer is well kept, meals are good-value pub favourites, dogs are welcome and the accommodation is very comfortable. What more could you want?

8 CASTLE BOLTON & REDMIRE

'My name is Sir Richard le Scrope and I have a licence to crenellate,' sounds like a line John Cleese could have uttered in *Monty Python and the Holy Grail*, but truth can be stranger than fiction. Sir Richard was the builder in 1379 and, like all 14th-century castle-builders, he needed a licence to put turrets on his towers.

Bolton Castle (DL8 4ET ✆ 01969 623981 ⌂ boltoncastle.co.uk ⊙ Mar–Oct) is a particularly rewarding place to visit, partly because it is so complete, but also because it is privately owned so hasn't had the corporate treatment some historic buildings suffer. The owner has considerable emotional investment in the place because, incredibly, the castle has remained in one family throughout its entire 600-year history. Tom Orde-Powlett, the present ninth Lord Bolton, is a direct descendant of Sir Richard the Crenellator. Incidentally, the building is Bolton Castle; the village it's in is Castle Bolton.

There is so little damage to the fabric of the building because the Royalist defenders surrendered after six months of passive siege in the Civil War, during another Pythonesque episode in the castle's history. Colonel Chaytor, the commander of the Royalists, apparently cut off his own hand and threw it at his enemies in an extreme gesture of defiance but, not surprisingly, this didn't work and the siege continued, with the defenders finally giving up after eating their last horse. The Scropes regained the castle after Cromwell's demise but moved out to the newly constructed luxury mansion of Bolton Hall near Wensley and the castle became a block of flats of sorts, with up to nine families living in it up until the 1940s.

Now uninhabited, the castle has been developed as an excellent visitor attraction, with the bulk of it restored and accessible. Much is made of Castle Bolton's most illustrious past resident, Mary, Queen of Scots, who spent an eventful six months here in 1568 after her capture by Queen Elizabeth's forces in Scotland. She was ostensibly imprisoned, but local Catholic sympathisers made her stay very comfortable, supplying cartloads of tapestries, Turkish carpets, luxury clothes and venison – certainly not the conditions that the wretches in the dungeons had to suffer.

The gardens have been relaid along medieval lines, including a herb garden, maze, bowling green, rose garden and what must be one of the most northerly vineyards in the country. Regular special events are held throughout the year, such as armada or medieval weekends, which involve lots of dressing up and period activities – the kids will probably love them, and you can leave them to it while you visit the gift shop and café.

"The gardens have been relaid along medieval lines, including a herb garden, maze, bowling green and rose garden."

A choice of two roads or two footpaths will take you downhill from Castle Bolton to its near neighbour, **Redmire**. What brings most people here is the **Wensleydale Railway**, this being the present terminus of the line. If you have arrived by rail, and have time to kill before your train back, a three-mile circular walk taking in the ancient sunken track of Thoresby Lane and Castle Bolton is an excellent way to do it.

THE WENSLEYDALE RAILWAY

⊘ wensleydalerail.com

'I have a dream,' one famous speech began, and so do the volunteers of the Wensleydale Railway Association. Their aim is to restore the rail link along the full 40-mile length of their beloved valley, from the East Coast Main Line at Northallerton, to the Settle–Carlisle line at Garsdale. This is not just a nostalgia trip by a group of middle-aged beardy types, or a cynical money-making tourist trap, but a genuine attempt to return the service that the local Dales people felt should never have been taken away. 'We'd love our railway to become the branch line it was in the 1920s and 30s,' said David Walker, one of the WRA volunteers, 'A thread linking all the communities of the dale from schoolchildren and commuters to tourists coming to visit this lovely part of the world.'

At present, 17 miles of operating line is marooned in the middle, between Leeming Bar and Redmire. Joining up the eastern end should

be the easiest task, as it's only five miles to Northallerton, and the track is still in place and used for freight transport – the MOD bringing tanks to Catterick Garrison in the main. The major long-term project will be the relaying of 18 miles of track from Redmire, the present terminus, to Garsdale Head. This would mean the reopening of stations in Askrigg and Hawes eventually, but the first goal is the next stop along the line after Redmire – Aysgarth.

'It's definitely a labour of love,' said David. 'None of us would put this amount of hard work in for free if we didn't enjoy it. It takes my head away from the day job and I've made all sorts of new friends – and contrary to popular perception, none of them are oddball eccentrics!'

¶¶ FOOD & DRINK

Bolton Castle Tea Room Castle Bolton DL8 4ET ⏱ 01969 623981. Basic, snacks-only café inside the castle (but free to enter).

Redmire Village Pub Redmire DL8 4EA ✆ 01969 629297 ⏱ thevillage.pub. Formerly the Bolton Arms, this was rescued by an American benefactor in Sep 2023 and is now a community-run pub doing proper beer and food.

9 BISHOPDALE

Few people are aware of Bishopdale. Even of those that are, not many stop to enjoy its delights, as they are usually on their way from Wensleydale to Wharfedale, or vice versa, on the B6160, which runs its length. The upper dale is almost-deserted sheep and walking country with a scattering of farms, but lower down there are three handsome villages of traditional stone cottages. **Thoralby** has a chapel and waterfall; **Newbiggin** has a pub; and **West Burton** is a veritable metropolis with all of the above plus school, village hall, general store, butcher's and gift shop. It also boasts one of the largest and most oddly shaped market crosses in the country, a strange stretched pyramid of a thing on the extremely spacious village green. What originally brought me to West Burton though was the same feature that attracted the landscape painter J M W Turner in the 19th century. Yards from the village centre, but hidden away in its own limestone amphitheatre, is **Cauldron Falls**, a beautiful cascade formed by Walden Beck's leap

◀ **1** Bolton Castle has belonged to the same family for its entire 600-year history. **2** The Wensleydale Railway. **3** Cauldron Falls, Bishopdale.

over a 15ft rock step. Good swimming can be enjoyed in the pool below when it's warm and quiet enough. A short stroll of a mile or so follows Walden Beck upstream from the waterfall to Cote Bridge, then back over fields or road to the village.

⊠ FOOD & DRINK

Fox and Hounds Inn West Burton DL8 4JY ✆ 01969 663111
⌂ foxandhoundswestburton.co.uk. A 17th-century building on the village green with quoits pitch adjoining. It is the social centre of the village with something going on most evenings, including darts and dominoes teams. Cask beers, John Smith's and Theakston, with other local guest ales. Very comfortable, dog-friendly accommodation. Good-value pub food; take-aways, too.

The Street Head Inn Newbiggin-in-Bishopdale DL8 3TE ✆ 01969 663282
⌂ thestreetheadinn.co.uk. A Grade II-listed coaching inn which has served travellers on the 'main' road between Wensleydale and Wharfedale for over 300 years. Food is traditional pub fare in hearty portions, especially the Sunday carvery, and there's a good range of mainly Yorkshire beers. Dogs are welcome in some areas. There's a choice of accommodation – en-suite B&B upstairs and the nearby 20-bed bunkhouse owned by the pub.

10 WEST WITTON

If you have seen the film *The Wicker Man* then the goings-on here one Sunday, every August around the 24th, will send familiar shivers down your spine. The name 'West Witton' is so innocent-sounding, and the local people are very decent really, but on St Bartholomew's Day every year they all take part in a ritual of barbaric pagan origins. It's called the Burning of Bartle and re-enacts supposed real historical events when a local criminal is chased, caught and burned at the stake in place of a sacrificial lamb. The route of the chase is recounted in a chanted verse:

> On Penhill crags he tore his rags
> At Hunters Thorn he blew his horn
> At Capplebank Stee he brak his knee
> At Grassgill Beck he brak his neck
> At Wadhams End he couldn't fend
> At Grassgill End we'll mak his end
> SHOUT LADS SHOUT!

To the accompaniment of a rousing cheer from the crowd, a straw effigy is set alight and everyone marches, singing, to the pub for a pint or two – it's very sinister stuff. This traditional ceremony has been carried out for at least 400 years and the villagers are very proud of it, so much so that the local youth club, with help from Rural Arts, North Yorkshire, produced a series of mosaic tiles telling the story. They are in place up on the hillside making up a trail which you can follow during a pleasant four-mile fell walk.

More gently, there's an informal croquet lawn at the west end of the village. Don't be surprised if locals invite you to join a game.

FOOD & DRINK

Fox and Hounds Main St ✆ 01969 623650 ⌂ foxwitton.com. A characterful 13th-century building housing a classic beer-drinkers' local, serving a variety of local cask ales and traditional pub grub.

Wensleydale Heifer Main St ✆ 01969 622322 ⌂ wensleydaleheifer.co.uk. I nearly didn't get past the tacky pub sign, and what a mistake that would have been. This is a fantastic fish restaurant in a pub, miles from the sea, not cheap but top quality: Wensleydale Brewery beer and in-house brews available. Also does luxurious accommodation.

LOWER WENSLEYDALE: WENSLEY TO BEDALE

11 WENSLEY

In 1956 schoolchildren made a strange discovery in Holy Trinity churchyard: a seemingly deliberately buried market cross. This odd ritual of laying to rest the symbol of a town's identity encapsulates Wensley's sad history and explains why Wensleydale is named after such a tiny village. In the 14th and 15th centuries this was the market town for the whole of the dale, but in 1563 the plague struck and Wensley was particularly badly hit. Most inhabitants died, others moved to

"In 1956 schoolchildren made a strange discovery in Holy Trinity churchyard: a seemingly deliberately buried market cross."

nearby Leyburn, and certainly no-one had any intention of visiting the market. There was probably nothing to sell anyway, the parish crop register noting grimly, 'This year nothing set down.' Wensley has never fully recovered its former importance and, but for Lord Bolton building his hall nearby, might have faded away completely. Today, however, it is one of the most appealing of the dale's villages, and well worth a visit.

A Ure-side stroll

❄ OS Explorer map OL30; start: Wensley bridge ♀ SE091894; 1½ miles; easy, with straightforward route-finding.

Very gentle walking starts from the bridge in Wensley, either up or down the nearby River Ure. If you head upstream (westwards) for a mile along the south bank and over Lords Bridge you can return via Bolton Hall, which isn't open to the public but a public footpath passes right in front of the hall – I'm sure Lord Bolton loves that!

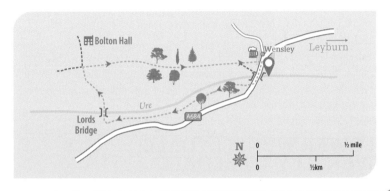

The old church is still there, and is well worth a visit for its remarkable medieval wall paintings: faded but chilling portrayals of St Eloi, and The Three Living and Three Dead. The graveyard's overgrown look, by the way, is deliberate rewilding, not neglect. Wensley also benefits from a village pub, and a Victorian watermill which now houses a traditional candle maker. **White Rose Candle Workshop** (✆ 01969 623544 ◇ whiterosecandles.com ⊙ 10.00–16.00 Wed–Sat) has been going since the early 1970s, producing traditional beeswax and other candles of all shapes, sizes, designs and scents. It is a fascinating experience, and one that I found strangely relaxing, to watch the candles being made. Admission is free and you can also enjoy the small waterfall by the side of the mill.

🍴 FOOD & DRINK

The Three Horseshoes DL8 4HJ ✆ 01969 622327 ◇ thethreehorseshoeswensley.co.uk. This cosy village inn is a beer-drinkers' pub with a good changing range of well-kept

Yorkshire cask ales and West Country ciders. Food includes homemade pizzas, and there's a fine view from terrace tables out the back.

12 LEYBURN

This pleasant and, seemingly, always busy market town is easily the largest settlement in this part of Lower Wensleydale though it has limited attractions of its own. I like Leyburn but I must admit I can't be entertained for very long within the town itself. It desperately tries to borrow a bit of history from Bolton Castle in its Leyburn Shawl story, where Mary, Queen of Scots was said to have escaped from Bolton Castle but dropped her shawl on the cliffs above Leyburn, thus betraying her whereabouts and causing her recapture. Wishful balderdash, I'm afraid; Leyburn Shawl Crag's name is much older than the Tudors and has its root in the word 'shielings' (shepherds' huts). Retracing the queen's supposed footsteps back along the Shawl top to the castle makes a splendid walk though, with glorious panoramic views.

No, Leyburn is not an historical centre but it is an effective service centre for the dale with a wide variety of shops. Among these is Wensleydale Longwool (⌂ wensleydalelongwool.co.uk), where knitters can buy yarn from the eponymous sheep, and locally made clothes made from it. A market takes place every Friday all year round with another on Sundays in summer. It also has one of the largest **antiques auction rooms** in the country in the form of Tennants (Harmby Rd ✆ 01969 623780 ⌂ tennants.co.uk). The town hosts the **Wensleydale Show** every August Bank Holiday Saturday, where every aspect of Dales life is on show.

Just downstream of Leyburn and Middleham, the River Ure is joined by the River Cover, the latter having just navigated the length of Coverdale, another little valley on a par with Bishopdale for unspoiled pastoral peace.

¶¶ FOOD & DRINK

Chambers Coffee House Market Pl ✆ 01969 625919. Great coffee, tasty soup, delicious cakes, patio tables, friendly service and good value. What's not to like?

Posthorn Tea Room and Café Market Pl ✆ 01969 622243. A friendly, Union-Jack-bedecked café serving light meals on patio tables in the marketplace.

Rupali Balti House High St ✆ 01969 624863. One of the best take-away curry houses I have encountered anywhere in Yorkshire.

Sandpiper Inn Railway St 01969 622206 sandpiperinn.co.uk Tue–Sun. One of Leyburn's oldest buildings is home to some of its best food, courtesy of host/chef Jonathan Harrison. Menus are based on local farm produce and game, expertly prepared and reasonably priced. Not especially a drinkers' pub unless your tipple is malt whisky, with over 50 to choose from.

13 MIDDLEHAM

Two miles south of Leyburn and perched on high land between the rivers Ure and Cover sits the village of Middleham. It has three links with royalty: the childhood home of a king; royal treasure; and the sport of kings, horseracing. The town is sometimes dubbed 'the Newmarket of the North', and is home to over 500 racehorses. Late morning is the best time to see them in the centre, when Middleham's 'rush hour' has a decidedly equestrian character.

A castle looms behind the market square, but these impressive remains are, in fact, Middleham Castle mark two: its predecessor is still visible as a mound on William's Hill just south and up the slope. Richard III was brought up here as a lad in the 15th century under the tutelage of the Earl of Warwick. It was then that he met the Earl's daughter Anne, whom he later married, thus inheriting the castle on Warwick's death. He became king on the death of his brother Edward IV in 1483 but his reign was a short and miserable one.

Within the space of two years his only son died in the castle aged 11, his wife went the same way the following year aged 28, and he also supposedly uttered those famous words, 'A horse, a horse, my kingdom for a horse,' at the Battle of Bosworth. He didn't get his horse and lost the battle, his kingdom and his life aged 32. We have Shakespeare to thank for the quote and the all-round impression of a vindictive, malicious and selfish character. Modern

"Richard III was brought up here as a lad in the 15th century under the tutelage of the Earl of Warwick."

historians are of the view that the Bard was trying to impress the reigning Tudors with his writing and that Richard was quite a nice chap on the whole. The villagers would certainly agree; their local king is still remembered with much affection and a requiem mass is said in the village church annually on 22 August, the anniversary of his death.

Following the dramatic discovery of the remains of Richard III beneath a car park in Leicester in 2012, a few contenders were put forward as

THE MIDDLEHAM JEWEL

A right royal treasure was found near Middleham Castle in 1985 by Ted Seaton, an amateur metal detectorist. He was about to pack up and go home when his machine picked up a faint signal from just over a foot beneath the soil surface. Ted dug out what he thought was an old compact box and took it home to clean. It was then he discovered what he had: a diamond-shaped gold pendant inlaid with a single sapphire and exquisitely engraved with a scene of the Trinity and a Latin charm against 'falling sickness' (epilepsy). The Middleham Jewel, as it has come to be known, was bought by the Yorkshire Museum in York for the tidy sum of £2.5 million. A replica is on display in the castle.

sites for the reburial, his childhood home in Middleham being one. In the end, Leicester Cathedral was chosen but many around here feel that the old king would have preferred Yorkshire soil and will be turning in his grave still.

An almost perfectly straight two-mile stretch of bridleway leads from Middleham over Low Moor to the west, and on the map it looks like a deserted trackway ideal for a peaceful walk or bike ride. If you do venture up, solitude you won't find but entertainment you will, as on most days, scores of racehorses thunder up and down it on their way to or from the old racecourse on High Moor. There hasn't been an official race here since 1873 but the training tradition, once started, continued. Today no fewer than 15 stables operate in and around Middleham, making it one of the biggest horse-racing centres in the country. If you want to see more than just the horses being walked around the lanes or cantering on the gallops, tours of the stables and more are available; meal or accommodation packages can be arranged too ($\mathscr{O}$ 07590 494644 $\mathring{\otimes}$ middlehamracingtours.co.uk).

🍴 FOOD & DRINK

Several pubs and a fish 'n' chip shop surround the square; the **Richard III** ($\mathscr{O}$ 01969 623240 $\mathring{\otimes}$ richard111hotel.co.uk) is a local choice for pub grub while **The Tack Room** ($\mathring{\otimes}$ 01969 622093 $\mathring{\otimes}$ thewensleydalehotel.com) offers upscale dining right in the centre, as well as boutique hotel accommodation. Just north of the square and in the shadow of the castle, the **Castle Keep Tea Room** (West End $\mathscr{O}$ 01969 623147 $\mathring{\otimes}$ castlekeeptearoom. co.uk $\odot$ 10.00–16.00 Thu–Sat, 10.00–noon Sun) is a cyclist- and dog-friendly local café with patio tables on a cobbled forecourt, proud of its freshly made sandwiches and barista coffee.

The Blue Lion East Witton DL8 4SN ☏ 01969 624273 ⌂ thebluelion.co.uk. Old coaching inn, an almost perfect blend of flag-floored, open-fired village pub bar and country house hotel. Excellent food and accommodation.

Cover Bridge Inn East Witton DL8 4SQ ☏ 01969 623250 ⌂ thecoverbridgeinn.co.uk. Another old coaching inn, gloriously situated on rivers Ure and Cover. Riverside walks from the door and fishing permits available from the bar. Good-value accommodation.

14 COVERDALE

Medieval monks and nuns sought out beautiful and isolated places for their abbeys and priories, so it's no surprise that ecclesiastical remains are scattered around Coverham and East Scrafton in this valley. Middleham Church is dedicated to the nun St Alkelda (page 106); perhaps she was a resident of the abbey in Coverdale. Little documentary evidence has been found concerning the Premonstratensian order (*Ordo Praemonstratensis*) that lived here – I suspect because few people could either spell or pronounce the name.

The Forbidden Corner

Tupgill Park Estate, Coverham DL8 4TJ ☏ 01969 640638 ⌂ theforbiddencorner.co.uk ☺ Apr–Oct daily, Nov–Christmas Sat & Sun; tickets must be booked in advance

West of Middleham, Coverdale's major attraction is the **Forbidden Corner**, a fantasy-based series of mazes and follies in the four-acre garden of an old racing-horse stables, Tupgill Park. It quite justifiably advertises itself as 'The Strangest Place in the World' and is brilliantly unique.

Although it regularly features on national lists of top days out, it was never intended to be anything more than a private family folly. It was the brainchild of the owner of Tupgill Park, Colin Armstrong, who in the 1980s teamed up with architect Malcolm Tempest to design a series of walled gardens, tunnels, grottoes and towers which linked into a three-dimensional maze for his family and friends to explore. As it developed it was opened to the public and its fame spread by word of mouth, to the point now where it can barely cope with its own popularity.

What makes it so good is that it is a genuine adventure. On arrival you are given a leaflet which is not a map, but a series of cryptic messages. 'All the clues to finding your way around are on the sheet,' a girl at the

---

1 View of Middleham from the castle walls. **2** Constable Burton Hall. **3** The entranceway to the Forbidden Corner, Coverham. ▶

KEVIN EAVES/S

SS

GODDARD NEW ERA/A

reception said, 'they're just not in the right order.' The entrance through the gaping mouth of a giant stone monster sets the tone, and away you go.

I first came here in the early days when my children were small and they absolutely loved it. We spent hours climbing, crawling, getting lost, studying clues, groping along dark corridors, planning routes from battlement viewpoints, getting lost again and finally finding the way to the underground temple. At times I was genuinely unnerved, for example by the revolving room with identical doors, and after two subsequent visits some secret corners have still managed to evade me.

This is a must-see place, especially if you have children, but I would strongly recommend coming at less busy times to make the most of the sense of exploration. Young children may find some parts scary, though these are easily avoided. For refreshment mid-journey, there's a kiosk selling snacks (there are also toilets), and there's a picnic and garden space near the entrance. Dogs are not permitted, except assistance dogs.

15 CONSTABLE BURTON

You'll find this village three miles east of Leyburn on the Bedale road. If you end up near Hull in East Yorkshire, your sat nav has taken you to Burton Constable not Constable Burton – an easy mistake, and you're not the first.

Here you'll find the Wyvill family home at **Constable Burton Hall** (⌀ 01677 450428 ◌ constableburton.com ◔ gardens mid-Mar–Sep; guided tours by arrangement). This Grade I-listed Neoclassical Georgian mansion stands in a large landscaped park. It is the park and gardens that most people come to visit, especially in springtime when they are at their best. The hall is still lived-in so is not usually open to the public but the honesty box entrance fee is worth it for the outdoor experience alone, particularly if you like your gardens less formal and with a few wild corners.

¶¶ FOOD & DRINK

Wyvill Arms DL8 5LH ⌀ 01677 450581 ◌ thewyvillarms.co.uk. An unashamedly food-orientated pub with a very good reputation for quality. Local provenance is a high priority, with herbs and some seasonal vegetables grown in the back garden. Beers served are also sourced locally and kept well. B&B accommodation is available with some very good-value offers.

16 JERVAULX ABBEY

HG4 4PH ⟨⟩ jervaulxabbey.com

This abbey suffered more than most under Henry VIII's violent Dissolution and, sadly, very little of it remains. It was a very influential daughter house of the Cistercian Byland Abbey, with the original French monks probably responsible for starting cheesemaking in Wensleydale. What remains today are peaceful and atmospheric ruins which the private owners have allowed to become overgrown by 180 species of wild plants – a lovely floral oasis. Entrance is every day of the year by honesty-box payment. You can cycle through the grounds.

Brymor Ice Cream

High Jervaulx Farm, HG4 4PG ⟨⟩ 01677 460337 ⟨⟩ brymordairy.co.uk

At High Jervaulx Farm, above the abbey, the Cistercian monks' dairy-produce tradition continues; not cheese nowadays but ice cream. Brymor Ice Cream is available throughout Yorkshire in over 25 flavours, from Amarena Black Cherry Whim Wham to Riggwelter (beer) Raisin Ripple, but what makes it so popular is its rich creaminess – how do they do it? The answer is pedigree Guernsey cows and lush Dales pasture. Brymor is one of the few on-farm producers of ice cream that only uses milk from the farm's own herd so they can guarantee the provenance of the product, and its richness – Guernsey cow's milk has one of the highest fat contents of any available. There are three ways you can sample the delights of rum and raisin, experiment with mocha almond crunch or remember nostalgic childhoods with traditional vanilla: you can look out for Brymor Ice Cream served in cafés and restaurants in Yorkshire, you can buy it from good delis and farmers' markets, or you can call in to High Jervaulx Farm and get it fresh. Either relax and eat it here in the conservatory or take it away along with some clotted cream and cheese if you wish.

17 BEDALE

Yet another town that dubs itself 'Gateway to the Dales', Bedale does have a justifiable claim as far as Wensleydale is concerned. If you enter the dale from the east, off the A1, or by train on the Wensleydale Railway, you will pass through this ancient market town.

Bedale is quite small and all the interest is concentrated on the long, thin marketplace, and the beck-side that runs parallel, so you can see

just about everything on a half-mile stroll up one and down the other. The best place to start is Bedale Hall at the top of the market, opposite the church, where the town's small, free **Bedale Museum** (✐ 01677 427516 ☉ Apr–Sep) is a collection of bygones amassed over half a century and featuring an 18th-century wooden fire engine; from the adjacent tourist office you can pick up a heritage trail leaflet. **St Gregory's Church**, looming from across the road, has a disproportionately large tower: this, the most fortified church in northern England, was refuge for the

"Wandering back up the cobbled marketplace gives the opportunity for some browsing, especially on Tuesday's market day."

townsfolk when the Scots came rampaging. Emgate leads from the 14th-century market cross down to the beck, which was part canalised in the 19th century to link Bedale with the River Swale, but abandoned when the railway arrived. The Harbour, a canal basin, is a reminder of these times gone, but nowhere near as impressive as the small square brick building on the far bank. This Grade II-listed castellated structure is unique: Britain's only remaining **leech house**, formerly a store place for apothecaries' wriggly medical helpers. There are pleasant picnic tables by the river, opposite.

Wandering back up the mainly Georgian, cobbled marketplace gives the opportunity for some browsing, especially on Tuesday's market day when the town's pubs are at their atmospheric bustling best too.

On the eastern edge of Bedale, **Big Sheep Little Cow** (Aiskew Watermill, DL8 1AW ✐ 01677 422125 ☉ bigsheeplittlecow.co.uk ☉ term-time Mon–Sun; school holidays Wed–Sun) is a bit of a 'Fast' children's attraction with an adventure play area and buggy rides, but its Slow credentials are earned with farm tours and home-produced Dexter beef and ice cream for sale.

⟨⟩ FOOD & DRINK

Buck Inn Village Green, Thornton Watlass HG4 4AH ✐ 01677 422461 ☉ buckwatlass.co.uk. Bedale's pubs have seen better days but this nearby option is worth getting to: a traditional locals' place by the cricket pitch. Beer from both Masham breweries plus micro-guests. Food is quality pub grub and good-value homemade pizzas. Dog-friendly B&B.

◀ **1** An autumn day at Thorp Perrow Arboretum. **2** The atmospheric ruins of Jervaulx Abbey.

Castle Arms Inn Top of the Green, Snape DL8 2TB ✆ 01677 470270 [f] castlearmssnape
☺ Tue–Sun. A friendly, low-ceilinged, flagstoned village pub, just south of Thorp Perrow
Arboretum. The menu is extensive, good value and top quality. Quiet annex B&B. Beer from
Jennings and Marston's.
Cockburn's Butchers Market Pl ✆ 01677 422126 ⌂ cockburnsbutchers.co.uk. A proper
butcher's, combining modern tastes with traditional quality. When in Bedale I can't resist
stopping here for a pie of some sort.
Institution Market Pl ✆ 01677 425541 ⌂ thisisinstitution.co.uk ☺ Tue–Sat. Relaxed
spaces indoors and out with imaginative breakfast and lunch dishes, plus grazing plates.
The North End Market Pl ✆ 01677 424922 ⌂ thenorthend.co.uk ☺ Mon–Wed, Fri &
Sat. At the top of the marketplace (technically 'North End'). Nobody pulls pork better, and
the ingredients for the café's enticing light meals and more substantial main courses come
entirely from local suppliers.

18 THORP PERROW ARBORETUM

DL8 2PS ✆ 01677 425323 ⌂ thorpperrow.com

What initially brought me to this place south of Bedale was joining a
fungus foray event, to learn the useful skill of how not to poison myself
eating wild mushrooms. In the process I was captivated by the autumn
colours of the trees and shrubs planted by the arboretum's creator, Sir
Leonard Roper, and also enjoyed a fascinating display of falconry at the
bird centre. Other regular events that take place include photography
courses, ghost walks, seasonal nature trails and outdoor concerts, and
you can call in to the arboretum's tea room and gift shop without paying
the entrance fee.

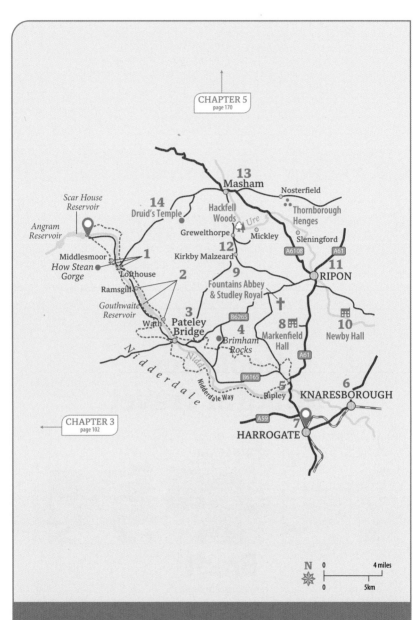

CHAPTER 5
page 170

Scar House
Reservoir

Angram
Reservoir

13
Masham

Nosterfield

14
Druid's Temple

Hackfell
Woods

Thornborough
Henges

Grewelthorpe

Ure

Mickley

Sleningford

A6108

A61

Middlesmoor
*How Stean
Gorge*

1

12
Kirkby Malzeard

11
RIPON

Lofthouse

2

9
Fountains Abbey
& Studley Royal

Ramsgill

*Gouthwaite
Reservoir*

Wath

3
**Pateley
Bridge**

B6265

8
Markenfield
Hall

10
Newby Hall

4
*Brimham
Rocks*

A61

N i d d e r d a l e

Nidd

Nidderdale Way

B6165

5

6

Ripley

KNARESBOROUGH

CHAPTER 3
page 102

A59

7

HARROGATE

N
0   4 miles
0   5km

NIDDERDALE, HARROGATE & AROUND

6
NIDDERDALE, HARROGATE & AROUND

With Caroline Mills

Swaledale, Wensleydale or Wharfedale would, I'm sure, be the first to be mentioned if someone was asked to name one of the Yorkshire Dales in a pub quiz. But Nidderdale? It tends to play second or even third fiddle to the better-known dales. It isn't actually in the area designated as the Yorkshire Dales National Park at all. Hence the main throng of tourists tends to bypass Nidderdale, heading straight for the national park: in Nidderdale, the absence of visitors is almost tangible.

It is indeed strange that Nidderdale hasn't been included within the park boundary. The spectacular countryside around the dale is designated as a National Landscape. The hills that fall across the border between national park and National Landscape status are the same hills making up the same landscape.

Yet Nidderdale is a game of two halves. To the northwest, and closest to the Yorkshire Dales National Park, lies Upper Nidderdale. It's an area that becomes increasingly rugged and remote the further back along the valley you go. It pulls you like a magnet, drawing you further into its midst, tempting you with an ever-changing panorama at every turn, rise and fall. With only one small road that leads to nowhere, the hills of Little Whernside and its giant neighbour Great Whernside creating a wall between Nidderdale and Coverdale, there is no through traffic, unless you happen to be on foot or on horseback. A string of pearly reservoirs line the route of the River Nidd from the foot of its source, Great Whernside. These watering holes, quenching the thirst of residents in far-flung Bradford, are interspersed with tiny hamlets.

It can feel isolated round here. In fact, England's remotest spot – as in 'furthest place from a tarmac road' – is in Nidderdale. In 2020 the Ordnance Survey pinpointed this to a bog on Riggs Moor, at ♥ SE030717.

So a good guess would be required as to why anyone should have set up camp in Nidderdale years ago but, now that they have, it's easy to understand – for its quality of life surpasses many others.

Further east, Nidderdale bottoms out, the hills recede and the land flattens. At least, the undulations are less undulating, the distance between villages decreases and the land becomes more cultivated. It's not until you reach **Knaresborough**, a good 30 miles from the river's source (and even longer if you stretched out the Nidd's meandering tendencies into a pencil-straight line), that you get any serious habitation – although the elegant town of **Harrogate**, joined at the hip with Knaresborough on its eastern side, now sprawls further north and west towards the edge of Nidderdale National Landscape with a plethora of housing developments.

Past Knaresborough, the Nidd continues for a few more meandering miles east before it disappears for good, its waters mingling with those of the more northerly Swale and Ure to form the mightier Ouse.

The Nidderdale National Landscape also swallows up the most southeasterly section of Wensleydale. Like its counterpart of Upper Nidderdale, the land furthest west begins harsh and inhospitable on top of Masham Moor before it drops down to greener pastures, great swathes of estate forests and a web of tiny tributaries that gurgle towards the Ure.

For this reason, Masham and Ripon, officially part of Wensleydale, are mentioned within this chapter but, for now, I'll stay with the upper reaches of Nidderdale before moving slowly southeast, just as the River Nidd does, towards Knaresborough and its neighbour, Harrogate.

SELF-POWERED TRAVEL

CYCLING

Nidderdale has a long tradition of cycling participation and competitive excellence. Indeed, Harrogate has staged major events, including two days of the 2014 Tour de France, and the 2019 UCI World Championships (during which it rained incessantly).

One long-distance bike route passes through the region, with a section of the 170-mile **Way of the Roses** (Sustrans route 688) meandering on (mainly) small country lanes between Pateley Bridge and Ripon, visiting both Brimham Rocks and Studley Royal.

TOURIST INFORMATION

Harrogate Royal Baths, Crescent Rd ✆ 01423 537300 🌐 visitharrogate.co.uk
🕐 Wed–Sat
Knaresborough Courthouse Museum ✆ 01423 866886 🕐 Wed–Sun
Masham Little Market Pl ✆ 01765 680200 🕐 Mon–Sat
Pateley Bridge Station Sq ✆ 01423 714953 🕐 Mon–Sat
Ripon Market Pl South ✆ 01765 604625 🕐 Wed–Sat

There are many popular road climbs. The moortop vault between Lofthouse and Masham, for instance, is a thrilling haul past reservoirs. Another favourite challenge is Greenhow Hill, rearing up from Pateley Bridge: avoid the busy main road, and take the quiet, winding parallel back-lane alternative to the south. A hidden tarmac gem is the service road from Lofthouse up the higher Nidd valley to Scar House Reservoir: it's closed to motor traffic but open to cyclists, so you have the scenic climb – and super downhill back – to yourself.

Visit Harrogate and Nidderdale National Landscape both have sections on their **websites** devoted to cycling but I don't think that the brilliant 🌐 hedgehogcycling.co.uk can be bettered. Local cyclist David Mitchell runs the site and gives thorough and up-to-date information on routes, shops, hire and general cycling issues.

The best family-friendly route in the region is the **Nidderdale Greenway**; the reopening of the old Nidd viaduct to walkers, bikes and horses has allowed access to a four-mile stretch of disused railway between Harrogate and Ripley. A rolling path continues to Clint, and there are plans to extend it further along the old railway to Pateley Bridge. The Greenway handily links up with another traffic-free cycle path called the **Beryl Burton Cycleway**, a 1½-mile route named after the seven-times world cycling champion and which connects Harrogate with Knaresborough along a stretch of traffic-free cycle path, avoiding the need to use the busy A59. One suspects the great Beryl might not have been that impressed, though – she was one of the toughest cyclists ever (of any gender) and, based on her 1973 record of 21 minutes 25 seconds for ten miles, it would have taken her a mere three minutes to cover the distance. She is celebrated in Knaresborough in a *trompe l'œil* window on High Street.

There is some opportunity for **off-road cycling** around the cluster of villages and hamlets on the eastern side of the dale, with gentler slopes and quiet country lanes connecting them, making it easy to join up the dots on the map. A few scenic, if arduous, bridleways high up on the moor may tempt the diehards, and there'll always be the odd pub or tea room on the way.

Group cycle rides around the Harrogate area

Formed in appreciation of a good cycle ride, **Wheel Easy** (*⌀* wheel-easy. org.uk) is a cycle group for keen or more casual riders that welcomes visitors to join rides. They go out every Sunday and Wednesday morning over distances from 15 miles upwards, sometimes staying out all day. Simply turn up at the Yorkshire Showground car park at 09.30 on Sundays and Wednesdays.

Said Malcolm Margolis, one of the organisers of Wheel Easy, 'Our name describes exactly what we do; we are all about enjoying a leisurely cycle ride, not about racing, so we really welcome anyone who is visiting the area to come on our rides with us and meet any number of our 250-plus members.' A list of rides is posted on the Wheel Easy website should you favour a particular route but, whichever one you select, you'll find some great cycling in good company.

HORSERIDING

SJ Equestrian of Warsill, near Ripley (*⌀* 07900 692250 *⌀* sjequestrian. co.uk) provides riding lessons, and can organise hack outs by arrangement.

WALKING

Nidderdale has some great walking territory, with spectacular views and scenery. There are opportunities for all, with many pre-planned short and medium-length routes across easy-going ground, which make good options for families. Wheelchair users can get out and about too at places like **Scar House**, where approximately two miles of the four-mile route around the reservoir is totally accessible. For walkers who like to stretch their legs, the **Nidderdale Way** trips its way over 53 miles of ground in a circular route that officially starts in Pateley Bridge. Complete it and you can buy a commemorative badge in Pateley Bridge's tourist office. It provides the opportunity to walk around the uplands that nurture the juvenile River Nidd and along the riverbank to the greener pastures of lower-lying land further east. The route quite deliberately wiggles about a bit to take in some worthwhile landmarks such as Brimham Rocks and Ripley Castle but also links up with other footpaths and bridleways for circular day or half-day walks.

The **Dalesbus Ramblers** ($\oslash$ dalesbus.org/friendsofdalesbus) organises a number of free, guided walks around the area that are all accessible by bus; simply catch the bus to the starting point. Harrogate and Knaresborough have some rewarding **town walks** too, covered in this chapter; they can be particularly good for those with mobility issues, taking advantage of tarmac footpaths and pavements.

UPPER NIDDERDALE: NIDD HEAD TO PATELEY BRIDGE

It makes sense to begin at the beginning – where the River Nidd dribbles out from the fells around Great Whernside. Here the land is harsh and inhospitable, where the only sign of civilisation is the odd farmstead over the top of Great Whernside in Coverdale. Much of this land has open access rights so you can walk across the upland freely.

The first sign of human activity in Nidderdale is a couple of miles downstream where the river flows through two reservoirs, first **Angram** followed by **Scar House**. Angram is the older of the two, completed in 1919, while Scar House was the last of the Nidd reservoirs to be built, in 1936. The stone to build the giant dams was quarried from around the valley either side of the reservoirs – it's still possible to see the scars – and just visible, poking through the grass like a line drawing, are the scratchy remains of the old village that once housed the 1,200 workers and their families while they built Scar House Reservoir.

Owned by Yorkshire Water, the two enormous lakes (Scar House is the larger of the two) supply Bradford via the Nidd Aqueduct. This is one of the most beautiful parts of Nidderdale to spend some time in; I love the circular walk around the reservoirs (page 212), where the view is constantly changing, as well as the light. Sheep hug the hillsides and stone walls criss-cross the landscape, the rough grasses and heathers providing a shelter for wildlife. Angram tends to be the livelier of the two, the wind whipping across the water that lashes at the dam wall. On the other side, with the river still only a trickle, Scar House is calmer. Its banks are shallower and have beach-like edges. From the top of the dam, you can look out over the wall to see just how high up you are

(216ft) from the valley floor; it does look a long way down, especially when you realise that you are looking into the top branches of the deep green pine trees of Scar Plantation below, which hides some of the workers' village now submerged by the very reservoir they built.

1 MIDDLESMOOR, HOW STEAN GORGE & LOFTHOUSE

Middlesmoor is the most far-reaching village along the Nidderdale Valley; there is no other habitation beyond except the odd lonely farmstead. To reach it by road, you need to climb the one-in-four gradient; the village is perched on top of a hummock, the ancient church of St Chad with its 19th-century castellated square tower acting as a guiding beacon to onlookers.

Scar House & Angram reservoirs circular walk

❀ OS Explorer map OL20; start: Scar House Reservoir car park ♀ SE066767; 5 miles, easy.

Beginning at the car park and toilets on the **southeastern point** of Scar House Reservoir, follow the tarmac track (owned by Yorkshire Water) that runs along the southern side. This section is popular with families as the walking is flat and easy, and children can zoom up and down on their bikes; it's also accessible for wheelchairs.

Continue past the end of Scar House Reservoir until you come to the **Angram Dam** where there's a small hut for shelter – watch out for sheep dung on the seats as woolly beasts shelter in it too! For a longer walk (an additional 2¼ miles), carry on along the shore of **Angram Reservoir** and keep following the route around its edge until you arrive on the other side of Angram Dam. This additional section has some rough and boggy ground and crosses two bridges over rivers.

Sticking to the Scar House circular walk, cross over the **Angram Dam** walkway, admiring the views across Angram Reservoir to both Great and Little Whernside. At the **northern end** of the dam, turn right and follow the path, now with grass under your feet rather than tarmac, along the upper reaches of Scar House Reservoir. It's from here that you get some of the best views of the reservoir and the valley running downstream, gaining a real impression of the remoteness of the area.

Cross over a **stream** and continue along the well-trodden path until you come to a **ladder stile and a gate**. You can **either turn right** downhill and then left to wander along the shore of the reservoir or you can climb over the stile on your left and turn almost immediately right to follow the bumpy stone track that runs parallel with the reservoir below you. I prefer this route

The alternative route to Middlesmoor is via the **Nidderdale Way**. Coming from the north you can pick up the walk at the southeast corner of Scar House Reservoir (close to the car park) and follow the path over In Moor. There's a punishing climb up the very rocky crag to begin but, once on top of the moor, the scenery is amply rewarding. As the reservoir disappears from view behind, the moor pans out, the purple heather in late summer an electrifying colour against a shiny blue sky. From here, the path cuts straight across the moor above the village giving views along the progressively greener Nidderdale Valley towards Gouthwaite Reservoir.

There are some wonderfully poetic names in this area. Look on a large-scale Ordnance Survey map and you come across places like Foggyshaw Barn, Limley Pastures, Beggar Moat Scar and Goyden Pot. Wackiest of

because you get better views along the valley both in front and behind, when you turn around for a passing glance from whence you came.

Arriving at the northern tip of the **Scar House Dam**, cross over the top of the dam to return to the start, not forgetting to look over the top of the dam wall for a glimpse of the valley floor below. The walk is four miles in total (just over six including a trek around Angram) and is a good family walk.

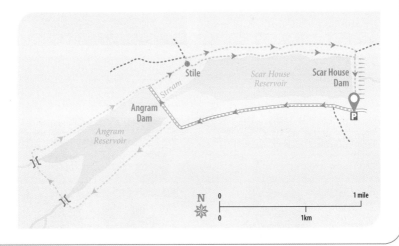

all for me though are Jenny Twigg and her Daughter Tib, a couple of eroded gritstone pinnacles on High Ash Head Moor, east of Lofthouse. From certain angles these huge blocks of rock are reminiscent of two stooping women, and I would love to know who the real Jenny and Tib were.

Next on the list of fanciful names is Hard Gap Lane, close to the village of Stean. Actually, Stean is no more than a few houses but what makes it famous is the 'Little Switzerland' of **How Stean Gorge**. This vast ravine with umpteen geological features is indeed impressive as a natural attraction, the waters of the How Stean Beck tumbling over giant boulders and smoothing the limestone into bizarre creations as it flows through the towering gap before wending its way to join the River Nidd. It's impressive enough to warrant Site of Special Scientific Interest (SSSI) status, but is privately owned: the fee to walk the half mile of specially constructed walkway is as steep as the rock faces. I prefer to avoid the fee and instead glimpse the gorge from the lane alongside up to Stean, and various footpaths, including the Nidderdale Way, that run alongside – and across – the beck.

"The waters of How Stean Beck tumble over giant boulders and smooth the limestone into bizarre creations."

That said, the How Stean Gorge activity centre (⌀ howstean.co.uk) offers a range of adventurous on-site options such as kayaking, abseiling, caving, canyoning, and even tackling their vertiginous via ferrata (one of only three in the UK, they say). If you prefer to look on from cosy safety, their fine café has a glass floor right over the gorge with giddy views down.

The first village to actually straddle the Nidd is **Lofthouse**, a good starting point for a number of walks, including a footpath that runs right alongside the Nidd. A short-cut narrow road across Masham Moor to the village of Masham also begins at Lofthouse. Even if you have no plans to go right across the moor (a nicely rugged and bleak stamping ground), take a moment to climb the steep **Trapping Hill** out of Lofthouse and look back along the valley towards Gouthwaite in the southeast and further round towards the hummock of Middlesmoor

---

◀ **1** Scar House Reservoir. **2** The village of Ramsgill. **3** The via ferrata at How Stean Gorge.
4 View towards Middlesmoor from Trapping Hill, Lofthouse.

in the northwest. The views towards the green pastures dotted with trees and the higher fells behind will leave a lasting impression on the mind.

¶¶ FOOD & DRINK

Useful for walkers is the **Crown Hotel** in the tiny village square in Middlesmoor (✆ 01423 755204), particularly welcoming with log fires on a frosty day. Lofthouse has its own pub, also confusingly called the **Crown Hotel** (✆ 01423 755206 ⌕ thecrownlofthouse.co.uk). Both pubs offer home-cooked food, serve ales brewed by the Black Sheep Brewery at Masham, and do B&B.

2 RAMSGILL, GOUTHWAITE RESERVOIR & WATH

Of all the villages in Upper Nidderdale, **Ramsgill** is the jewel. It sits at the northern head of Gouthwaite Reservoir, a grouping of comfortably proportioned stone cottages. The houses are centred around a large, immaculately kept green and a harmonious church. At its head is the striking old shooting lodge that is now the Yorke Arms, cloaked with ivy. Sadly it's no longer open as a restaurant, offering only closed-doors fine dining for groups. Also in the village, open by appointment, is the Ramsgill Studio (✆ 07968 524443 ⌕ sarahgarforth.co.uk). This small art and craft gallery exhibits the work of Sarah Garforth, a painter and printmaker with a contemporary style, inspired by the local landscapes.

"This one is long, sleek and dark, where the movement of the water is minimal except on the stormiest of days."

This village also makes a good base for a walk, the Ramsgill Beck playfully splitting the village in two, the halves joined by a tiny bridge. Wander over a second bridge that crosses the Nidd a little north of Ramsgill and follow the road to the hamlet of **Bouthwaite**. From there, on slightly higher ground, you get wonderful views towards Ramsgill with the River Nidd and Gouthwaite Reservoir in the foreground. You'll also cross the ghostly tracks of the old railway that once supplied the workers building Angram and Scar House reservoirs with materials.

Gouthwaite Reservoir, also supplying Bradford with water, is not a bit like its more northerly cousins. This one is long, sleek and dark, where the movement of the water is minimal except on the stormiest of days. At its head, close to Ramsgill, the reedy banks provide housing for nesting waterfowl while, two-thirds along the western side, a platform has been set up for birdwatchers to sit and view the mannerisms of the native and migrating wildlife that call the reservoir home, if only for a season.

The Nidderdale Way follows right along both sides of the reservoir while the Dales Explorer Bus (page 34) stops opposite the viewing platform at weekends. There's also a pleasant picnic spot across the road, next to a small and unobtrusive car park.

At the southern end of Gouthwaite Reservoir lies the tiny hamlet of **Wath**, again just a few houses, this time spread out like beads along a ribbon above the river. The Nidd flows past, the Nidderdale Way following it.

¶¶ FOOD & DRINK

Sportsman's Arms Hotel Wath HG3 5PP ✆ 01423 711306 ⌂ sportsmans-arms.co.uk. Fantastic location and a beautiful building both inside and out; the gardens, adjacent to the river, make the most of the surrounding scenery. Reservations recommended for the restaurant, which offers Whitby lobsters in summer. Accommodation too.

3 PATELEY BRIDGE

For many visitors to the area, Nidderdale begins and ends at Pateley Bridge. It's as if they arrive in the town, and leave without going any further up the valley. Oh, what they miss, but Pateley Bridge is a very good start.

The small town is flanked on both sides by sharply rising, beautifully green fells, the Nidd adding a very pretty decoration to the town's beauty. It is Nidderdale's gateway – there is no other route to Upper Nidderdale other than through the town – so it remains an important 'capital' to both visitors and local communities alike. Pateley Bridge is home to the annual **Nidderdale Show** (⌂ nidderdaleshow.co.uk), a major rural event in the area's calendar, held every autumn in Bewerley Park. It is a fantastic day that, perhaps more than anything else, epitomises the beating heart of Nidderdale and what it means to live and work in the area.

Much of Pateley's interest lines the High Street which rises steeply from the bridge over the River Nidd that gives the town its name – a quaint assemblage of little shops and eateries leaning on each other's shoulders as they climb the hill. Among these is **The Oldest Sweet Shop in England** (⌂ oldestsweetshop.co.uk), on the corner of Church

NIDDERDALE LLAMAS

Kiln Farm, Wilsill, Pateley Bridge HG3 5EF ✆ 01423 711052 ⊘ nidderdalellamas.org

I first met Jack and Ike when they were three years old, Ike likened to a stroppy teenager despite his age. Louis was a little younger, just two years old, while Ted was the baby at 15 months, desperately trying to be more grown up like his friends. This is not the result of something in the Nidderdale water, creating a male baby boom at the hands of Suzanne Benson, though these are her babies of a sort. These are her llamas, reared and trained for pack trekking through some of the most inspirational countryside you're ever likely to see in England while with a llama. And if there is ever a perfect way to take things slowly, this has to be it.

Nidderdale Llamas is based at Kiln Farm in Wilsill, a tiny hillside village between Pateley Bridge and Summerbridge. It's run by Suzanne Benson who fell head-over-hooves in love with llamas when she discovered their intelligent and loving character. I discovered this character too when I took Jack and Ike out for a walk on one of Suzanne's llama treks through Nidderdale.

You don't ride llamas, but you walk with them and they carry your stuff while they amble along at the pace set by you – and sometimes by them, should they find an irresistible blade or two of grass to eat on the way. I found it to be one of the most gentle and sociable ways to explore the countryside, strolling at a pace far slower than I would go during a normal hike across the hills. Having first met the llamas in their own environment and been given the opportunity to handle them before setting out on our walk, I felt confident that I knew their personalities a little bit. That tiny speck of knowledge grew into a real bond with Jack and Ike, my llamas for

Street, with one of the largest selections of old-fashioned teeth-rotters and filling-pullers you're likely to find anywhere. Personally I can never resist the sherbet lemons.

The Old Workhouse: Nidderdale Museum

King St, HG3 5LE

Up the hill from the town centre, this austere Victorian building is now home to a hub for arts, crafts and heritage. The **Nidderdale Museum** (✆ 01423 711225 ⊘ nidderdalemuseum.com ☉ Summer 13.30–16.30 Tue–Sun; winter (closed Dec) Sat & Sun) catalogues the grim goings-on in the building's past, among other things. It is an absolute gem, run by volunteers, and a bargain for families – children accompanied by parents enter free – and you will quickly become drawn into the fascinating world of Nidderdale life. Each exhibition is split into themed the day, something that is quite common as Suzanne explained during our trek.

'Llamas are very intelligent creatures. They will look you up and down [indeed they did], weigh you up as to whether they can be mischievous while in your care and will work with you as you walk. They are very easy to handle. We have had a very elderly woman who came to trek with the llamas and, likewise, a wheelchair-using visitor who was blind. There was something about the llamas' instinct, they could sense that they needed to be even more gentle and considerate than they usually are and the visitors, despite their challenges, found a true bond with their llamas.'

Kiln Farm is high on a hill and looks straight across the dale. Other than short walks around the farm, the llamas are trekked along footpaths and bridleways in the area. It's great to be able to learn about the animals as you trek and, because of the slow pace, Suzanne can point out all the beauty of the Dales as you go. Part way through the trek, the llamas are given their break and you get the refreshments that they have been so considerately carrying. One of the longer trekking options is to Brimham Rocks.

Suzanne tailors each trek according to the people that are booked. Therefore, it is not possible to simply turn up to the farm unannounced to look at the llamas (the chances are, they won't be there), or to expect a trek immediately. It's not advisable for children under ten years to trek with a llama because of the pace ('young children tend to get bored with the slow speed,' says Suzanne) but children from the age of 12 will easily be able to lead a llama, so long as they have an accompanying adult with them. Don't be surprised if you find yourself talking to the animals!

rooms exactly as you would anticipate finding them. The cobbler's shop, the joiner's shop, agriculture room, Victorian parlour, workhouse and general store, all bring the area to life, with implements and exhibits donated by local people. There is a very authentic feel to it all. Set aside at least an hour, but don't be surprised if you find yourself there for considerably longer.

Coldstones Cut

Coldstones Quarry, Greenhow Hills HG3 5JQ ⊘ thecoldstonescut.org

This is a staggering place in more ways than one, as you have to walk nearly half a mile and climb 150ft, from Toft House car park, to even see it. When you get there though, what you see will take what's left of your breath away. It is the biggest sculpture in Yorkshire – a monumental piece of public art, like a small Aztec fortified town somehow teleported

to the Dales, that allows you to scale a series of platforms and view the huge working quarry below, and Nidderdale in the distance. From an original idea in 2006 by the quarry's owners, Hanson Aggregates, it took the designer Andrew Sabin three years to complete before its opening in 2010.

FOOD & DRINK

Cocoa Joe's High St ⊘ cocoajoes.co.uk. Opposite Kendall's Butchers, a nirvana for fans of the wonder bean and very popular with locals: large range of hot, cold and flavoured chocolate drinks, and artisan confectionery. Take-home DIY kits also available.

The Crown High St ⊘ 01423 313910 ⊘ thecrowninnpateleybridge.co.uk. The standard local ales (Timothy Taylor's, Dark Horse, Theakston), plus food, rooms, outside tables, and even an art gallery.

Whittaker's Distillery Dacre Banks HG3 4HQ ⊘ 01423 781842 ⊘ whittakersgin.com ⊙ noon–17.30 Wed–Sat; tours every 13.30 and 15.30 Thu–Sat. About four miles outside town, then a mile up a picturesque farm lane, is this artisan ginmakers (with their first whisky due to be ready in 2024, joining Yorkshire's two other single-malt producers). The shop sells spirits and hampers, and there are tasting tours.

The Willow Restaurant Park Rd ⊘ 01423 711689 ⊘ thewillow-restaurant.com. Just off High Street, down a tiny alley, Margaret, the owner and cook at The Willow, has been producing hearty, traditional English fare for over 20 years. The quality of her roasts, pies, fry-ups, cakes and cream teas is as high now as it ever was.

EASTERN NIDDERDALE

East of Pateley Bridge, the land doesn't exactly flatten out but it's not quite so harsh and inhospitable. The hills and valleys begin to look vividly green, the stone walls that turn the hills into pastures, creating geometric patterns, all the more noticeable. Due east of Pateley Bridge is the extraordinary geological spectacle of **Brimham Rocks**. North and south of these mammoth natural sculptures are two clusters of villages, some of which, in the southern cluster, lie in the Nidd's valley, tucked up against the sides of the river; others cling to the sides of the hills. The northern cluster, centred around **Galphay** and **Kirkby Malzeard**,

◄ **1** Coldstones Cut, near Pateley Bridge, is the biggest sculpture in Yorkshire.
2 The Oldest Sweetshop in the World can be found in Pateley Bridge. **3** Trekking with llamas in Nidderdale.

lie in the Nidderdale National Landscape but the streams and rivulets that drift through them link up with the River Ure, after its journey through Wensleydale.

4 BRIMHAM ROCKS

If there is ever a place to take children for some good old-fashioned life-building skills, Brimham Rocks is it. These giant stacks of millstone grit, carved by glaciation, erosion and any amount of geological disturbances over more years than one can contemplate, certainly focus the imagination, and they make fantastic climbing frames. Sure, it may well frighten parents, anxiously watching as their children hurtle from one giant stack of boulders to the next, oblivious to the potential pitfalls – literally – but it is a breath of fresh air to find a place where nature prevails and children can pretty much do as they please. They can stand and climb without red tape and risk assessments, and appreciate the magnificence, and significance, of the landscape without 'Don't' signs littering the place; the only warning is that things might be a bit slippery and you need to be aware of sudden drops. We've had magical times with my children there, jumping, climbing, respecting and appreciating.

Perched nearly 1,000ft above sea level on the heather-cloaked Brimham Moor, the rocks also provide primeval-feeling views across Nidderdale. The area around them is designated a Site of Special Scientific Interest (SSSI) for its surrounding plant life. Secret paths dart this way and that, the bracken and the rowan trees fighting for space, their late summer show of red berries exploding with colour against the lichen-covered darkness of the rocky giants.

The National Trust owns the site and entrance is free, with just a small charge for parking (free for NT members); there's a small refreshment kiosk on site. You can access the rocks at weekends by using the Dales Explorer Bus (page 34) from Pateley Bridge; the Nidderdale Way passes over Brimham Moor too.

5 RIPLEY

As the Nidd runs its course towards Knaresborough, the dale broadens, turning from bleak moorland to shallow hills dotted with farmsteads

---

1 Stunning Ripley Castle. 2 Brimham Rocks – nature's climbing frames. ▶

and small villages. This is perhaps the kind of landscape that most would associate with the Dales – a gentle river of no great size and a rolling countryside of emerald green that's broken up by stone walls built to a Dales spec.

Ripley, three miles north of Harrogate, is one village that surpasses all others in this area as a magnet for visitors, thanks to its charming, period-estate-village square. The signs at its edge announce that the place lays claim to Ripley's famous ice cream, and you can indeed enjoy it at the sunny tables outside the village shop. But it's **Ripley Castle** (✆ 01423 770152 ⌖ ripleycastle.co.uk) for which the place is best known. It is the rather beautiful home of the Ingilby family,

"Giant Wellingtonia stand alongside oaks and sweet chestnut trees vying for the biggest and knobbliest girth prize."

who have owned it for over 700 years; Jamie and Sarah currently run it. While the interior is attractive and the associations with British history are impressive, it's the exterior that appeals to me: the walled gardens with their huge herbaceous borders, the kitchen garden full of rare varieties of fruit trees and the pleasure grounds, with two shapely lakes, silted up from a beck that runs into the nearby Nidd.

The grounds have that archetypal estate feel, planted with specimen trees that defy age. Giant Wellingtonia reach for the sky alongside oaks and sweet chestnut trees vying for the biggest and knobbliest girth prize, their trunks showing more warts and pimples than the foulest of imaginary characters.

On your way out, take a peek inside **All Saints' Church**. It has the most beautiful Victorian ceiling, decorated like a piece of fabric with a repeat pattern in simple reds and greens, embossed with gold. Look for the deliberate mistake in the panel on the right-hand side, fifth along from the end and second up from the bottom: subtly missing leaves and spurs supposedly emphasise human fallibility against God's perfection.

Ripley Show is a traditional agricultural and horticultural get-together on a mid-August Sunday (⌖ ripleyshow.co.uk).

ⵏ FOOD & DRINK

Ripley has plenty of snacking and cake opportunities. The village store offers pies and drinks; the church runs an informal pop-up café on Thursdays; and just inside the castle precinct is both a fine tea room and a barista café, **Grindhus**.

The Boar's Head Hotel Main St, HG3 3AY ✆ 01423 771888 ⌂ boarsheadripley.co.uk.
Housed in a fine building (note the arched windows) in the centre of the village. Refined
dining in either the restaurant or the bistro. Sir Thomas Ingilby, owner of Ripley Castle, often
personally selects the wines for the wine list. Accommodation available in very comfortable,
and dog-friendly, rooms.

KNARESBOROUGH & HARROGATE

6 KNARESBOROUGH

It's hard to tell what is the dominant feature of Knaresborough, a town
that perches on a steep bank above the River Nidd. Is it the river itself,
the huge viaduct (potentially the best-known feature as its vista is
regularly used to promote the town), the ruined castle that just about
stands above the river, or is it actually the town's most famous and oldest
tourist attraction, Mother Shipton's Cave, tucked away out of sight?

Most of the town sits to one side of the Nidd. On the other are the
remains of the ancient Forest of Knaresborough. The woods, which
include hornbeams, oak, ash and beech trees that smell like peaches
when you wander through them, screen **Mother Shipton's Cave** and
the bizarre well that turns everything to stone – including numerous
hanging teddy bears – and has been drawing visitors since the early
17th century. The beech trees are considered to be such fine specimens
that every single one has a preservation order placed upon it and the
Forestry Commission has filed a seed bank for future plantings. You
do have to pay to wander through the woods (accessed at the entrance
to Mother Shipton's Cave) but, running alongside the river, there's an
arresting view of the town and a nice picnic spot too.

On entering Knaresborough, either by train over the **viaduct** high
above the river – what an eye-opening introduction to the town – or by
other means, I think the most prominent feature is actually the number

KNARESBOROUGH BED RACE

Knaresborough is famed for its annual Bed
Race (⌂ bedrace.co.uk), a real community-
spirited athletic event with the subtle
difference of pushing a decorated bed
through the streets! It might not make it
as an Olympic sport, but at least there is
somewhere to snooze after all the strenuous
activity. It's usually held every June, and most
competitors take a dip in the Nidd during the
closing stages of the race.

of **black-and-white chequered buildings**. It's a significant trademark of the town and the mysterious reason behind them makes it all the more intriguing. I've received all kinds of answers when enquiring around the town, including some kind of relationship with the chequered flag used to signal the end of a grand prix! But the most plausible answer is likely to be that the checks used to denote licensed premises (hence pub names like 'The Chequers Inn'); consequently, in Knaresborough it then became fashionable to paint your house black and white, explaining why there are so many. Oddly, these mono houses look right, yet could you imagine if anyone tried to paint their house similarly elsewhere? There could be uproar among neighbours.

"At the upriver end of Waterside there's a wishing well, but fulfilment can't be guaranteed."

Close to the river, and the viaduct, is one of these chequered houses, the **Old Manor House**. Built in the 12th century, it is where Charles I and Oliver Cromwell signed the treaty that ended the English Civil War. The ancient **Knaresborough Castle**, positioned high above a bend in the river, played its part in the war too, with a Parliamentarian siege on the Royalist camp. It is now officially owned by the King, although an overnight stay by His Majesty in this tumbledown residence might not have quite the same appeal that it once had for many of his forebears. It is, however, the best place to snap a photo of the most traditional of Knaresborough scenes, overlooking the river and the viaduct.

Wandering along **Waterside**, naturally by the river, gives you a real feel for the town, a tiered system of beautiful terraced houses each with a miniature garden. You can hire a rowing boat here too, to appreciate the river from another perspective. At the upriver end there's a wishing well, but fulfilment can't be guaranteed. There are several options to reach the main town area from Waterside but they all involve a good climb, including the steep steps up to the castle, from where you can see the old mill on the opposite side of the river. The fields around Knaresborough used to be filled with the daily flourish of hazy blue flax and the mill was appointed by Queen Victoria to supply linen for all the royal palaces.

◄ KNARESBOROUGH: **1** The grand railway viaduct towering over boaters on the Nidd. **2** Mother Shipton in her eponymous cave. **3** The 600-year-old Chapel of Our Lady of the Crag. **4** Black-and-white chequered buildings are a prominent feature of the town. **5** No chance for a snooze during the annual Bed Race.

The old town is centred around the **marketplace**, still in weekly use for the Wednesday sales, and the **High Street**. I love the centre. It has higgledy-piggledy house roofs and narrow streets that radiate from the centre like spokes on a wheel. Look out for some unusual windows around the town; the 'Town Windows' project is a collection of public art that uses the *trompe l'œil* effect – at first glance you'll believe that someone really is hanging out of a window. That 'someone' is actually one of a dozen or so characters from the town's past (plus a giraffe and a zebra) and they're used to brighten up some of the blank windows in the town's Georgian buildings.

One of these historical figures is Blind Jack. Born in 1717, Jack Metcalf lost his sight as a child through smallpox yet went on to become a reputed fiddle player and a pioneer in civil engineering, constructing 180 miles of roads throughout Yorkshire. He can be seen playing his fiddle from an upstairs window in the pub that bears his name, in the market square. But you can also sit next to him, again in the marketplace, where the bronze figure of Blind Jack rests on a bench, his measuring wheel propped up by his side.

One of Knaresborough's more contemporary places to visit is **Henshaws Arts and Crafts Centre** (⊘ henshaws.org.uk) on Bond End (the A59 towards Harrogate). This complex has a circular brick turret-like entrance sandwiched between high stone walls, which makes it feel as if you're entering through a castle keep. Inside, shops sell crafts made by Yorkshire residents who have visual impairments and learning difficulties, a wonderful sensory garden that can be appreciated and enjoyed by all, and a gallery café. The centre also runs a whole range of arts workshops that anyone can join, and runs events through the year, like the Urban Beach in August, when tons of sand are shipped in.

"The peace is sublime while the town continues daily life on a clifftop above. This is the ancient Pilgrim's Way."

A wander down to the River Nidd and along Abbey Road follows the river for a mile (coming to a dead end) past private riverside gardens; the peace is sublime while the town continues daily life on a clifftop above. This is the ancient Pilgrim's Way and tucked back into the rock, about half a mile downstream from the castle, is one of the sweetest, tiniest chapels that you will come across, the 600-year-old **Chapel of Our Lady of the Crag**. Look for too long at the river and you'll miss it, the powder-blue door is the only clue to its existence. Beside it is a beautiful rock garden, the most restful place to sit in the town. A mile further along the riverside, hidden away down in the cliff face by the water's edge and accessible by a narrow footpath, is **St Robert's Cave**, which served as the hermit's home around 1200. Across the bridge on the opposite bank, a quarter-mile walk away, is **'Knaresborough Lido'**: a short stretch of the Nidd ideal for a (free) summer dip. Don't swallow the water though – it can be mucky. The adjacent **Watermill Café** is open every day.

¶¶ FOOD & DRINK

For its size, Knaresborough is blessed with more than its fair share of good pubs, at least ten of which serve locally brewed cask beer. A short stroll from the railway station along the High Street, down Cheapside and Briggate and back along the riverside, passes pretty much all of them so you can take your pick.

Blind Jack's Marketplace ⊘ blindjackspub.co.uk. No food, but everything a town boozer should be, with an excellent selection of beers, a cosy ambience and lively banter, traditional pub games, and a *trompe l'œil* of Jack himself. Dogs welcome.

The Cross Keys Cheapside ⊘ 01423 863562. Lots going on in this beer drinkers' local run by the Ossett Brewery, with live music every Saturday night, a popular quiz on Thursdays, and monthly Northern Soul nights. A wide range of real ales is always on offer and dogs are welcome.

McQueens Café High St ⊘ 01423 860089. With its lavishly decorated walls crammed with collectibles, this is like an eccentric Continental backpackers' café. A warm welcome, good quality food and drink and free Wi-Fi.

Mother Shipton Inn Low Bridge ⊘ 01423 865638 ⊘ mothershiptoninnlowbridge.co.uk. This 16th-century building by the river feels more like a country pub, especially by the roaring fire or out in its beautiful beer garden. Meals are an interesting mix of traditional and international cuisine. Cask ales.

Riverside Café Waterside ⊘ 01423 546759. No-nonsense dog- and cycle-friendly café in a great location.

Two Brothers Grill and Pizzeria Castle Courtyard ⊘ 01423 869918 ⊘ twobrothersgrillandpizzeria.co.uk. Exceptional service, quality pizzas, pasta dishes and burgers; very good value for money.

7 HARROGATE

Where York has history and Knaresborough has old-world charm, Harrogate has elegance. My father used to say that it was easy to imagine

HARROGATE FLOWER SHOWS

With such a floral tradition, it comes as no surprise that Harrogate is renowned too for hosting one of the most important events in the gardening calendar, particularly in the north. The spring (at the Great Yorkshire Showground in April) and autumn (at Newby Hall in September) Flower Shows (⬧ flowershow.org.uk) attract thousands of gardeners, many of whom return home from the shows laden with plants and having filled their heads with advice from specialist plant societies and gardening experts.

Unless you're planning on purchasing a lorry-load of plants, you can travel to the showground by shuttle bus directly from the town centre, running from Station Parade.

Miss-Marple-like elderly spinster ladies daintily sipping tea out of bone china cups and nibbling on cucumber sandwiches while discussing society life. Even today the centre of Harrogate is about refinement.

Harrogate's appearance owes much to the kind of visitors it has been able to attract over the centuries – wealthy and noble society from across Europe in search of cures for ailments from the town's spa water. They brought money into the area and with it an air of decadence. Today the town regularly features on top-ten lists of the best places to live.

The vast open expanse right in the centre of town is **The Stray**, an important part of Harrogate community life where joggers breathe a cleaner air, and any number of weekend football matches for all ages take place. An act of parliament created the park in the late 18th century, fixing its size at 200 acres, which must be maintained today. There's no doubt that it enhances the look of Harrogate and in winter, when the trees that line its perimeter twinkle with fairy lights, it takes on a magical quality.

Floral Harrogate

Harrogate is famed for its gardens. The town regularly wins national and regional awards for its floral displays and the volunteer organisation behind it, **Harrogate in Bloom** (⬧ harrogateinbloom.org.uk), has a wealth of community projects to ensure that everyone, of all ages, can take part and be proud of their success. Flower-spotting walks with downloadable audio guides are occasionally put together for summer: Google 'Harrogate Floral Trail' for the latest.

The most celebrated promenading spot of them all is the **Valley Gardens**. Year-round colour here is more than vibrant, a classic spa-town garden with giant specimen trees, lawns, and flower borders that show true dedication from their gardeners. Seasonal displays of autumn crocuses and dahlias are replaced with deep red holly berries, much appreciated by the garden's birds whose songs fill the air. Jungle plants hover above streamlets, and alpine rockeries make way for formal rose beds, while a giant and ancient wisteria slithers its gnarled trunk up the pillars of a walkway like a serpent. Explore and you may find the Japanese Garden and New Zealand Garden.

One footpath through the gardens is named the **Elgar Route**, commemorating Sir Edward Elgar's love of Harrogate; the composer visited many times between 1912 and 1927 and would walk regularly in the Valley Gardens. The first provincial performance of his Second Symphony was held in the town in 1911.

Music lovers can enjoy Sunday afternoon concerts in summer at the bandstand, in front of the striking Sun Pavilion on the north wall, along which runs a colonnade.

"Music lovers can enjoy Sunday afternoon concerts in summer at the bandstand, in front of the striking Sun Pavilion."

The Royal Horticultural Society's northern home at **Harlow Carr** is huge and shows all the professionalism that you would expect from the nation's largest gardening organisation. The 58 acres of visitable gardens, demonstrating a huge range of microclimates from subtropical to alpine, is a popular attraction for coach parties; the UK's longest streamside garden is here. However, it is also a trial site, where plants and gardening techniques are assessed for their suitability in a northern climate. The stunning contemporary acclimatised alpine greenhouse and a Learning Centre (built from sustainable materials and with a zero-carbon footprint) keep Harlow Carr special. The new café offers fine terrace views over the site and freshly-picked produce from the gardens themselves.

Bus 6 or S6 goes to Harlow Carr from Station Parade; visitors arriving at the gardens by bus receive discounted entry. Alternatively, you can take the very pleasant 1½-mile marked walk through the Valley Gardens and Harrogate's **Pinewoods**, a woodland that's filled with sycamore, birch and rowan as well as pine trees.

In late April and early May, The Stray becomes a miniature Japan, when two avenues of **cherry trees** blossom in full, fluffy pink glory. Bring a picnic and join the gently partying groups out on the grass lawns to enjoy one of Britain's best *hanami* (cherry blossom viewing) opportunities.

A spa town

Tewit Well, the original iron- and sulphur-rich spring that began Harrogate's fortunes as a spa town, is found within The Stray but other locations around the town also have waters bubbling up from the deep. One such place is the **Royal Pump Room**, the refined-looking black and gold building close to the Valley Gardens. It houses a museum exhibiting the history of the town as a spa and you can drink a glass of what is allegedly Europe's most sulphurous spa water if you feel you must. It tastes absolutely disgusting (by which token we can assume it's good for you) and a sulphurous smell pervades the air outside.

Close by are the **Turkish Baths** (01423 556746 turkishbathsharrogate.co.uk), a place to unwind in the same way that society did in the 19th century, though with a few modern alterations and luxuries. Restored in 2004, the baths are one of the most historically complete of their kind remaining in Britain. With a Moorish design, the Islamic arches, decorated pillars, glazed brickwork walls, painted ceilings and terrazzo floors are a work of art, and that's before you've dipped a toe into the plunge pool or laid your head on a soft pillow in the rest room. You can simply turn up to use the Turkish Baths but it's well worth booking one of the many spa treatments in advance for a truly rejuvenating experience.

Bettys & Taylors of Harrogate

The very first thing that comes into my head when I think of Yorkshire is **Bettys**, a Yorkshire institution. It is a world-renowned family empire of elegant tea rooms and a few other things beside. Although now very much a 'Yorkshire thing', the story actually began in Switzerland. Orphaned under tragic circumstances, a young Fritz Bützer, the son of a Swiss miller and master baker, came to England in 1907 to find work. Getting on to the wrong train in London, he found himself in Bradford without the means to return. After many years of hard work and dedication to learn the art of chocolate-making, and a certain amount of moving around Yorkshire, he anglicised his name to Frederick Belmont, moved to Harrogate and opened a café with an emphasis on fine quality, from the furnishings to the food and drink, and the service. All of this

HARROGATE: **1** In bloom: the Valley Gardens and Festival Pavilion. **2** The Royal Pump Room. **3** Mercer Art Gallery. **4** An institution: Bettys Café Tea Rooms. ▶

SS

SS

SS

TRAVELLIGHT/S

finery was bait to tempt Edwardian Harrogate's high-society visitors – and it worked.

Ninety years on, Frederick Belmont's nephew Jonathan Wild, together with his wife Lesley, are semi-retired from owning and running the place, but there are still plenty of Wilds on the board. There are now six tea rooms in Harrogate, York, Ilkley and Northallerton, each with a very special, individual character and ambience. Having bought out the long-time tea and coffee merchants **Taylors of Harrogate** (world-famous for 'Yorkshire Tea') in the 1960s, every aspect of the Bettys business today is maintained with the highest standards. For example, in the craft bakery where all the Bettys products are made, housed in a beautiful 'Swiss chalet' in Harrogate, every process is done by hand, whether it's making speciality breads ready for baking in the traditional brick oven, creating the most divine cakes, tarts and biscuits, or making the very finest chocolates.

"Every process is done by hand, whether it's making speciality breads, the most divine cakes, or the finest chocolates."

A visit to Bettys for afternoon tea is a must-do for many, but the queues can be notoriously long. The wait will be shorter at the light, airy and modern branch at Harlow Carr (page 231) than at the more traditional main Harrogate branch.

I paid a visit to **Bettys Cookery School** (Harlow Carr ✆ 01423 814016 ⬦ bettyscookeryschool.co.uk), based opposite Bettys craft bakery in Harrogate. It was set up by Lesley Wild in 2001 and has the enviable resource of being able to draw on the talents of the craftsmen, bakers, confectioners and cooks who work for Bettys. They still look to their Swiss–Yorkshire heritage for inspiration and it's this that really makes the courses unique and inspiring.

I joined in with the school's pinnacle course, the ten-day 'Bettys Certificate Course', which covers just about everything you need to know for a really firm grounding in cooking, from knife skills and pastry techniques to chocolate-making, taught by one of the master chocolatiers from Bettys bakery.

The school kitchen is incredible, a room that is inspiring to cook in before the lovely staff have even said a word. However, it is the warmth of the tutors that make the school and the teaching so special. Friendliness abounds but they are helpful and non-judgemental too, turning the most nervous, or newest, of cooks into confident cooks. The most experienced of chefs will gain something from one of their cookery courses too, even if it's simply a fantastic day out and meeting new friends. Of the 'pupils' on the Certificate Course that I attended, some were local to the area while others had made it their holiday in Yorkshire and were full of praise for the school. With breakfast, lunch and dinner thrown in, who could ask for more? The school is also very keen to encourage young cooks. Richard Jones, the cookery school manager who pops around to chat while you're cooking, said: 'Inspiring children to cook is one of the main reasons that Lesley Wild wanted to set up the school. We offer courses that will ensure that children can cook a proper meal, not simply fairy cakes.'

Personally, I can't wait to return for other practical one-day courses – anything from preparing supper parties, and pasta making (I need to hone the skills that I learnt on the last course), to cooking with chocolate. But there are two that really grab my eye. One is entitled the 'Greek Odyssey', taking students back to those idyllic Mediterranean holidays, and the other is 'Yorkshire Breads', learning to bake traditional loaves and pikelets. I can't think of a better souvenir of Yorkshire.

Harrogate & art

While its sulphurous waters have brought fame to the town, its connections with the arts are lesser known, although one rather famous crime writer did put Harrogate in the headlines. The **Old Swan Hotel**, close to the Valley Gardens, was the bolthole for Agatha Christie in 1926. A nationwide search for the author was launched following her disappearance but she was found ten days later having checked into the hotel under a pseudonym. It was a plot to match any of her thrillers, involving secret affairs, revenge and the possibility of murder; the mystery remains

"It was a plot to match any of Agatha Christie's thrillers, involving secret affairs, revenge and the possibility of murder."

as to why she chose to disappear, but it was possibly revenge against her husband who had just announced his secret affair with another woman – her disappearance cast suspicious rumours that he had murdered her.

Between the hotel and the Valley Gardens is the **Mercer Art Gallery** on Swan Road (✆ 01423 556188 ☉ Wed–Sun). This Neoclassical building is home to Harrogate's fine art collection of 2,000 works,

An easy bike ride in Harrogate, Ripley & Knaresborough

✻ OS Explorer map 104 (and very briefly, 99); start and finish at Harrogate train station

📍 SE304553; 19 miles; easy; almost all on car-free paths or quiet lanes

It may be less than 20 miles and have only a couple of mild hills, but with so much to see and do en route this trundle can easily take all day. It's suitable for families, with a bit of care on the few short stretches of busy road – walk along the footway if necessary (small children can ride them). Otherwise, though, it's a lovely mix of gentle, car-free riding.

Start at **Harrogate train station**. From Platform 3, follow signs for NCN67 (National Cycle Network route) to Ripley. Once through Asda's car park, you follow a smooth car-free tarmac track out of the town. Stop to admire artworks celebrating local heroes, gaze over the Nidd and distant countryside from a lofty viaduct, and – if your bike and sense of adventure is up to it – ride some of the informal MTB jumps in the woods near the riverside, right next to the path. As you enter **Ripley** you pass a monument to the 2014 Tour de France, which went by here. (You'll pass some public toilets, too.) The village is an Italianate gem: explore the castle, visit the church, and relax with an ice cream or snack in the filmset-pretty square.

From Ripley, retrace your pedal-strokes back towards **Harrogate**. Where the path crosses the lane half a mile after the viaduct, turn left along the **Beryl Burton Cycleway** to **Knaresborough** (don't ride as fast as she did), where a pub beer garden offers refreshment. The lane becomes a bike-only path with glimpsed views over distant hills before it plummets through woods down to Knaresborough (take care!). At **Mother Shipton's Cave** (page 225) turn left over the bridge, then immediately right up lovely **Waterside** (page 227) under the grand viaduct. To access the town centre (or train station, if you want to return to Harrogate), push up steep **Water Bag Bank**, just before the viaduct. Go as far along Waterside as you want (perhaps even to St Robert's Cave, page 229) before turning round and returning to the bridge. There are toilets here.

Cross the bridge and, at **Mother Shipton's Cave**, carry on straight up the busy A59. It's best to walk up the footway on the right-hand side – it's only a short distance to a segregated bike path back on the left-hand side. Keep riding on the path until the high street of **Starbeck**, a suburb of Harrogate. Freewheel down over the railway crossing and turn left, following the cycle-route signs to Showground. After turning left and going on the main road for a few yards, use the crossing just after the roundabout to enter a small **park** on the right. In the park, branch right just before the play area (beware: there's no direction sign). Now follow the Showground signs again. You arrive there once you turn right just after **Sainsbury's**.

Prominent in the middle of the vast, rolling (and probably empty) **showground** is the excellent deli-restaurant-café **Fodder** (page 238), which you cycle right past. Keep on, following signs for the **Yorkshire Event Centre**; but once at the centre, turn left up the permissive path. At the hilltop junction here, there's a dry-stone-wall seating area with viaduct views, a good spot for a snack. Further on, at the 'crossroads' in a wood, turn right, staying on the permissive path, and follow NCN67 signs for the **station** back across The Stray and back to your train.

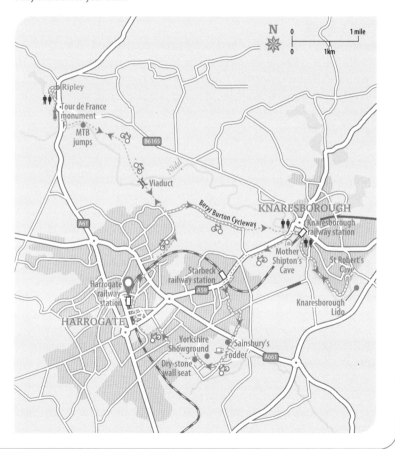

although these are not on permanent display. It's only a small gallery, free to enter, and exhibitions change regularly. On display are works by local artists, photography, national touring exhibitions and themed displays of prints, paintings and drawings taken from the permanent collection.

To enjoy art and the company of others, the **Arts Society Nidd Valley** (⊘ theartssocietyniddvalley.org.uk) holds monthly lectures on a wide range of themes and subjects, using experienced and knowledgeable public speakers. Informal lectures are held every third Monday of the month at Christ Church Centre on The Stray; a small donation is requested per visitor.

🍴 FOOD & DRINK

Bean and Bud Commercial St ✆ 01423 508200 ⊘ beanandbud.co.uk ⊙ 08.00–16.00 Mon–Sat, 10.00–16.00 Sun. The name refers to coffee beans and tea-plant buds. This place is a hot-beverage connoisseur's paradise, serving a huge range of rotating teas and coffees from around the world. The cakes, bakes and pastries to go with them aren't bad either.

Bettys Café Tea Rooms 1–3 Parliament St ✆ 01423 814000 ⊘ bettysandtaylors.co.uk ⊙ 09.00–17.00 Sat, 09.00–16.30 Sun–Fri. The ultimate dining experience in Harrogate, even if it's just for a cup of tea while listening to the resident pianist or people-watching through the plate-glass windows. Visit the Montpellier Bar (closest to the entrance) for a menu of sandwiches and mains, or the tea rooms for full-blown at-table service and a more traditional tea-room menu (that includes some Swiss favourites too, of course). For a fantastic cup of tea, you can't beat the Tea Room Blend. It's not the cheapest place in town, but you're paying for the whole ambience as well as top-quality food. Freshly made breads, cakes and biscuits as well as Bettys teas and coffees can be bought in the shop too.

Drum and Monkey Montpellier Gardens ✆ 01423 502650 ⊘ drumandmonkey.co.uk. Atmospheric little restaurant specialising in really good seafood.

The Fat Badger White Hart Hotel, Coldbath Rd ✆ 01423 505681 ⊘ thefatbadgerharrogate.com. Harrogate is not renowned for its pubs but this one within the White Hart Hotel deserves a mention for the range and quality of both food and local cask beers to enjoy inside or al fresco.

Fodder Great Yorkshire Showground, HG2 8NZ ✆ 01423 546111 ⊘ fodder.co.uk. This fantastic farm shop is owned by the Yorkshire Agricultural Society; 85% of the products on sale are made, baked or grown in Yorkshire. There's an environmental and sustainable ethos behind the whole business, from the main building to educating children on where food comes from. There's a great on-site café too.

Hales Bar Crescent Rd ✆ 01423 725570 ⌂ halesbar.co.uk. The oldest pub in Harrogate and it looks it (in the best possible sense). Edwardian décor and original gas lighting, great food and drink, and a 'secret garden'.

The Harrogate Tea Rooms Westminster Arcade, Parliament St. One of my local contacts told me to come here if I wanted the 'Bettys' experience minus the queues and the hype, and there's no doubt that this is a top-quality traditional English tea rooms. As to which is the better, I couldn't possibly say.

Weetons 23–24 West Park ✆ 01423 507100 ⌂ weetons.com. Owned by local farmers, it's a fantastic food hall, deli, butcher's and bakery opposite The Stray. It sells lots of seasonal Yorkshire produce including Ampleforth cider and a Triple Curd Cheese, made with milk from their own dairy herd. There's also a good, bustling, on-site café.

NORTH FROM HARROGATE TO MASHAM

While the A1 carves up North Yorkshire, slicing between the Yorkshire Dales and the North York Moors, the Ure Valley to the west of the road is far from dull with a string of attractive properties, market towns and satellite villages making the most of their rural location.

8 MARKENFIELD HALL

01765 692303 ⌂ markenfieldhall.com ⊙ selected afternoons (check website)

A mile or so off the A61 and three miles south of Ripon, this is a strikingly well-preserved – and most beautiful – medieval house, describing itself as 'the loveliest place you've never heard of'. Markenfield Hall is most definitely someone's house, and that is why it works its spell on me. (The utility room claims to be the country's only example of both Norman-era double-vaulting *and* plumbing for a dishwasher, for example.) With the exception of a spot of tinkering over the centuries, it has remained largely unaltered since it was built in the early 14th century for the de Markenfield family. Completely surrounded by a fashionable moat (it wouldn't keep out many marauding armies) and walled courtyard, this wonderful, crenellated pile has seen a remarkable and tragic history, its walls, rooms and tiny chapel playing a major part in the 1569 Rising of the North, a battle in direct rebellion to Henry VIII's dissolution of the monasteries. This caused the house's – and the family's – downfall.

Today Markenfield Hall is once again owned by descendants of the Markenfield family who have restored the magnificent Great Hall.

Standing in the courtyard, listening to the vividly recounted events that befell the property while glancing at the giant petals bursting open on the magnolia that climbs the wall by the entranceway, you can almost hear the whispers and the chatter of aggrieved Catholics plotting against the forwarding armies.

Markenfield Hall's tiny chapel, restored alongside the Great Hall, is remarkable too, especially given its past history: it is licensed to hold both Roman Catholic and Protestant services. However, because of its size, the congregation is limited to a mere dozen or so people.

The hall is only open to the public by guided tour on certain afternoons throughout the year, when you can visit the courtyard and four rooms (including the Great Hall and chapel). I urge you to visit but it's advisable to check the website for opening times. The Ripon Rowel Walk runs past the moat and gatehouse. Some tours include tea and cake at the end, but there's no café or other refreshments available.

9 FOUNTAINS ABBEY & STUDLEY ROYAL

HD4 3DY ✐ 01765 608888; National Trust

The remains of the Cistercian foundation of **Fountains Abbey**, four miles southwest of Ripon (buses run from Ripon, Leeds and Harrogate) and just a few fields away from Markenfield Hall, constitute the ultimate romantic ruin. Yes, it would be wonderful to see it as it once stood, but there's a certain charm in willowy grasses and ivy growing out of the roof, wild figs sunning themselves in the abbey courtyard and every crevice and archway stuffed with wild scabious waving in the wind that blows along the valley of the River Skell, the soothing sound of its waters rushing past the ruins to the adjacent Fountains Mill.

The Cistercian monks certainly knew how to pick a good location. We have Henry VIII and his iron will to crush Catholicism to thank (if you can really use the word) for the flora and being able to watch the birds flutter in and out under the vaulted arches of the old refectory. There's a steep climb beyond the river valley but take a wander up to the secret lookout named Anne Boleyn's Seat (is that title given in jest with a hint of irony?) and you'll appreciate all the more how magnificent the abbey would once have been.

---

1 Newby Hall and gardens. 2 Markenfield Hall. 3 Exploring the Muniments Room at Fountains Abbey. 4 Fountains Abbey. ▶

DEBUSSY/S

JIMMONKPHOTOGRAPHY/S

ANNA MOORES

NICOLO' ZANGIROLAMI/S

From Anne Boleyn's Seat you can take any number of paths to visit **Studley Royal**, the formally landscaped 18th-century water park that uses the Skell for its feed. The park was begun by John Aislabie after expulsion from Parliament for his part of the South Sea Bubble scandal in 1720, with the abbey forming part in the vista. His son William completed the scheme – evidently the family had much more skill at landscaping than financial management. The design of the wider estate incorporates the **Deer Park,** where you are virtually guaranteed to see some antlered beasts. Once when I visited, the lower branches of the trees around **St Mary's Church**, within the grounds of the estate, were getting a very good pruning. The church itself is a visual treat inside, with an extraordinarily ornate 1870s interior by William Burges (best known for his adornments to Cardiff Castle), and featuring depictions of angelic musicians and carved parrots against a gorgeous background of red and gold.

You can also **walk** into Studley Royal via public footpaths, in particular the delightfully secretive Skell Valley, with its quaint 'packhorse bridges' (Victorian recreations rather than medieval survivors). The estate village of Studley Roger, just west of Ripon, is a useful starting point.

FOOD & DRINK

The licensed restaurant at Fountains serves homemade dishes from locally sourced produce. Bus travellers are entitled to a free cup of tea or coffee in the restaurant on presentation of a bus ticket. Farm-produced ice cream can be had just up the road in Risplith (⊘ gandts.com ⊙ Wed–Sun).

The Sawley Arms Sawley HG4 3EQ ⊘ 01765 620642 ⊘ sawleyarms.co.uk. Gastropub a couple of miles from the Abbey with locally sourced classic specials, and prices to match. Not a place for dogs or muddy boots.

10 NEWBY HALL

⊘ 01423 322583 ⊘ newbyhall.com ⊙ Apr–Sep

Arriving by car, bike or on foot (the Ripon Rowel Walk runs close to the estate), you enter through the majestic parkland, dotted with giant oak trees, under which cattle and sheep graze. After an eternally long driveway, you're greeted with the great Georgian brick façade of the hall, an imposing front entrance that looms large. There are guided tours of the house, and you can wander around the equally impressive gardens, split into themed 'rooms' with one of the longest herbaceous borders you're likely to encounter. The gardens are mostly accessible for wheelchairs.

It's the extras that help to keep a place like Newby Hall financially viable, but all too often the added 'attractions' of miniature railways, adventure playgrounds and craft fairs can detract from the beauty of this place. Newby's website has event listings and a site map so you can choose a date and a route to best suit your interests.

Shopping and dining are possible at Newby Hall but, oddly, you have to pay for entrance to the gardens to access the shop or restaurant. However, the closed pub nearby at Skelton, the Black Lion, may reopen as a community-owned enterprise in 2024.

11 RIPON

Apart from York, the North Yorkshire area boasts another, often overlooked city. Ripon is smaller than most towns, with a great history and that characterful atmosphere that provincial market towns seem to acquire. It owes its status to its huge cathedral, one that dominates its surroundings and is vastly out of proportion to the city's size, a sign of the cathedral's importance. You can see **Ripon Cathedral** as you approach from the surrounding roads – and the chances are you will approach the city this way, for the railway no longer reaches Ripon. Your only other option is by boat – either on the River Ure or on the Ripon Canal, itself a tiny 2½-mile spur that enters town off the Ure. Thursday is market day in the central square, and the town hosts various festivals during the year, from poetry (Sep) to international classical music (⌀ riponinternationalfestival.org ☉ Aug–Oct).

THE RIPON HORNBLOWER

The horn in Ripon's coat of arms celebrates a remarkable ritual that has happened at 21.00 every evening since the year 886. The hornblower, one of a rotating team of men and women in period dress, stands at the four corners of the marketplace obelisk and sounds a blast at each. Having engaged with visitors, the hornblower contacts the mayor (by text these days) and blows three more times before announcing 'The watch is set!' Originally, the blower was known as the wakeman, a kind of Saxon nightshift policeman. The ceremony even continued during Covid lockdowns, but at the hornblowers' homes. It's not the only long-running tradition here: since 1367, every Thursday at 11.00, a costumed bellringer has formally opened the market in the main square.

GORDON BELL/S

M BARRATT/S

JULIAN ELLIOTT/S

SS

SS

Ripon Cathedral

⌂ riponcathedral.org.uk

The official title for Ripon's most imposing structure is 'The cathedral church of St Peter and St Wilfrid'. It was Wilfrid who ordered the building of a new church (new in AD672, that is), the crypt of which forms the basis of today's cathedral. It is the oldest existing crypt in England and has been a place of Christian pilgrimage for over a thousand years because of the saint, even though his remains are buried beneath the cathedral altar. Built to resemble Christ's tomb as Wilfrid imagined it, the crypt is a tiny, whitewashed room with a ledge for a candle; so very different to the embellishments and adornments that grace the building above. One visitor asked, as he squeezed down the narrow, dimly lit staircase, 'Is this it?' Indeed, that is all you get, except for a sense of over a thousand years of history.

The cathedral is at the centre of Ripon life, just as it has always been. Its history lies within the tombs – the remains of ancient families of significance, such as the Markenfield family from nearby Markenfield Hall (page 239). But, like many huge medieval cathedrals, it also fulfils the differing roles today of art gallery, concert hall and meeting place, alongside being the 'mother church' for the Leeds Diocese.

Perhaps that perplexed crypt visitor found more of interest in the cathedral's soul-stirring spaces upstairs, particularly in the quire. A bizarre moving wooden hand below the organ there serves as remote-control conductor, and the fantastic misericord carvings are said to have inspired *Alice's Adventures in Wonderland* author Lewis Carroll – they include a rabbit disappearing down a hole and a pig playing bagpipes.

Ripon's museums

⌂ 01765 690799 ⌂ riponmuseums.co.uk ⌂ mid-Feb– end Nov: Courthouse Museum & Prison and Police Museum 13.00–16.00 daily; Workhouse Museum 11.00–16.00 daily

Opposite the cathedral is the **Courthouse Museum** (Minster Road), one of three museums linked by their subject matter; the others, five minutes' walk away, are the **Workhouse Museum** (Allhallowgate) and the **Prison and Police Museum** (St Marygate). The titles are a dead giveaway to the

◀ RIPON: **1** Marketplace. **2** Kirkgate wends its way towards the mighty cathedral. **3** The Workhouse Museum. **4** The interior of the cathedral. **5** At 21.00 every evening since 886 the hornblower sounds four times.

buildings and their contents, but they have played an important part in the history of the city. Ripon maintained independence from the rest of Yorkshire until 1888, so it had to provide its own law and order. In the courthouse (operational until 1998), you can stand in the dock and listen to a court session where petty thieves were sentenced with deportation to Australia. In the virtually complete workhouse, you encounter first-hand the brutal segregation between ruling and ruled classes, while the prison has some horrific tales of punishment and regime, all the more terrifying when the five-inch-thick door is slammed shut. You can peer into the master's study, pantry and inmates' dining hall to get the full picture.

Walking around Ripon

Wandering around Ripon is a pleasure. It has an eclectic mix of both stone and brick buildings of every conceivable style and yet, owing to the nature of the materials used, even recently built houses seem to blend in well with the existing structures and streets. If you fancy a quiet stroll, head to the **Ripon Spa Gardens**, a small but verdant oasis. The main entrance (wheelchair accessible) is on Park Street, with other, stepped, entrances off Skellbank. A combination of flower borders, grassy picnic spots and mature trees centred around a traditional bandstand provides somewhere to munch a pork pie from Appleton's (see opposite).

The **River Laver** runs through the centre of the city, joining up with the River Ure on the outskirts, and the **Ripon Canal** runs adjacent to the Laver, on the opposite side of the Boroughbridge Road. The **canal basin**, accessed off Bondgate Green and Canal Road on foot, is hidden away and looks rather lonely despite being only five minutes' walk from the town centre. Just to the east of the canal is **Ripon Racecourse** (⊘ ripon-races.co.uk ⊙ May–Sep), one of Yorkshire's nine.

"The marketplace and cathedral are a good a place to begin a walk. A set of waymarked routes begins at the cathedral."

The **marketplace and cathedral** are as good a place as any to begin a walk. A set of waymarked routes begins at the cathedral itself. The **Sanctuary Way Walk** is based upon the times when Ripon looked after its own law and anyone within the Sanctuary Boundary, indicated by a series of posts (one of which still stands today) was granted overnight sanctuary. Markers have been installed, not so much to grant sanctuary to tourists, but to encourage walkers around the town and its outer limits through the countryside. The full circuit is ten miles long but there are shorter walks that visit historically important locations. If you're here at the end of July or early August, you won't be able to miss St Wilfrid's Procession (stwilfridsprocession.com), Ripon's grand annual street carnival.

You can pick up a walking route map from the tourist information centre on Market Place, or from the Ripon BID office nearby on Westgate.

For a much longer walk, the **Ripon Rowel Walk**, which passes the cathedral, uses 50 miles of existing public rights-of-way or permissive paths on a wander through the extended countryside around Ripon. En route, you walk through beautiful villages and some gentle countryside, past river valleys, lakes and historic buildings such as Markenfield Hall (page 239) and Fountains Abbey (page 240). The most accessible bit of it is the three-mile stretch that follows the full length of the Ripon Canal towpath towards Newby Hall (page 242).

FOOD & DRINK

There has been something of a boom in Ripon's café culture. North Street, a continuation of Fishergate, appears to be the centre of it.

Appleton's Market Pl 01765 603198 Mon–Sat. Pork butcher's selling the most fantastic pork pies.

Chimes Café Kirkgate 01765 606167. A very welcoming coffee shop with a cute courtyard, in the cathedral's shadow – hence the name. Exotically flavoured scones are a speciality.

Storehouse North St 01765 600088 storehouseripon.co.uk. Comfy, relaxed local restaurant favourite for lunches, dinners and weekend brunches. Expect the likes of swordfish and rhubarb panna cotta rather than fish-and-chips and apple crumble.

Oliver's Pantry North St 01765 607548 oliverspantry.com. A quirky café with excellent Slow credentials. Wholesome, locally sourced food and delicious cakes, loose-leaf teas and house-roasted coffees.

The One Eyed Rat Allhallowgate 01765 607704. A popular town boozer; no food but great local cask beers, and a courtyard with covered seats.

Realitea North St 01765 609887 riponrealitea.co.uk 17.00–19.00 Tue (bookings only), 10.00–15.00 Wed–Sat. Classy tea room with authentic, homemade (Anglo-)Indian dishes and cakes, and a 'British Raj High Tea' experience.

Wakeman's House Café Market Pl 07866 226014. Lively, friendly local café in a genuinely old, half-timbered building named after the town's hornblower (page 243). Their homemade cakes and scones are legendary.

The Water Rat Bondgate Green ✆ 01765 602251 ⊘ thewaterrat.co.uk. Near the town centre but hidden cosily on the riverside, with tables by a footbridge in sight of the cathedral. Good-value pub meals and local cask ales.

12 WENSLEYDALE IN NIDDERDALE: KIRKBY MALZEARD & AROUND

🏠 **The Ruin**

Within the Nidderdale National Landscape a cluster of villages and hamlets here are not directly on the well-known tourist trail, which is partly what makes their character so appealing. This is an area to savour on a bike, along quiet country lanes and through sleepy villages like Laverton and the Grantleys. Riverside scenery doesn't come much better than the couple of miles of the River Ure between Mickley and Sleningford Mill, and nearby **Nosterfield Lakes Nature Reserve** is a haven for wetland wildlife (page 18). Very close to Nosterfield, and very obvious on the OS map, is one (or is that three?) of the most important prehistoric monuments in the country: **Thornborough Henges**, a trio of huge, Neolithic earth circles. The middle one is the best to visit, with information panels and access gates, but car parking is almost non-existent. Bus 150 between Ripon and Richmond stops here, though.

"This is an area to savour on a bike, along quiet country lanes and through sleepy villages."

The henges are thought to represent the stars of Orion's belt. By a neat coincidence, it is possible to see the real thing, the constellation of Orion that is, at **Lime Tree Observatory** (✆ 01765 839837 ⊘ limetreeobservatory.com ☺ by appointment; occasional events) in the village of **Grewelthorpe**, just up the road. The serious 24-inch reflecting telescope takes advantage of the area's dark skies, and its planetarium puts on impressive cinematic shows. The farm grounds have a modest scale model of the solar system to walk round.

Barely a mile further up the lane is another farmer's private project that's turned into a public attraction. The **Himalayan Gardens** at Hutts Farm (✆ 01765 658009 ⊘ himalayangarden.com ☺ mid-Apr–Jun Tue–Sun & Bank Hol Mon; Jul–Oct Wed–Sun & Bank Hol Mon) are a 46-acre delight that exploits the Himalayan-foothills-like microclimate here. In among the exotic plants and trees, prayer huts, pagodas and bridges, are over 90 sculptures from round the world, including a miniature Stonehenge and a giant pineapple – the Dales' own sculpture park, to rival Yorkshire's more famous one outside Wakefield. There is also a fine café on-site (for garden visitors only).

If I had to pick one village to be representative of this little corner of Wensley-cum-Nidderdale, it would be **Kirkby Malzeard**, a buzzing mini-metropolis that manages to keep a pub, village store, butcher, fish and chip shop and garage all going. A small reading room offers free Wi-Fi and a coffee machine if you need to sit out a shower. Two historic buildings here are St Andrew's Church and the Mechanics' Institute, a fine Victorian edifice which doubles as the village hall.

A great circular walk starts just west of Kirkby Malzeard called the **Crackpots Mosaic Trail**. It's 6½ miles long and is based around **Dallowgill**, an area known for its Iron Age forts. The trail is based upon a community project set up in Kirkby Malzeard when a group of residents calling themselves 'The Crackpots' created a series of mosaic pictures depicting local flora and fauna that can be found along the way These 22 mosaics have been placed around the trail and make excellent waypoints as well as bringing in a treasure hunt – great with children. A walk map and guide can be downloaded from the community website ⌀ kirkbymalzeardarea.org.uk.

SWINTON PARK COOKERY SCHOOL

Swinton Park, near Masham HG4 4JH ⌀ 01765 680900
⌀ swintonestate.com/cookeryschool

A part of the spectacularly imposing Swinton Park hotel just outside Masham (page 250), the cookery school here is open to both day visitors and hotel residents alike. Housed in the renovated Georgian stables overlooking the crenellated castle entrance, this is a cookery school with a difference.

The kitchen has quite an informal, homely feel, like a personal farmhouse kitchen complete with a huge Aga as the centrepiece. Students prepare and cook food around a giant central table, topped with a slab of smooth granite just waiting for some pastry and a rolling pin. After the hard work has been done, you adjourn to the cookery school's fine dining room (not your average school dining room), where the food that you prepared is served to you. If you have a partner who has been keeping well out of the way for the duration of the course, they can join you in the dining room to taste your culinary delights.

Day courses cover all kinds of tastes and techniques: there's a bread-making course, or you can learn how to make the ultimate Sunday lunch, and they run children's cookery courses too, including private family tuition for groups of two adults and two children who like to cook together.

NIDDERDALE, HARROGATE & AROUND

 SPECIAL STAYS

The Ruin Hackfall, Grewelthorpe HG4 3DE ☎ 01628 825925 ⌖ landmarktrust.org.uk. Don't be put off by the title: a 'ruin' this definitely is not. Built in 1767 as a banqueting house and tastefully refurbished, it's a folly-like pavilion, a mix of reimagined Gothic and Romanesque. The setting is wonderful: perched on a clifftop, it overlooks the most picturesque meanders of the Ure Valley. Access is via a rough track, and the footpath from your door takes you along the ridgetop and down to the lost-world magic of Hackfall Woods. The Ruin is supplied with electricity, underfloor heating and water, but don't expect too much of the 21st century: there's no TV or Wi-Fi. The rooms are unconnected, so you have to venture outside to go between them. Nocturnal flits across the moon-bathed terrace are part of the appeal though.

¶¶ FOOD & DRINK

Queen's Head Kirkby Malzeard ☎ 01765 658497. Unless Grewelthorpe's defunct Crown Inn has been rescued by a community buyout when you read this, this is the only pub in the walkable area round here. Usual local cask ales, pub grub, live music, and a beer garden out back.

13 MASHAM

⋏ Swinton Bivouac

I can't understand why the small market town of Masham (pronounced 'Massam') doesn't make it into the Yorkshire Dales National Park. To me it is the epitome of Dales life, a town with true community spirit that holds its traditions dearly while moving forward.

I often judge a town by its shops. From them, you can tell the character of the place. In Masham the supermarket (a Co-op) does not dominate, but is discreetly round the side. Instead, tucked between a line of old stone houses just off the market square, is a bakery, a butcher's and a greengrocers, one after the other. The square itself is more of a car and motorbike park most of the time, but the lanes and valleys off it are a pleasure to amble round. Showing the community spirit here, a local fundraising effort has enabled the town to buy the library and tourist information building for the public good. One of the initiatives was a cowpat sale, which delivered over £6,000!

1 The Black Sheep Brewery, Masham. 2 Stargazing at the Lime Tree Observatory. 3 The Sheep Fair in Masham. 4 The Druid's Temple, near Masham. 5 The Himalayan Gardens at Hutts Farm. 6 A folly at Hackfall Woods – visitors can stay at The Ruin. ▶

For one weekend a year, usually the last one in September, all this peace and quiet goes out of the window when the annual **Masham Sheep Fair** (⌗ mashamsheepfair.com) is held. The original event took place back in the 1980s to celebrate the town's previous, dwindling, dependence on sheep and to raise money for African farmers. This one-off festival was so successful it was made into an annual event featuring not only the traditional showing of breeds, but also sheepdog demonstrations, a woollen-craft competition, fleece stalls and the ever-popular sheep races. It all takes place in Masham's huge marketplace which was built to house thousands of sheep in the heyday of the auction marts, so coping with 500 animals for the weekend is relatively straightforward. 'It's bad enough clearing up the muck from 500, so I shudder to think what it was like when there were so many,' said Susan Cunliffe-Lister, the event organiser, and now deservedly Dame Susan. 'Apparently, back then, they used to make the town's elderly people clear up… we don't do that anymore!'

"It all takes place in the huge marketplace which was built to house thousands of sheep in the auction marts' heyday."

Masham is officially part of Wensleydale, bordering the **River Ure**, though it is many miles from the area that most think of as being Wensleydale, around Hawes. The Ure by now is a sizeable river, a rowing boat or a swim required to get from one bank to the other. On entering Masham from Ripon, you cross over the Ure before it flows past the recreation and cricket grounds. Sitting listening to the river gurgling behind you, this is an idyllic place to pause for a while or catch up on a few runs, the cricket club regularly serving afternoon teas at weekends during a match.

The breweries

Beer has placed Masham on the map. The older of the two breweries is **Theakston** (☎ 01765 684333 ⌗ theakstons.co.uk), renowned for its quirkily spelt 'Old Peculier' ale. Established in 1827, the brewery is still under the ownership of the Theakston family, although a brief spell with a multinational conglomerate before being bought back by the Theakstons split the family. From the visitor centre, named the **Black Bull in Paradise** (you'll find out why when you visit), you can take a guided tour of the old Victorian brewery concluding, naturally, with sampling a wide range of their ales in the visitor centre taproom. Though

SWIFTS IN MASHAM

Another local speciality that the town has taken to its heart is its colony of swifts. These fabulous birds nest under the eaves of many of the taller buildings around town and on warm, still evenings in summer they fill the sky over the marketplace, feeding on insects. Their presence is celebrated in the **Masham Swifts Town Trail**, a guided route around town with ten swift-themed pieces of artwork to find en route. Pick up a map from the tourist information office (page 209). A swift webcam inside the local church lets you watch the birds at ease.

what really interests me is the cooperage, with the brewery having one of the few remaining craft coopers in the country; it's fascinating to see how they make the traditional barrels.

However, there is another side to the story of brewing in Masham. When Theakston was sold to an international corporation for a while, it caused friction within the Theakston clan and one family member, Paul Theakston, decided to go it alone. He set up a rival brewery in the town using traditional brewing methods. With Masham's long association with sheep (a traditional sheep fair is still held annually in the town, see opposite), and the background to the brewery's formation, it was named the **Black Sheep Brewery**. It too is now a massive part of Yorkshire life with worldwide fame. Financial challenges in 2023 threatened it, but corporate manoeuvres kept it going and Theakston family members still serve as CEO and board members. As with their rival, you can take a tour of the brewery here and compare notes of the two brewing houses, although there should be no industrial espionage required; the family members have now 'kissed and made up'!

 SPECIAL STAYS

Swinton Bivouac Masham HG4 4JZ ℘ 01765 680900 ⬙ swintonestate.com/bivouac. Glamping options with meadow yurts and woodland tree houses (plus lofts and other bricks-and-mortar options) in the 20,000 grand acres of Swinton Estate. Lord and Lady Masham's stately pile is just round the corner; but the Bivouac's rustic setting in the hills of Lower Wensleydale feels reassuringly off-grid and tranquil. And ecological too, because the estate prides itself on its green credentials. Slow exploration is easy, thanks to woodland and moor biking and walking trails that start right here. The good on-site café provides a refuelling stop, and if you fancy fine dining and a classy bar later on, that's available nearby on the estate.

🍴 FOOD & DRINK

Black Sheep Brewery Visitor Centre 🖉 01765 680101 🖰 blacksheepbrewery.com. On the site of the brewery (you can smell the hops as you enter, and the water comes from their own borehole), there's a bistro serving food all day. As you would expect, the bar serves the full range of the brewery's ales, including seasonals, promotionals and specials.

(Johnny Baghdad's) Café on the Square Market Pl 🖉 01765 688809. A venue with a definite hippy vibe – colourful and welcoming. Food has a Middle-Eastern feel and vegetarians are very well catered for. Excellent range of gluten-free cakes.

Where There's Smoke Silver St 🖉 01765 689000 🖰 wts.restaurant. Alias 'WTS', this is really fine dining without a hint of snootiness, serving locally produced ingredients superbly cooked over coal. Booking essential for this highly rated Slow-food experience.

The White Bear Hotel 🖉 01765 689319 🖰 thewhitebearhotel.co.uk. The Theakston brewery tap, curiously situated right inside the Black Sheep Brewery site. Full range of Theakston beers, excellent food, and dog-friendly B&B accommodation.

🛍 SHOPPING

Masham Gallery 24 Market Pl 🖉 01765 689554 🖰 mashamgallery.co.uk ◷ Mar–Dec Tue–Sun; Jan & Feb by appointment only. Artist-run creative centre of mainly printmaking and ceramics. Work by over 120 artists featured, plus regular events and exhibitions.

14 DRUID'S TEMPLE

West of Masham, a narrow lane rising from the village of Ilton heads up into forest plantation and abruptly stops. Follow the remaining track, on foot or by bike, and very soon you may find yourself blinking in disbelief at a bizarre curio known as the Druid's Temple, which is the folly of all follies: a scaled-down Stonehenge plonked amid the trees. Actually, it's Stonehenge with knobs on – more lintels than the real thing, and a stone table, cave and altar to boot. Only it's far from prehistoric, having been created by the local landowner, William Danton, in the 1820s as a job creation scheme. He even engaged someone to play the role of a hermit, though it's said that whoever took on the role didn't stick it out for long before going slightly off the rails.

INDEX

Entries in **bold** indicate major entries; those in *italics* indicate maps.

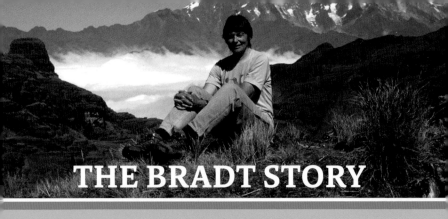

THE BRADT STORY

In the beginning
It all began in 1974 on an Amazon river barge. During an 18-month trip through South America, two adventurous young backpackers – Hilary Bradt and her then husband, George – decided to write about the hiking trails they had discovered through the Andes. *Backpacking Along Ancient Ways in Peru and Bolivia* included the very first descriptions of the Inca Trail. It was the start of a colourful journey to becoming one of the best-loved travel publishers in the world; you can read the full story on our website (**bradtguides. com/ourstory**).

Getting there first
Hilary quickly gained a reputation for being a true travel pioneer, and in the 1980s she started to focus on guides to places overlooked by other publishers. The Bradt Guides list became a roll call of guidebook 'firsts'. We published the first guide to Madagascar, followed by Mauritius, Czechoslovakia and Vietnam. The 1990s saw the beginning of our extensive coverage of Africa: Tanzania, Uganda, South Africa, and Eritrea. Later, post-conflict guides became a feature: Rwanda, Mozambique, Angola, and Sierra Leone, as well as the first standalone guides to the Baltic States following the fall of the Iron Curtain, and the first post-war guides to Bosnia, Kosovo and Albania.

Comprehensive – and with a conscience
Today, we are the world's largest independently owned travel publisher, with more than 200 titles. However, our ethos remains unchanged. Hilary is still keenly involved, and **we still get there first**: two-thirds of Bradt guides have no direct competition.

But we don't just get there first. Our guides are also known for being **more comprehensive** than any other series. We avoid templates and tick-lists. Each guide is a one-of-a-kind expression of an expert author's interests, knowledge and enthusiasm for telling it how it really is.

And a commitment to wildlife, conservation and respect for local communities has always been at the heart of our books. Bradt Guides was **championing sustainable travel** before any other guidebook publisher. We even have a series dedicated to Slow Travel in the UK, award-winning books that explore the country with a passion and depth you'll find nowhere else.

Thank you!
We can only do what we do because of the support of readers like you – people who value less-obvious experiences, less-visited places and a more thoughtful approach to travel. Those who, like us, take travel seriously.

Bradt GUIDES
TRAVEL TAKEN SERIOUSLY